D0920936

PUTA LIFE

JUANA MARÍA

PUTA

SEEING LATINAS,

DISSIDENT ACTS A SERIES EDITED BY MACARENA GÓMEZ-BARRIS & DIANA TAYLOR

RODRÍGUEZ

LIFE

WORKING SEX

DUKE UNIVERSITY PRESS DURHAM AND LONDON 2023

Library of Congress Cataloging-in-
Publication Data
Names: Rodríguez, Juana María, author.
Title: Puta life : seeing Latinas, working
sex / Juana María Rodríguez.
Other titles: Dissident acts.
Description: Durham : Duke University
Press, 2023. | Series: Dissident acts |
Includes bibliographical references and
index.
Identifiers: LCCN 2022039256 (print)
LCCN 2022039257 (ebook)
ISBN 9781478019497 (paperback)
ISBN 9781478016854 (hardcover)
ISBN 9781478024118 (ebook)
Subjects: LCSH: Hispanic American women
in mass media. | Women in mass media. |
Sex workers in mass media. | Prostitutes—
Public opinion. | Feminist theory. | BISAC:
SOCIAL SCIENCE / Feminism & Feminist
Theory | SOCIAL SCIENCE / Human Sexuality
(see also PSYCHOLOGY / Human Sexuality)
Classification: LCC P94.5.W65 R63 2023
(print) | LCC P94.5.W65 (ebook) |
DDC 305.48/868073—dc23/eng/20221121
LC record available at
https://lccn.loc.gov/2022039256
LC ebook record available at
https://lccn.loc.gov/2022039257

Cover art: Self-portrait by
Vanessa del Rio.

Duke University Press gratefully
acknowledges the support of the
University of California, Berkeley,
Townsend Center for the Humanities,
and the Andrew Mellon Humanities
Research Fund, which provided funds
toward the publication of this book.

CONTENTS

▼

Epilogue: Toward a Conclusion
That Does Not Die or a Subject
That Is Allowed to Live

ACKNOWLEDGMENTS

This book was conceived in an instant to surface a word that was always there, but it was produced through the slow, meditative exercise of sitting with images and words between the demands of an overburdened life, translating the feelings they conjure into a book to hold. I was joined in this regular writing ritual by two of my most cherished friends, amantes de lengua e imaginación: my forever academic boo, Emma Pérez, who inspires me to live out my best adventures; and Achy Obejas, my discerning queer Cuban critic and confidant. Once I began writing and sharing, I benefited from a crew of friends and interlocutors who made the work better and kept me moving forward. My sister-comrade Leigh Raiford is a coveted reader and my emergency evacuation plan; she added life to this project, and that made all the difference. Judith Butler was one of my earliest academic supporters; today I revel in their warm friendship, their easy kindness, and their everyday brilliance. Over the years, Caren Kaplan and Eric Smoodin have shared copious amounts of food, scholarly insights, and personal counsel with me, and I plan to spend a lifetime repaying their many acts of generosity. My friendship with KT Thompson has realigned all I know about intellectual intimacy and care; I am happy to keep learning. Nicole Fleetwood is a beautiful, bountiful source of motivation and encouragement; she helps me reimagine what academic work can do and inspires me to live out loud. Julian Carter is a queer creative beloved who is known to appear out of nowhere, like a rainbow, to share wild ideas. As a femme friend and a world-making scholar, Beth Freeman offers me regular life-affirming lessons in the immense design of things. The imprint of my queridísima homie Xandra Ibarra and our many conversations about the politics and flesh of puta life permeate this work; gracias, mujer. Manuel Cuellar, Giancarlo Cornejo, and Iván Ramos each contributed to this project in both tangible ways, through gifts of language and bibliography, and intangible ways, through the affections they generously bestow on their former teacher; they are each trusted readers and valued friends. My most lavish thanks to la divina Marisa Belausteguigoitia, who always adds the D.F. sizzle; to Amalia Cabeza for her powerful scholarship on sex work, her many years of friendship, and her generosity in sharing both; to Deborah Vargas, a longtime friend and fellow sucia lover; to Laura Gutiérrez, who made my Mexican adventures extra magical and whose insights on rumberas were so generative to my thinking. Love and propers to Marcia Ochoa, who has long loved and supported my puta ways and is always there for the afterparty; and to Yolanda Martínez-San Miguel, my perfect match and a phenomenal friend. #Bi4Bi love and pink appreciation to mi queridísimo Mauricio Ilan Carrión for bringing new meaning to care, cake, and planetary light. My thanks to Julia LaChica, who keeps making my world more beautiful, and to Claire Jeannette for bringing the calm and clarity. These extraordinary humans have each supported me in my efforts to live my best puta life. I am overwhelmed with gratitude for all the ways they accompany me in the everyday urgency of surviving the present and finding joy in the cracks.

I had the pleasure of working with three extraordinary research assistants on this project—Michelle Velasquez Potts, who accompanied me on an archival trip to Mexico (a.k.a. the Femme Empowerment Tour); Marlyn Zuno, a Berkeley undergraduate who was outstanding beyond belief and helped me stay organized, focused, and on schedule; and Jacqueline Serrano, who provided me with a great start to organizing an unruly archive. Un saludo caluroso to Victoria Soto, a young scholar at the Universidad de Puerto Rico en Rio Piedras, who helped me out in a pinch by sharing her own extraordinary research. All are a testament to the power of Latina brilliance and public education. A solidarity shout-out to my fellow writers on Writing Every Day, where we keep showing up for ourselves, each other, and the practice. Translation is its own love language; special femme appreciation to Aspa Chalkidou for making me glow in Greek; Sabine Fuchs for introducing me to German butches and femmes; and mi querido Santiago Castellano por tantos gestos bonitos.

As a graduate student at Columbia University, I had the distinct pleasure of watching porn and discussing visual representations of sex in a class taught by Anne McClintock; her daring and her influence helped make this work possible. The friendships that I formed during my time at Projecto ContrSIDA por Vida (PCPV) remain some of the most impactful of my life; love to all the PROJECTO putos, putas y putes on both sides of queer heaven. I offer gratitude and glory to the genius of Samuel R. Delany; his work changed my understanding of what written language could do and what a sexual life could be; I remain a student of his presence. The brief, quirky, and queer friendship I shared with Lauren Berlant was a heady thrill: Rest in Brilliance. I still miss José Esteban Muñoz, but I imagine him hovering nearby awash in the gossip and grime of it all, looking for someplace else to go. Love and ease to my given family on both sides of the many borders that separate us. My beautiful, kind, smart, and loving son, Mateo, is the gift that keeps giving, the baby turtle that is always swimming at my side. Thank you for all the ways you love me.

As friends and scholars, the following people have buoyed me when I needed to believe: José Quiroga, Jillian Hernandez, Margaret Rhee, Alani Hicks-Bartlett, Omise'eke Natasha Tinsley, Milena Britto, Marco Antonio Flores, Larry La Fountain-Stokes, Santiago Castellanos, Joshua Javier Guzmán, Christina León, Summer Kim Lee, Julia Chang, Jaime Cortez, LaMonda Horton-Stallings, Mireille Miller-Young, Kemi Adeyemi, Kareem Khubchandani, Tavia Nyong'o, Cole Rizki, Jessica Pabón-Colón, Lázaro Lima, Laura Luna, Jennifer Tyburczy, Ricardo Ortiz, Susan Stryker, Patrick "Pato" Hebert, Roy Pérez, Cathy Davidson, Anita Mannur, Dean Spade, Leticia Alvarado, Alexandra Rodríguez deRuiz, Macarena Gómez-Barris, Diana Taylor, Raquel Gutierrez, Moi Santos, Ricardo Bracho, SA Smythe, Jina B. Kim, Jafari Allen, Alison Kafer, Ren Ellis Neyra, Josh Kun, Ronak Kapadia, Ianna Hawkins Owen, Susana Vargas, Leticia Sabsay, Greta LaFleur, Nguyen Tan Hoang, Sara Kessler, Mary Pat Brady, Anwar Uhuru, Dredge Kang, Debanuj Dasgupta, Anna Elena Torres, L. B. Johnson, Mayela Rodríguez, Maya Sofia Oliver, Fred Moten, Ann Cvetkovich, Karen Tongson, Eng Beng Lim, Kyla Wazana Tompkins, Micha Cárdenas, David Findley, Ara Wilson, Cathy Hannabach and the exceptional team at Ideas on Fire, Gabe Rosenberg, Harris Scott Soloman, Ulrika Dahl, Paul Joseph López Oro, María Teresa Mendez Baiges, Isaias Fanlo, and Diego Falconí Trávez. Warmest greetings and gratitude to the new friends I found in Berlin: Sin Morgana, Sabine Hark, Halil Dk Sugar, Ben Trott, Berit Ebert, Ben Miller, Thomas Castañeda, Carol Scherer, Caitlin Hahn, Amy Kurzweil, Bertrall Ross, Joy Milligan, Ladee Hubbard, Lan Samantha Chang, and my beloved Channing Gerard Joseph.

At UC Berkeley, I benefit from the friendship and good cheer of so many wonderful colleagues. Extra special thanks to Abigail DeKosnick, Dareick Scott, Poulomi Sahar, Damon Young, Julia Bryan-Wilson, Wendy Brown, Mel Chen, Michael Cohen, Nadia Ellis, Natalia Brizuela, Brandi Cantonese, Kris Gutierrez, Lisa Garcia Bedolla, Salar Mameni, Raka Ray, Cristina Mora, Roshanak Kheshti, Laura Nelson, Eric Stanley, Raúl Coronado, and Ula Taylor. Unending thanks to Keith Feldman, who exemplifies the spirit of collegiality. Working with Sandra Richmond has transformed my relationship to the ugly details of administrative life to make everything better; no words can account for all the ways her labor makes my own possible. Dewey Saint Germaine, Laura Jimenez-Olvera, Charisse Dyer, Uilani Hunt, and Latonya Minor all work hard to brighten the halls where I work.

Teaching makes you smarter. Endless gratitude to the many students whose engagement has enriched my own in innumerable ways; special thanks to Caleb Luna, David Pham, Fernanda Cunha Rivera, John Mundell, Sofi Chavez, Alan Pelaez Lopez, Jess Dorrance, Juliana Fadil-Luchkiw, Lázaro González González, Juan Manuel Aldapa Muñoz, and Julia Havard.

On Twitter and in the world, I have been schooled by a whole host of sex workers and their advocates who have helped keep it real, urgent, and relevant to the daily assaults on sex worker lives, protections, and dignity that happen around the world every day. Special love and deep appreciation to Courtney Trouble, Dorian Katz, Jiz Lee, Jessica Sage, Cris Sardina, Olivia Snow, Lola Davina, Lexi Dark, the Desiree Alliance, the Global Network of Sex Work Projects, Casa Kúa, Hydra Cafe, El/La Para TransLatinas, and the many local chapters of Sex Worker Outreach Projects.

Special thanks to Ken Wissoker for his belief in this project and to the hardworking staff at Duke University Press for their help moving it along. Eternal gratitude to dedicated librarians and archivists everywhere, but especially to Lillian Castillo-Speed and the entire staff at the Ethnic Studies Library at the University of California, Berkeley; to Ilya Oehring and the enterprising librarians at the American Academy in Berlin; and to Natalia López López of the Instituto Nacional de Salud Pública in Mexico, who was a wellspring of warmth, collegiality, and invaluable research assistance.

This work was nurtured by provocative engagements with audiences at the American Academy in Berlin; Brown University; California College of the Arts; Columbia University; Indiana University; Miami University; New York University; Northwestern University; Rutgers University; San Diego State University; Smith College; Tufts University; Universitat Central de Catalunya; University of California, Riverside; University of California, San Diego; University of California, Santa Cruz; University of Georgia; University of Illinois; Universidad de Málaga; University of Maryland; University of Miami; University of Michigan; University of Oregon; University of Texas; Washington University; Wesleyan University; and Yale University. At Berkeley it was supported by the Latinx Research Center, the Center for Race and Gender, the Othering and Belonging Institute, a Project Grant of the Townsend Center for the Humanities, and the Andrew Mellon Humanities Research Fund. The final manuscript was completed while I was in residence at the American Academy in Berlin. Equal parts exhilarating and restorative, my stay in Berlin was a gift of time and release from the usual pressures of academic life that changed me in the best ways and cast new horizons for whatever is next in my own puta life. Finally, I offer gratitude to the luminous wisdom of the Universe that one dark night reached back to touch my outstretched hand and remind me of all the ways we remain united in its radiance.

INTRODUCTION

Puta Life: Seeing Latinas, Working Sex takes as its subject a range of texts that silently or loudly attach the word *puta* to a face, a form, a fugitive gesture captured in a frame. As an intellectual project of inquiry and imagination invested in exploring this enduring figure of latinized feminine excess, this book probes a wildly capacious and curiously curated collection of images to search for the ways that Latina sexual labor becomes a visual phenomenon. Sex workers hold a special place in the visual archive—they function as the unnamed muses and mistresses to a host of mostly male artists and photographers. In the archives of criminalization and social welfare, the puta's face is presented as a warning, a subject of state and social surveillance. In the realm of popular culture and media, sex workers function as an endless source of prurient fascination; the puta's voice narrates the cautionary tale of dangerous desires or the titillating details of those who get paid to do something most of us do for free. As archetypical figures, putas function as screens for a whole host of anxieties and desires about money, sex, and power. Encumbered with the double burden of being desired and vilified, sex workers function as an endless source of inspiration and concern for those who wish to possess, rescue, or venerate them; to know the sexual secrets they harbor or the indignities they have endured. Crafted in the crevices between image and voice, the real and the imagined, *Puta Life* asks how stigma sticks to flesh.

Erving Goffman (2009) begins his influential treatise *Stigma* by reminding us that stigma emerges as a visual phenomenon. According to the Greeks, stigma refers to "bodily signs designed to expose something unusual and bad about the moral status of the signifier" (1). Conceived of as a "bodily sign," a visual marker of deviance, the social stigma that attaches to sex workers is intended to be seen, visible to those publics authorized to cast judgment. But in order to be recognized, viewers must be instructed in what to look for, trained in identifying aberrant sexuality. Visuality is what binds the social stigma of sexual deviance onto the body of the sex worker, but it also allows all of us who fall under the scrutinizing gaze of moral judgment to become suspect carriers of the moral deficiencies sexual labor is intended to represent. The sexualized availability and aberration that is forever attached to racialized bodies crystallizes in the archetype of the puta. This book, formed in the interstice between visual and textual forms of biographical representation, asks: What does it mean to be the visual target of gendered scrutiny and racialized surveillance? To be the source of so much fantasy and speculation? What does it mean to live a sexual life in public? To be seen and assumed known?

La "P" de Puta

Puta's most recognized translation is the English word *whore*, and like *whore*, it is most frequently used as a slur to shame and stigmatize, intended to castigate rebellious forms of sexual expression, particularly in feminine subjects. As a word, *puta* can stand in for sex worker, prostitute, hooker, slut, or bitch, and sometimes it is used to simply mean woman. When it is gendered in the masculine as *puto*, it can reference male sex workers but most frequently collapses into simply a synonym for faggot, another femininized subject of unrestrained and shameful sexuality. But reader, you already know this; the Spanish word *puta* needs no translation. Like the word *macho*, that other term for excessive latinized gender, *puta* has already entered the official lexicon of American English; the *Oxford English Dictionary* tells us so: "puta, n. In Spanish-speaking countries or parts of America: a prostitute; a promiscuous woman, a slut." And like those it is intended to describe, the word *puta* has been known to circulate. As an intended insult in any language, the word itself packs quite a punch. Pronouncing it requires you to push out your lips to force out the air of the "pu" followed by the hardest "ta" that presses tongue against teeth.[1] As an oral performance, the word is often spit rather than spoken, hurled in the direction of the suspected violator of gendered propriety.[2]

The quotidian uses of the word *puta* occupy a conflicted, contradictory, and at times comical space in both Spanish and Portuguese, and the complexity of its signification serves as an apt metaphor for the ways feminized gender is understood in Latin America and its diasporas. By itself, *puta* can be used as an intensifier to express frustration or anger at a situation, similar to the way *damn* or *fucking* might be used as an adjective. Gendered in both masculine and feminine forms, it can serve to cast a negative inflection, *puto trabajo* (damn job) or *puta policía* (fucking police), but the word can also signify something quite wonderful, depending on context. A phrase such as *¡Qué puta suerte!* (What fucking luck!) can hold either a very positive or a very negative connotation depending on context, in ways that mirror the context-driven meanings that the phrase might hold in English. One of its most popular forms is *hijo de puta* (son of a bitch), or frequently *hijo de la gran puta*, which adds an additional element of grandeur in its invocation of abjection. The phrase *puta madre* combines the terms *whore* and *mother* and brings together the binary designations to which Latinas are routinely assigned and functions precisely in this contradictory fashion, where *puta madre* can be used to mark something that is extraordinarily good or extraordinarily bad.[3] This contradictory range of potential registers of signification is central to constructions of Latina sex workers and Latinas who work sex. As a category of human subjects, putas are activated discursively as objects of scorn and social rejection but also as spectacular fantastic projections of corporeal desire and sublime sexual possibilities.

Despite the decidedly derogatory associations of the word, many sex worker activists in Latin America have taken up the term *puta* in an effort to reappropriate the word's significance. Gabriela Leite, the grand dame of the sex worker movement in Brazil, states, "Eu gosto da palavra puta desde sempre. Eu acho uma palavra sonora e quente" (I have always liked the word *puta*. I think it is a word that has a nice sound and it's hot) (fig. I.1).[4] As an activist, Leite understood the power and significance of claiming puta as an identity, arguing that "precisa ter identidade, aí a gente muda alguma coisa" (we need to have an identity, then we'll change something) (Murray 2013). In 1996 San Francisco feminist performance artist Loana Valencia, known as La Sinvergüenza, or shameless one, coined the acronym P.U.T.A., Porque Usted Tiene Animo (Because you have spirit/courage), defining *puta* as "a woman who loves sex and is *never* afraid to admit it" (1996).

FIG I.1 ▸ Gabriela Leite in the documentary *Um Beijo para Gabriela*, 2013.

FIG I.2 ▸ Mural in front of the offices of the Programa de Estudios de Mujer y Género at the Universidad de Puerto Rico, Rio Piedras, 2017.

As with the resignification of the word *queer*, these activists and artists have taken up the word *puta* as a symbol of their refusal to be shamed and as a way to claim a politicized identity. As with *queer*, the linguistic possibilities for *puta* resonate expansively, even as subtleties emerge within specific local vernaculars (fig. I.2). For example, the slogan "Puta feminista" activates a double valence by transforming an invective imagined as very bad, a fucking feminist, into something very good, a feminist puta. Once again, two feminine subject positions imagined as being opposed to one another are united and related: puta feminista. Similarly, the slogans of the sex worker rights movement frequently rework offensive phrases to highlight the hypocrisy of systems of gendered sexual control: for example, changing the ever-popular insult *hijo de puta* (son of a bitch) by declaring, "Las putas insistimos los políticos no son nuestros hijos—solo utilizan nuestros servicios" (Putas insist politicians are not our sons; they only use our services).

As sex workers have crafted a political identity deserving of civil rights, some have also sought political office to highlight the ways they have been disenfranchised.[5] As early as 1991 Claudia Colimoro, a sex worker and feminist organizer, ran on the slate of the Partido Revolucionario de los Trabajadores (PRT, Revolutionary Workers' Party) during the 1991 Mexican parliamentary and municipal elections on a platform that included the decriminalization of sex work and protection for people with AIDS (Kuppers and Thow 1993, 93).[6] In 2010 Leite ran for a congressional seat in Brazilian parliament with the slogan "Puta deputada" (Puta congresswoman). When Ángela Villón, a sex worker and founder of Miluska, Vida y Dignidad (Miluska, Life and Dignity), Peru's first organization advocating for sex workers, ran to be a congressional representative in Peru in 2016 and again in 2021, she defined herself as "una puta decente" (a decent puta) who wanted to represent Peru's sex workers and make Congress into a respectable brothel, to foreground the corruption and duplicity of the state (fig. I.3).[7] In one interview, Villón appears with her now adult son, an aspiring musician, who declares that he appreciates all the ways his family has benefited from his mother's economic contributions. In another interview, Villón proudly declares, "*Puta* es sinónimo de libertad" (*Puta* is a synonym for freedom) (AP Archive 2016). Like these other women, Jacqueline Montero, another former sex worker, who was successfully elected to the Chamber of Deputies in the Dominican Republic, refused to be shamed for her work or her life (fig. I.4). Instead, in an early political rally she declared, "I come from sex work, and this is my power. This is not a weakness" (Ashly 2021). In her successful campaign, she situated these demands within a larger framework of sexual autonomy and protection for vulnerable communities, tweeting out a photograph of herself at a Pride event with the words "feliz con la cominidad [*sic*] GLBT" (Montero 2017). Once elected, Montero introduced legislation against the discrimination of LGBTQ communities, sex workers, and people with AIDS. As political candidates choosing to elevate issues of gendered violence and state impunity, these figures offered a face, a voice, and an experience that exceeded the fantasy and gossip that surround puta life. By taking up the name, they refused the stigma.

When activated politically, putas seem happy to claim LGBTQ rights as part of their party platforms; however, most contemporary mainstream LGBTQ organizations remain less enthusiastic about supporting the decrim-

FIG I.3 ▸ Ángela Villón's campaign flyer, 2016.

FIG I.4 ▸ Jacqueline Montero's campaign flyer, 2017.

inalization of sex work publicly. However, queers have always formed part of sex worker economies and the social movements to address the injustices leveled against them. Gay and trans sex workers were primary targets of the police raids that would come to be known as the Compton's Cafeteria riot (1966) and, later, the Stonewall riots (1969), foundational events viewed as igniting the contemporary LGBTQ movement in the United States. And even as sex workers like Sylvia Rivera, Marsha P. Johnson, Tamara Ching, and Felicia "Flames" Elizondo are frequently lauded as queer pioneers for their roles in these historic acts of resistance, their relationship to sex work remains under continual erasure in many contemporary accounts of their lives. After Stonewall, Sylvia Rivera and her friend Marsha P. Johnson went on to form Street Transvestite Action Revolutionaries (STAR), a group whose mission included providing support services to other trans women and transvestites, many of whom were similarly engaged in sex work.[8] That erasure, born of a desire to appear more acceptable and respectable, was powerfully called out by Rivera when she addressed the crowd at New York City's Christopher Street Liberation Day March in 1973 (fig. I.5). In that speech, she railed against the ways those in attendance had seemed to have forgotten their "gay brothers and sisters in jail," speaking directly to ways the emerging gay and lesbian movement was intent on ignoring the criminalization and police violence that surround sexual commerce. In a later

FIG I.5 ▸ Street Transvestite Action Revolutionaries at the Christopher Street Liberation Day March, 1973. Photograph by Leonard Fink. Provided by The Lesbian, Gay, Bisexual, Transgender Community Center.

interview, conducted by another transgender icon, Leslie Feinberg (2017), Rivera stated, "We always felt that the police were the real enemy."

Police violence is often the culminating result of how social stigma gets codified into state policies and local disciplinary practices, and this is powerfully evident in relation to the treatment of sex work. Nevertheless, laws regarding the commercial exchange of sex and their application vary widely within the Americas, and often within individual countries. Unlike in most of the United States, sex work is generally not illegal in Latin America, even as many municipalities and countries actively regulate the commercialization of sex work by using zoning laws to establish red-light districts, requiring sex workers to register with municipal health departments, enacting prohibitions against the establishment of brothels, and prohibiting sex workers from accessing worker benefits and social resources from the state where these are available.[9] Even in a political climate like the United States, where notions of individual freedom are canonized, entrepreneurialism is exalted, and commerce is king, sex work is never framed as an expression of corporeal autonomy, sexual freedom, or promising commercial opportunism. In *The Political Imagination of Sexual Freedom*, Leticia Sabsay (2016, 97) writes, "Sex work is an area that marks the limits of what we understand as sexual freedom and democratic ideals, highlighting the sociopolitical models of sexual respectability and the exclusionary imaginaries that configure hegemonic notions of diversity, recognition, and autonomy." What does not change, across the hemisphere, and perhaps across the world, is that sex workers are always seen as a stigmatized population that must be identified in order to be criminalized, controlled, or disappeared. Even when they are begrudgingly accepted by law, they must continue to be scorned by society, limited in their freedom to extract money from their bodies.

The hypocrisy that defines sexual morality saturates the scene of sexual regulation and control. Because, despite the ways they are routinely vilified and shunned, historically sex workers throughout the Americas have also been imagined to form part of the fabric of everyday life, part of the necessary social structure that organizes gendered life under patriarchal rule. Brothel owners, one of the few occupations that offered economic independence and power to women, were once recognized public figures who might wield a measure of political and social clout, if not public respect. For example, Isabel Luberza Oppenheimer (1901–74) owned two prosperous brothels in her hometown of Ponce, Puerto Rico, from the late 1930s until the mid-1960s that were well documented in the local press, and she

FIG I.6 ▸ Isabel Luberza Oppenheimer, also known as
"Isabel la Negra," ca. 1920.

eventually became something of a local icon (fig. I.6). Dubbed "Isabel la
Negra," she has been celebrated in music, literature, and folklore, and today a street sign commemorating her is located in the neighborhood of
San Antón, near her once famous brothel—Elizabeth's Dancing Club.[10] But
as with so many putas, the origin story behind Isabel's turn to sex work,
the source of both her wealth and her local fame, is mired in the calam-
ity of love and loss across the borders of race and class, ensuring that any
perceived economic power that sex work might afford its practitioners be
mired in shame and stigma.

In the canons of Latin American letters, the prostitute as tragic protagonist reaches back to the 1902 naturalist Chilean novel of urban despair
and moral degeneration that bears my first name, *Juana Lucero*, by Augusto
d'Halmar.[11] Here, written in a masculine voice dripping with self-absorbed
pity, heavy with the melancholic weight of impossible longing, d'Halmar
([1902] 1998, 225) writes of the aesthetic beauty buried deep in the interior of a puta's soul: "Y ni ese aire ni esa luz hacen distinciones entre el
alma de un poeta o de una prostituta" (And neither that air nor that light
make distinctions between the soul of a poet or a prostitute). The famed
Colombian Nobel laureate Gabriel García Márquez titled the last novel

he was to publish *Memoria de mis putas tristes* (*Memories of My Melancholy Whores*) (2006), even as putas figure prominently throughout so much of his work, most notably in the short story "La increíble y triste historia de la cándida Eréndira y de su abuela desalmada" ("The Incredible and Sad Tale of Innocent Eréndira and Her Heartless Grandmother") (2005). That story tells the sad, tragic, and magically fantastical story of a grandmother prostituting her granddaughter to repay an impossible debt, and the many lovers who try to rescue the young woman from her doomed existence.[12] And of course, *telenovelas*, that most popular form of Latin American entertainment, have long used the tragedy and allure of sex work as a narrative standard because, even when it is not seen as a crime, sex work is always seen as a disgrace, a cautionary tale that needs telling and that everyone wants to hear. As early as 1986, Brazil broadcast the wildly popular eighteenth-century historical drama *Dona Beija*, which was remade in Colombia as *Doña Bella* in 2010. In fact, in recent years we have seen an explosion of films and television shows that feature sex work. In Brazil, *O Negócio* (2013–18), *Me Chama de Bruna* (2016–19), and the latest entry in the sex worker genre, *Rua Augusta* (2018–), have all garnered national attention. The Colombian *Sin senos no hay paraíso* (2008–9) was a sensation throughout the Spanish-speaking world and spawned numerous spinoffs. In the United States, fictional series such as *The Deuce* (2017–19), *The Girlfriend Experience* (2016–), and the American–British collaboration *Harlots* (2017–19) have emerged alongside an outpouring of documentary projects such as *Cathouse: The Series* (2005–14), *Hot Girls Wanted* (2015), and *OnlyFans: Selling Sexy* (2021).

The other side of romanticized sensationalism, however, is misery, exploitation, and depravity. In discussions of "white slavery" of the previous centuries or the current media frenzy around sexual trafficking, the hysteria that revolves around sexual labor is generally organized around a discourse of youthful innocence and victimization that is always racialized and gendered. When young women of color turn to sex work, they are deemed the promiscuous and immoral products of perverse sexual cultures that don't respect the sanctity of marriage, the moral virtue assigned to monogamy, or the value attached to virginity. These discourses affirm the heightened human value of young, white, able-bodied women and the fetishization of virginity as they deny the other social and economic circumstances that lead diverse people to sex work. In the United States and Europe, the language of sexual trafficking has been powerfully marshaled to make all sex work subject to increased state and public surveillance. And discourses around trafficking are particularly perilous because they are so easily appropriated to restrict migration itself.

In her indispensable text on the subject, *Sex at the Margins: Migration, Labour Markets and the Rescue Industry*, Laura María Agustín points to the ways that migrant sex workers form part of larger unprotected informal economic sectors such as farm laborers, domestics, service workers, and street vendors that rarely receive the kind of sensationalized attention as sex work. Like my own text, she focuses her attention on women "because women provoke the scandal" (2007, 11).[13] She writes, "Women who cross borders have long been viewed as deviant, so perhaps the present-day panic about the sexuality of traveling women is not surprising" (40–41). More disturbing still, recent US-based ad campaigns designed to enlist the public to end sex trafficking frequently list the Department of Homeland Security, the same federal department responsible for immigration enforcement and deportations, as the organization to call if you suspect someone is being trafficked.[14] In recounting the personal and structural factors that drive women to migrate, Agustín reminds us that "the myriad possibilities for being miserable at home are forgotten" (45). As social projects of reform, addressing the quotidian harms of everyday misogyny always seems less compelling than rescuing the ideal of a girlish sexual innocence that so few of us ever experience. In their emphasis on protecting youth and innocence, these campaigns seem to imply that sex workers disappear after the bloom of youth expires—that they assimilate into respectable or impoverished lives or that they meet predictably tragic ends. This compulsion to protect the innocent also serves to condemn those deemed guilty, allowing concerned citizens to wallow in the prurient details of youthful female sexuality while ignoring the exploitation of other migrants or the everyday violence that women, girls, and other feminized bodies of all ages are subjected to at home and abroad—familial violence, domestic violence, police violence, state violence, or the ongoing benign neglect that comes from being seen as wholly disposable.

When not viewed as hapless victims, sex workers are depicted as manipulative sexual agents, diseased and dangerous social parasites from which the public needs to be protected.[15] In her essay "Ruminations on *Lo Sucio* as a Latino Queer Analytic," Deborah R. Vargas (2014, 724) offers lo sucio as a way to account for the dirty sensory pleasures of nonnormative sexualities of those "deemed collateral genders within a social world invested in the fiscal benefits of normative sexual intimacies." Not only are putas imagined as "collateral genders," imprudent and dangerous, but sex with sex workers is imagined to be dirty, shameful, and taboo and often desired for precisely those reasons. That sex work frequently engenders contact across differences of color, class, age, size, or ability forms part of the visual scandal, producing the juxtaposition of two bodies that are misaligned in the cultural imagination of acceptable erotic pairings. Moreover, sex work's structure of negotiation and the possibilities it offers for sexual explorations that exceed social norms around appropriate sexual partners and practices make all sex work inherently queer, adding to both its allure and its vilification. Nevertheless, sex work exists within particular dominant structures of exchange, in which one person offers a service and the other person purchases it. It is still work for one person and a commodity for another. Standing outside the gates of normative sexuality, reproductive citizenship, and demure expressions of gender, putas are always imagined as sucias, "always weary of the heteronormative temporality of love as defined by guarantees, for-sures, and forevers" (Vargas 2014, 723). Instead, sex work functions as outside heteronormative marriage (even when sex workers are married) but also adjacent to it, as the understood release valve for the tedium of monogamy. Even as they might be stigmatized as women not worthy of being wives because they charge for their affections, they are also rarely recognized as workers.

When sex enters into the desires of capitalism, an ordinary human activity becomes transformed into something else. For some, sex is perceived as a basic necessity, something that one must acquire at whatever cost the market dictates and the paycheck affords. For others, sex can become a kind of luxury service: sex so special it is worth paying for, offering a precious opportunity to luxuriate in the forbidden and fantastic. The sex that is presumed to transpire in sex work is never about reproducing normative demands organized around seduction, romance, monogamy, marriage, procreation, and durational care even as it might flirt with these as performative postures. While all the prevailing racialized gender norms of every era are replicated and perpetuated within these sexual economies, sex work is also a place where niche markets for all that falls outside societal norms can also thrive. Color, size, age, ability, and the particularities of embodiment matter—but so too do attitude, style, and experience. Putas understand that their desirability is always dependent on the marketplace of sexual possibilities, of finding the right audience or client for the particular attributes they possess or are able to perform. Putas, more than most, also understand that desirability and appeal change with time: the materiality of the body and the bounce that collagen provides fade with age; joints start to break down along with possibilities for pleasure, even as the sexual tricks we have learned and the erotic imagination that worldliness provides fuel new possibilities.

Always coveted as much as they are scorned, putas are rumored to have a kind of elevated sexual magic, charismatic prowess, and serious bedroom skills that set them apart from other women; they are said to know how to captivate and control masculine subjects and everyone else. The providers of initiation and the holders of secrets, they are accustomed to being repositories for the shameful desires of others. It is no wonder then that sex workers occupy so much real estate in the furtive spaces of our erotic imaginations; they traffic in the promise of sexual pleasure and satisfaction as a form of leisure and entertainment against a narrative backdrop of shame and abjection. The price for their sexual freedom, however, is always imagined to be tragedy. In locating the roots of whorephobia, Lola Davina (2020) declares, "To civilians, [sex workers] don't seem 'real.' They're objects of fantasy, or revulsion, or some confusing mix of the two. Our humanity is obliterated." Davina's comment crystallizes how the fantastic projections cast onto sex workers are directly related to the real-world violence to which they are continually subjected.

Working Sex Work

Within the world of academia and public policy, numerous investigations of sex work have approached the subject from a range of disciplinary locations: local histories of prostitution; ethnographic studies of sex workers; legal, public health, and public policy approaches; and sociological studies of individual actors and social movements. In these accounts of sexual labor, the definition of sex work determines who is imagined as the object of inquiry; those that work in street-level sex work, pornography, strip clubs, massage parlors, and escort services are generally understood as performing different forms of erotic labor, even as the risks, labor, and legal status of these jobs differ dramatically across and within specific localities. Pornography, in all its varied forms, is also generally understood as sexual labor. But porn is a billion-dollar transnational industry that employs editors, distributors, writers, photographers, bouncers, booking agents, tax accountants, and landlords; are they sex workers too? If the definition of sex work is limited to those who exchange sexual labor for money, might we need to think more expansively about what constitutes sex? Would this include any number of dominatrixes whose only touch might be the sting of their words or their whips, or the arduous labor of OnlyFans content providers who have no flesh-to-flesh contact with their clients? If just "talking" about sex is considered sex work in one instance, are the vocalized sexual narratives we share within the context of a therapeutic exchange, a staged performance, or academic discourse also forms of sexual labor? And if we interrogate the limits and possibilities of the category of sex, might we also need to investigate what constitutes work, remuneration, and payment? How might the sexual labor we perform within romantic relationships, including marriage, also function as a kind of sexual labor, performed in exchange for social status, jewelry, or domestic harmony? Even in these noncommercial contexts, when is sex about mutual aid and shared pleasure and when is it a transactional exchange performed across uneven registers of power?

In recent years, there has been a flourishing of books that highlight the first-person voices and perspectives of current and former sex workers to define the meaning of their own lives.[16] What these texts make abundantly clear is that sex work is never a single thing even when it is always work. In the introduction to *We Too: Essays on Sex Work and Survival*, Natalie West (2021, 10) writes, "Without seeing sex work as work, sex workers cannot be seen as laboring subjects in need of rights, not rescue." This refusal of "rescue" also functions to call out attempts to study and represent the diverse conditions, attitudes, and motivations that define sex worker lives absent the voices and theorizations of sex workers.[17] In her contribution to the collection *Coming Out like a Porn Star*, edited by queer porn icon Jiz Lee, Zahra Stardust (2015, 305) asserts that they are "not a walking research project to appease the voyeurism and sexual tourism of middle-class careerist professionals who want access to our sexual communities while avoiding stigma and protecting their reputation." Stardust, West, Lee, and many others are themselves actively involved in writing and theorizing the conditions of their lives and their labor. This new generation of texts by and about sex workers makes a resolute effort to include the diverse voices of sex workers and former sex workers who are Black, Indigenous, nonwhite, immigrant, disabled, trans, homeless, queer, nonbinary, undocumented, and survivors of sexual and domestic abuse. The force and range of the stories recounted in these texts illuminate how varied the experiences of sex workers are, making clear how the terms, risks, and potential rewards of sex work need to be situated within the context of each individual's particular frame of reference. Like the biographical accounts I present in my own text, these first-person accounts refuse the false binary of happy hooker or hapless victim that have dominated public debates about the decriminalization of sex work and instead insist on the messy affective, material, and psychic realities these representational accounts leave out.

Addressing the stigma that surrounds puta life is also about addressing the stigma of those willing to pay the price for someone else's sexual labor. While some of these first-person accounts expose how sex work can be dehumanizing, exploitative, and too often seen as a license for nonconsensual forms of sexual violence, other accounts highlight how sex work can also be tender in its clarity of intimate care, lasting in its commitments, elevated and valued precisely because it is negotiated and paid for. Clients, always imagined as male, are generally portrayed as pathetic and undesirable losers rather than as people in search of sexual attention, satisfaction, or care. What might it mean to imagine that sexual touch might be something that those of us who are female or femme can also purchase, that those poorly equipped to navigate sex in the marketplace of normative desirability might also have a right to access? That rather than waiting to be asked for sex, or relegated to giving rather than receiving, those of us who are unchosen in these economies of desire can also seek out, negotiate, and value for ourselves the sexual pleasures offered by the touch of another? If we can agree that sexual labor, intimate erotic care, and those who perform it are valuable, might we allow ourselves to imagine that we too should have access to that care?

Inquiries, Investments, and Interventions

As a project of academic inquiry, my own text steers clear of making any truth claims about sexual labor or attempting to represent its many articulations. Instead, I am invested in exploring how these images are cast onto all of us who are female and femme, sexual and unashamed. Surrounded by an infinite archive of spectacular sexuality—putas exist in every small town and big city; they come in all sizes, colors, and ages—curating a visual dossier for its investigation becomes a random and imprecise affair. Be advised, the images and stories I have assembled are decidedly skewed, motivated as much by my own desire to find pieces of myself in the archive as by any futile interest in representing the possibilities that Latina sexual labor might conjure. I look not to unpack the intentions of those who dwell on either side of the lens, or to decode the secret meanings buried in the image, but because something in the frame has reached out to touch me. This is an academic project born of identification and desire, each chapter an opportunity to dwell in the fantastic and quotidian associations of puta life.

Constructing a visual genealogy of puta life allows us to see how and where this figure has emerged across historical and geographic sites. The images I have collected for this project span continents and centuries; they track the routes and traces of colonialism and empire to highlight the dominant aesthetics associated with puta life and offer glimpses into the erasures that they expose. In providing a visual referent for what a sex worker "looks like," images perform the visual terms of recognition and identification. On screen, the puta takes shape as a voluptuous, exotic, sexually alluring, racially ambiguous temptress; her corpulent flesh a corporeal marker of her abundantly licentious sexual appetites and her insistence on satisfying them.[18] However, the necessary visual counterpart to these figures who might be saved or seduced is the Black crack whore, la india puta working border cantinas, the down-and-out trans hooker—distorted, dehumanized figures deemed too damaged to warrant anything other than pity, those whose disappearance and death come to be expected as the inevitable order of things. These figures saturate the airwaves, despised as much for their race and poverty as for their vocation as sex workers.

Against these decidedly distorted projections of puta life, I probe the biographical encounters with the women we find there, washerwomen and porn stars, sexiles and strippers, starlets and masked wrestlers. As we roam through this archive of putería, this project attempts to remain attentive to the space that exists between what is known—a name, a location, words penned in a ledger or spoken to whoever asked—and what is unknown. We begin with photography, the techne of visual representation that ushers us into a scopic episteme of knowledge production. Where once gossip carried messages of who did what to whom in exchange for what, now it is the advance of technology that adds ever increasing layers of sensorial data about the sexual lives of others. Photography, promising the veracity of the real, comes to produce its own regimes of sexual surveillance and spectatorship, ones that reproduce the very power dynamics they instantiate. Photography fixes the fantasy of the sex workers into an image, a stance, a look, a gesture—offered as evidence of the puta's scandalized identity. As a static image, it allows us to stare fixedly on her face and form to ponder her hidden supernatural sexual powers or the imagined buried traumas that she carries.

The image, codified through visual conventions, becomes the template that teaches us to see sexual deviance, desire, and daring and in doing so attempts to fulfill its role in identification. Technological innovations stitch additional layers of signification onto her form; the voice we might hear in a written account becomes animated in video or audio recordings, adding new sensory details to the perceivable presence of the subject framed in time. The photo shoot becomes a prerequisite for the feature profile of journalism; the graphic presence of the subject of life writing is taken as the necessary evidence of the veracity of their experience, and a prior reliance on testimonial translations is transformed into livestreamed accounts of political urgency. Today, in the digital age of sensorial overload, an endless stream of family portraits, "selfies," and visual documentation on social media function to produce an overabundance of highly curated biographical data, and life stories become told and retold through various multi-medial forms of documentation and archived across a range of platforms.

Even when surrounded by a cornucopia of images, a cacophony of words and information, what might these accounts reveal about the psychic contours of our own sexual lives, let alone that of others? Despite attempts to categorize its enunciations or decode its mysteries, the vagrancies of sexuality are imagined as unseen and unknowable, even as they are glimpsed in fleeting gestures and guileful looks. Invoking the mysteries of sexuality conjures the irrational logics of desire, fantasy, and fear, and an unruly carnal archive of memories and sensations, affirming Gayle Salamon's (2010, 47) assertion that "sexuality is a matter not of seeing but of sensing." But even as the secrets of sexuality are forever kept out of view, the desire to see and extract a hidden interiority remains entangled with our scopic desires. Sex workers, who must often live their sexuality publicly in order to exact a profit, are forever invited to satisfy the visual appetites for knowledge about sexuality, paid for a glimpse into the powers of seduction, charm, and erotic expertise they are rumored to possess.

If sexuality is envisioned as always on display and yet never fully seen, race functions as that which is imagined as always already known and available for visual capture. In her work *Imprisoned in a Luminous Glare*, Leigh Raiford delineates how "the visual field counts as one of the most difficult places to dislodge the relation between the biological 'fact' of race, the cultural 'truths' those bodies possess, and the technologies of vision that bind these two together in ways that erase their own labor" (2013, 235–36). Ethnographic portraiture has instantiated a particular fascination with the spectacle of sexualized racial difference and has installed its own visual conventions of representation rooted in the colonial archive.[19] For Latinas, for whom the fiction of race and its attendant material consequences exist in a register of meaning that is multiply coded by national imaginaries, historical context, phenotypical legibility, classed aesthetics, and ethnic stereotypes, "seeing" racialized difference requires us to inhabit the uncertainty that latinidad offers as a visual signifier.

The question of how we "see" latinidad remains particularly vexed for scholars of visuality, particularly absent linguistic cues or national markers. Latinidad, because it can include those marked legally or socially as Black, white, Asian, or Indigenous, and is very often a mixture of these elements, is always about reading beyond these readily produced categories of phenotypic difference and reading into the ways that localized racial logics emerge within the particularities of each encounter. Forged through colonial conquest, slavery, miscegenation, and migration, visual or linguistic markers that signal latinidad might be perceived in aesthetic, corporeal, and linguistic performances, but legibility already depends on access to specific cultural codes. Rather than an attempt to assign discernible truths about race, gender, or sexuality to the images I engage, I follow Nicole Fleetwood's (2011, 20) formative work in *Troubling Vision*, where she focuses instead on how "the markings and iterations of blackness are manifested through a deliberate performance of visibility that begs us to consider the constructed nature of visuality." Like Raiford, Fleetwood's insistence on exploring *how* meaning becomes attached to "bodies, goods, ideas, and aesthetic practices in the visual sphere" (20) helps us consider how as spectators we search for signs of racialized and sexual meaning, how we assign deviance or desirability, and how the visual uncertainty that comes to define both latinidad and sexuality merge in powerful ways through the figure of the puta.

In their eloquent introduction to a special issue of *Women and Performance Studies*, Joshua Guzmán and Christina León (2015, 272) offer lingering as a mode of engagement, "a granting of permission to slow down the work of understanding *latinidad* and instead to dwell in the space of its many times and places." Lingering as a method seems ideally suited to engage the multidimensional vectors of legibility that surround the convergence of sexual labor, visual culture, and latinidad that my wayward archive demands. As the images I encounter circulate across geographically and historically bound sites in Europe and the Americas, from Alicante to Havana, from Spanish Harlem to Mexico City, they become suspect vectors for representing subjective racialized experience. But if lingering serves as "an impetus for us to rethink theory from the pleasures the aesthetic realm can afford," it also becomes an occasion to stare down the violence and abjection that cultural production also lays bare (Guzmán and León 2015, 274).

Puta Permissions, Puta Poetics

A puta methodology inspires capacious desires, but it must also wrestle with the limits placed by law and ethics. Whether as a photographer or as a writer, to think about representation is to think about the granting of permission: the stated or unstated permission to look, to linger, to record, to circulate, and to transform the meanings that images might convey. This project has been defined by permissions, ones that are free and accessible, and others that require payment to people or institutions who may or may not have secured their own permissions from models and subjects. Permission and consent serve as complicated synonyms for a process where one allows access to one's body and one's labor but perhaps also to one's intentions, yearnings, and agonies. Permissions last; they endure after the moment in which they are given, able to determine the medium and scope of where the image may travel or how it will be known. Copyright law tells us that permissions eventually expire, at which point we can take all that we want. The historical images in this book, produced in another moment under unknown circumstances, are burdened with this freedom to use freely. It is my task to hold these images of uncertain provenance more tenderly, to treat them with an additional level of care in the hope that in my own acts of recovery, the spirits they hold might recognize a kindred soul.

While these archival images, particularly those taken from the state's repository of criminalization, might seem to require another set of ethical imperatives to account for the social pressures and constraints that define the subject's entrance into the visual field, the truth is that many of the faces presented in this book were in one way or another compelled to appear, compelled by the state, compelled by virtue of the instructive gaze of another's technology of capture, compelled by economic forces and social restrictions to offer their image in exchange for shelter, money, and the possibility of a life. Therefore, as author, I have to account for the social pressures and constraints that define the puta's entrance into the archives of visuality; I am tasked with representing the contradictory truths of pleasure and violence, coercion and agency, conjecture and verifiable detail that I am able to gather from the documented remnants of puta life. In photography, it is the point of view of the photographers that is captured in the frame—their desires, anxieties, and motivations that are on display—even when they are serving as documentarians for hire. Much like the consent that one might offer within a sexual exchange, contractual or otherwise, our consent to be photographed never assures that we will be satisfied with the outcome or the feelings the image might inspire. Consent functions as a temporal construct; we consent to something that is about to happen, about a future that has yet to arrive, a future where the image might become a cherished paper memento held between aging hands or proof of a past we had longed to leave behind.

The temporal complexities of consent do not only apply to images, however; they also hover around the voices that have also been recorded to account for the subject's presence. In my text, scraps of biographical documentation are pieced together: sometimes there is a name, a marker of space and time; sometimes we hear a voice, answering a question or demanding an audience. While some of the women I present within these pages were obligated to give testimony, others stumbled into a scene of representation, ready or not, to deliver an account of their lives. At times, we hear the tiniest twinkle of her voice recovered in dusty folios; others silently smile and pose in front of the lens of someone else's camera; and there are those who enter the scene full blown in living, moving color, speaking directly to us—because sometimes putas have a lot to say. Yet, even when I have their words, I know that their language, like my own, is trapped within narrative frames shaped by an imagination of the possible, incapable of capturing the fullness of their lives, their aspirations, or their authorial intentions. An absence of all that they are, and the excess of all we might imagine them to be, hovers around any encounter. Even as this book is my attempt to hold the weight and promise of others' words and worlds with tenderness and care, attempts at representation invariably falter. Caught between this pressure to appear and the desire to be fully seen, I search for those moments where narrative voice and visual representation collide to spark something else, when the subject emerges to provide her own poetic projections of puta life. And in this encounter with the faces and words of others, known and unknown, I also reckon with my own affective attachments to these figures, my own associations, academic and otherwise, with the weight and possibility of puta life.

In her formidable essay "Venus in Two Acts," Saidiya Hartman (2008, 3) offers us "critical fabulation" as a means to craft an account of the female slave that offers more than the scraps of documentation scattered in the archives of dominance, to write a "counter-history of the human, as a practice of freedom." In that essay, Hartman presents two questions that have guided my own methodological engagement throughout this project: "How does one revisit the scene of subjection without replicating the grammar of violence?" (4) and "How can narrative embody life in words and at the same time respect what we can not know?" (3). These questions warn us about the treacherous terrain of representation; they gesture to how our own authorial desires for something that might exceed the possible hovers over the words and images we might encounter in the pages of someone else's mapping of the world. If we understand that social relations take place within a field of power, Caribbean theorist Édouard Glissant invites us to rethink the underlying dynamics of our encounters with alterity. Glissant is less invested in being faithfully represented than in affirming his resistance to having his difference determined. In his text *The Poetics of Relation*, Glissant deploys the idea of opacity as a way to resist the move to know, comprehend, and capture the Other. He writes, "Agree not merely to the right to difference but, carrying this further, agree also to the right to opacity" (1997, 190). Yet, even as "respect[ing] what we can not know" and "the right to opacity" become the correctives for modernist fictions of transparency and knowledge production, these authorial practices stage the fraught encounter between what we might see in an image and the interpretive practices, born of our own scopic desires and horizon of possibilities, that we might bring to them (Hartman 2008, 3; Glissant 1997, 190).

In the "ruins of representation," there is feeling, the felt presence of a life that has left its trace in the archive; the scent of the subject's spirit that wafts out to bury itself inside us, the essence of a life force that endures.[20] Recognizing one's "right to opacity," acknowledging all that we will never know, does not assuage the desire to see ourselves represented or to find connection with the lives of others, near and far. And it does not lessen the risk of trying to do the urgent work of forming enduring political bonds with others. Judith Butler (2005, 136) writes, "We must recognize that ethics requires us to risk ourselves precisely at moments of unknowingness, when what forms us diverges from what lies before us, when our willingness to become undone in relation to others constitutes our chance of becoming human. To be undone by another is a primary necessity, an anguish, to be sure, but also a chance—to be addressed, claimed, bound to what is not me, but also to be moved, to be prompted to act, to address myself elsewhere, and so to vacate the self-sufficient 'I' as a kind of possession."

Butler urges us not only to allow ourselves to be undone but to use the undoing of our singularity as an opportunity to act, to make our relation to the world about an ethics of engagement. That representation is flawed, that it is dangerous, that it is susceptible to causing harm, does not mean we should refuse its potential to change how we see ourselves, others, and the worlds we share. Because even when it fails in its efforts to depict what exists outside of us, representation offers an encounter with alterity capable of transforming how we know, feel, and move in the world. Formed in the chasm that the juxtaposition of image and voice pry open, the tension that binds interiority and surface together, my hope is that the staged encounters with puta life that my work offers will inspire us all to care more about the lives of sex workers and commit ourselves to reimagining the material and psychic conditions of their lives.

Against the rigid demands of knowledge production, *Puta Life* sways among the visual, the textual, and the haptic to reach for those traces of felt possibility that might inspire more ethical forms of relation and care. It offers an invitation to look and linger, not to know and understand but to feel and sense the weight of puta life, to be touched and therefore changed. In the process, this book enacts the ways these shadows and reflections of a life function as encounters with our own edges, swerving around the attachments, identifications, and traumas of our own corporeal embodiments and intimate histories. As a methodological mode of interpretation, abiding in the sensory spaces that feeling pries open performs its own refusal of transparency; it asserts a kind of knowledge production that is at ease in unknowing and a methodological reckoning with unruly practices of succumbing to sensation, memory, and imagination. Caught in the space between the right to opacity and the promise of critical fabulation, *Puta Life* performs the impasse between knowing and unknowing, between seeing and sensing.

Autobiographical Interlude

José Esteban Muñoz (2020, 51) reminds us that "our affect does not simply flow out of us but instead tells us a story about our relationality to ourselves and also to groups." In a book that is focused on the fascination and affective attachments that sex workers inspire and the impossible desires for recognition that representation offers, this brief pause is an opportunity for me to address my own puta life. Like so many other feminine subjects, by the time I became a teenager, I had already been warned about not dressing like a puta by my mother; hailed as a spic slut by my peers; ogled, pinched, groped, and treated as an object for someone else's pleasure by the adult men around me. In other words, I had already been assigned this category of female by the world and only had to decide my relationship to her. As a light-skinned Latina, I might have been able to pass into the white, working-class suburban ethnic community that my multigenerational Cuban family would eventually move into—except for my name, which would generally be pronounced as "Wuana do you wanna?"; except for my family who never learned English, placed a shrine to Santa Barbara in front of our house, slaughtered chickens in the yard, and hosted loud drunken Latin dance parties that always seemed to end with the cops at our door; except for my refusal of the rules of decent, delicate, and demure that were intended to define acceptable white American girlhood.

I came into sexuality in a moment after women's liberation and before AIDS, a time of sexual adventure and risk taking. Pornography was my guide and bisexuality my default position. As a teenager, casual sexual exchanges served as a kind of deliverance from the banality associated with high school romance, and I was lucky to have lovers—male and female— who were as eager as I was to explore the possibilities for pleasure that sex offered. I found an inner sense of power and control in my teenage ability to seduce others, especially older adult men, and associated sex not with the security of marriage and family but with the imagined erotic adventures promised by *Penthouse Forum*, *Playboy*, and *Cosmopolitan*. The porn of that era offered flat color layouts of airbrushed women spreading wide for the camera, talking about their hobbies and their major in college. Porn encouraged my youthful experiments with bodies and pleasures—adding props, positions, and a new vocabulary of filthy words to my growing repertoire of sexual experiences. But what intrigued me, then and now, were the stories—confessions of taboo encounters, sexual infidelities, office parties gone wild, unexpected pleasures with uninvited strangers, and the thrills suggested by new locations, new partners, and previously unexplored sexual practices. These stories, often inserted as letters to the editors and frequently narrated in a feminine voice, told of the exploits of women who had succumbed to the temptations of the flesh, who had strayed off the path to respectability, and who were writing the *Forum* editors to seek advice, absolution, or an audience.[21] These teenage sexual incursions to experience what existed outside of heteronormativity functioned as some of my earliest adventure narratives of puta life and added an element of intentionality that worked to dislodge, or at least loosen, expectations about "natural" or "normal" sexual practices.

In high school, politics—of the feminist, anti-colonial, and revolutionary persuasion—arrived in the form of a Sephardic Jewish girlfriend with Communist parents. At fourteen, I joined the Young Workers Liberation League, the junior division of the Communist Party USA (Angela Davis was our fearless leader), and found another way to understand my family's complicated relationship to Cuba as well as the political climate swirling all around me. As I walked the hallways of my high school, alternately called a lezzie, a spic, a slut, and a commie, I was aware that I was leaving something behind, that there was a danger to being named, identified, singled out for exclusion from the civil society offered by high school life. Yet I sensed a certain power in not caring, secure in the knowledge that revolution was right around the corner, that a bright, colorful, queer sexual future was waiting for me if only I was brave enough to seek it out. Even as I would be frequently reminded by my very closeted girlfriend that homosexuality was just another manifestation of bourgeois decadence, coming into revolutionary consciousness and queer sexuality together instilled in me the belief that another world was on the horizon. I surmised that in exchange for respectability, a nice white middle-class boyfriend, and a future suburban life, I could have freedom, not just the pleasure of my own body but the self-assigned authority to explore the meanings and limits of my own desire, to change the rules of what the future could be. In my teenage imagination, the hypercommercialized projections of (white) women's liberation and sexual freedom offered by porn became intermingled with the revolutionary adventures of Assata Shakur, Emma Goldman, Angela Davis, and Lolita Lebrón. These were women who lived their lives outside the dictates of normative gendered expectations, who knew what they wanted, what they believed in, and who went for it, no matter the price. Now, the slurs that had once been used to define me became sites of identification and possibility, the very things I wanted to grow up to be. And so began my puta life.

Although I had started my sexual explorations with other switchy teenage lovers, once I made my way to the Warehouse, the local gay bar in Hartford, Connecticut, I started to develop more refined erotic attachments and began to seek out more experienced partners capable of providing me with the advanced lessons in sexual education that I craved. For me that meant older, more seasoned butch lovers, people who had spent time "in the life" and could introduce me to these new erotic worlds of carnal rapture; I was fifteen at the time.[22] Gay bars have long been sites where all sorts of underground sexual possibilities flourish, and the disco era brought with it a new sonic vocabulary for the queer sexual cultures that were exploding into public view. Lost in the beat of a funk-fueled dance floor, gyrating to Prince's "Controversy," Donna Summer's "Bad Girls," and Rick James's "Super Freak"—gay bars epitomized the dream of living otherwise. Many of the first dykes I met at the Warehouse worked the massage parlors and strip clubs around Hartford, and I was fascinated by these women who had sex with men for money, and with women for pleasure. To a radical feminist, this arrangement seemed like the most perfect kind of subversive gender rebellion, even if, according to my Communist comrades, sex workers would have to be reeducated after the revolution. Occasionally these women would bring their johns to the queer club to party in our underworld playgrounds fueled by desire, disco, and the dark. Some of these women became my friends, and others would occasionally become my lovers in the lust- and drug-fueled parties that seemed to happen every weekend. Part of that queer initiation process was a visit to a local sex shop. In a time before you could buy sex toys online, before streaming porn and internet chat rooms, local sex shops with neon XXX in the windows were where you went to buy dildos, poppers, and smut. Walking into these stores with the windows blacked out to protect the identities of those inside also served to remind you that you shared consumptive habits with those marked as lowlifes, perverts, queers, and freaks by dominant society.

These early lessons in sexual politics and the sexual communities that emerged around them further fueled my interest in those who got paid to have sex. As a young person already engaged in illicit and illegal sexual encounters—that is, underage sex with friends and strangers, sometimes for drinks or drugs, sometimes for a place to crash, and usually just for the thrill of it—I quickly learned that my sexuality had a value that could be traded. The summer before my senior year in high school, I was trying to save money for a road trip with my older butch lover and began to consider sex work as a fast cash option to supplement the savings from my minimum-wage job. Several of my friends from high school had already discovered that they could earn quick money giving blow jobs to the men who frequented the train station in downtown Hartford, and I admit it sounded tempting if somewhat scary. At twenty-five dollars a blow job, I wasn't sure the hassle and the risk were worth the money; as a teenager, I already had a lousy job I hated. As luck would have it, that summer I was solicited to engage in another kind of sex work, a kind of sexual labor that I would keep returning to throughout my life: I got paid to *talk* about sex.

After seeing more than a few of my friends drop out of high school because of pregnancy, or suffer through the ordeal of securing abortions, legal but still expensive, I started taking my classmates to the local Planned Parenthood clinic; I was their number one recruiter. That summer, Planned Parenthood offered me $150 to talk to parents and social workers about the sex I was having as a bisexual Latina teenager. I jumped at the chance. As a sexually audacious and politically empowered proto-feminist, I had expected that my first encounter selling my sexuality for cold hard cash would leave me feeling sexually empowered and liberated. But I admit that after two hours of sharing my experiences to aghast parents, troubled social workers, and concerned health providers, I went home feeling dirty and ashamed. That said, the money was good.

Moving to San Francisco in the mid-1980s, just as the devastation of the AIDS pandemic's devastation took hold, I encountered thriving sexual cultures and more queer bodies to explore them with. The AIDS crisis made talking explicitly about the sex we were having and wanting to have a matter of life and death and sparked public and private conversations around risk, vulnerability, and consent along with global movements that challenged the stigma that surrounds both sex and disease. Having already produced and exchanged dozens of dirty Polaroids with friends and lovers, when I was asked to pose for the raunchy and celebrated lesbian erotic publication *On Our Backs*, I was more than eager to sign on. To be clear, I didn't pose for money but just because someone asked, eventually enlisting my BFF Julia Sumi LaChica to join the photo shoot. There is a certain undeniable vanity associated with puta life, a kind of sexual audacity that assumes that others might be so beguiled by the sexy that you have to deliver that they would be willing to pay for it—as a photograph in a magazine, as a scene in a movie, or as a set amount of time in your company. However, the photos themselves were uninspired; it was an early nineties aesthetic of femme-on-femme sex. Sexually tame and visually mundane, we did not make the cover. The truth is there wasn't a whole lot of chemistry; we were best friends feigning sexy for the camera in our best thrift-store lingerie (fig. I.7).[23] The spread was labeled "Las Chicas," a reference to both her last name and a way to mark the scene as something other than white for a magazine that had a complicated relationship with racialized sexuality. There is nothing about the photographs that is particularly exceptional, but I do remember a certain femme sense of vanity when a

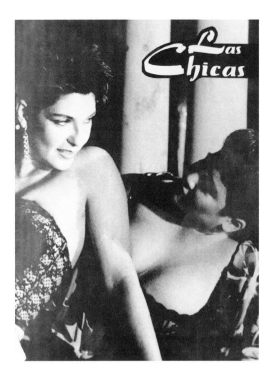

FIG I.7 ▸ "Las Chicas" spread from *On Our Backs* magazine, July–August 1990. Photograph by Myra Fourwinds.

handsome butch approached me on the San Francisco Municipal Transportation Agency (MUNI) and asked if I was the girl in the *On Our Backs* spread. During this time, and before and during graduate school, I also published an s/m-themed short story, led sex-positive workshops for Latinas for the HIV-prevention agency Proyecto ContraSIDA por Vida, wrote a sexy bilingual safer-sex guide for dykes, and generally found other ways to turn sexual experience and a willingness to be publicly perverse into a marketable skill. The truth is, once you succumb to the hail of puta, once you have had enough rumors, ex-lovers, and naked pictures circulating in the world, the stigma stops mattering as something that can be used against you, even as you notice all the ways it sticks to your skin.

My final year of graduate school, I moved to Iruña (Pamplona) in Spain's Basque region chasing love and foreign adventure, an opportunity to live an elsewhere I knew little about. Welcomed into a community of faggy Basque activists along with a few unshaved hippy heterosexual feminists, I became immediately self-conscious of all the ways I stood out visually and otherwise—phenotypically not that different from others in the Spanish state, my accent, my aesthetic, and my way of moving in the world marked me as mismatched from the available categories of female gender in the region. My age marked me as no longer belonging to the category of señorita even as it was also clear that I had not ascended to the status of señora, that dignified, matronly figure seen throughout Spain with matching leather purse and shoes. Even after abandoning any semblance of high heels to navigate the cobblestone streets of my new ancient neighborhood, I didn't look the part of the environmentalist/Basque separatist/squatter/feminist/ gay activist types who constituted my social sphere. I was also not Roma, that despised category that lives under perpetual suspicion and who are similarly identified by sartorial aesthetics, social practices, and geographic location. Because the voice hangs in the air, sending coded sensory signals to those within its range, in the market, in the club, on the streets, those around me knew I was from their colonized elsewhere—sudaca—like the telenovelas; others could name it more precisely, cubana, because they had already visited my island home and fallen in lust. In Spain, my voice served as an irrefutable marker of my difference—inmigrante, sudaca, cubana, puta.[24] During my year in Iruña, I was propositioned three separate times for sexual labor, including once by an older, slightly masculine woman who shyly approached asking how much. These encounters all happened in the daylight, based as much on my assumed status as an immigrant sex worker as by the audacity that is required to be a woman alone in public. But most times, I simply heard the word puta whispered around me—at the bakery, in the café, in the street—suggesting the sexual acts that I was invited to perform.

In Spain, as in other parts of Europe, immigrant women, particularly those marked as Black or from countries associated with the African diaspora—cubanas, dominicanas, brasileñas—are always assumed to be working sex, ogled with unrestrained lust and unquestioned sexual suspicion.[25] In fact, cubanas are so fetishized that we even have a sexual act named for us: *una cubana* refers to stimulating a penis by squeezing it between corpulent breasts.[26] In Spain, regardless of where I was in the city or what I was wearing, being identified as cubana meant stepping into a visual and auditory category that was firmly entrenched and totalizing. Moving back to an increasingly gentrified San Francisco, I rented an apartment in the Tenderloin, an area popular with sex workers and their clients, and I would be repeatedly asked—How much? In both places—here and there—I was identified by how I looked and where I was located in someone else's spatial mapping of a world of erotic possibility.

The truth is, I have been called puta more times than I remember. I have been called puta because of how I look and where I wander; because

FIG I.8 ▸ Author at the Folsom Street Fair, San Francisco, 2011.

FIG I.9 ▸ Author en route to Kit Kat Club, Berlin, 2021.

of who and what I desire and because of who and what I refuse. And I have answered, cultivating an aesthetic and an attitude from the impossibility of being otherwise. Maybe you have seen me grinding out my puta passions on a dance floor, being scandalous with strangers at San Francisco's kinkiest block party or in a Berlin dark room (figs. I.8 and I.9), or documenting my amorous misadventures on the socials. More shameful still, perhaps you recognize my aging face from the numerous dating apps that I turn to in the hope of getting lucky. More likely, however, is that you have seen me on your campus lecturing about cybersluts, sodomites, sexual futures, or puta life, fulfilling (or not) your expectations of what a puta with a PhD and a government job might look and sound like. In fact, as an academic who has created a reputation for herself as a scholar of sexuality, I have been rewarded in unexpected ways for writing explicitly about my own erotic archive even as I have no doubt also been dismissed or excluded from other opportunities. These too are forms of sex work, and ways of working sex, pleasurable, profitable, and dangerous in different ways and to different degrees.

The differences matter. While this project is invested in dismantling the stigma that surrounds sex work by highlighting the wide variety of practices that constitute erotic labor, it is also committed to challenging the hierarchies that assign differential moral and legal value to that work. While I have frequently been able to extract monetary value from my sexuality in a variety of ways, because I have never been economically dependent on criminalized work to pay my rent or feed myself or my child, I have never had to fear being arrested for doing my job; I have never been denied citizenship, a job, an apartment, or state benefits for engaging in sex work; I have never had my assets seized because they were procured through illegal means; I have never had my bank account or social media accounts closed because I was suspected of engaging in illicit activity; I have never had to worry about my adult son being arrested for procurement because he benefits economically from my work selling sex. These are some of the current realities faced by sex workers worldwide, made more pernicious and obscene through laws such as SESTA/FOSTA in the United States (Stop Enabling Sexual Trafficking Act / Fight Online Sex Trafficking) (2018) that make websites responsible if third parties post ads for illegal activity on their platforms, including consensual adult sex work.[27] In the United States, the shutting down of websites offering sexually explicit material on Backpage, Craigslist, Tumblr, and Patreon, and a brief ban of the website OnlyFans, has accentuated the precarity of sex workers seeking out sources for independently controlled income and has resulted in more dangerous working conditions for all involved in the industry.[28] The result of these bans reach far beyond commercial sex work, impacting the creative production of all sexually explicit artists and performers, including those whose art practices might not be recognized as connected to sex work, and numerous artists have already had their accounts blocked (Holmes 2021). The laws and regulation that surround commercial sex work function to discipline the sexual expression, pleasures, and possibilities of all of us, but the harms they inflict are always differentially experienced, governed by the preexisting hierarchies of power and privilege that swirl all around us.

Puta Mourning, Puta Life

Drawing on a language of affect and aesthetics to bear upon understandings of gender, age, race, sexuality, labor, ability, and migration, *Puta Life* aims to intervene in public policy debates around the criminalization and stigmatization of sex work by foregrounding the lives and experiences of women whose work has been sex. In this way, it joins Amnesty International, the United Nations, Human Rights Watch, and the World Health

Organization to support the decriminalization of sex work worldwide and to argue that laws that criminalize sex work put those involved in the sex industry at increased risk of a variety of harms. Today, sex workers face a worldwide epidemic of violence and murder; sex workers are routinely hunted and harmed by those who understand that the value of their lives is, more often than not, deemed negligible, insufficient to warrant concern, let alone protection or justice.

The stigma that conditions the violence against sex workers is the same stigma that structures the response to those violations. Whether in discussions of the Asian American female victims of a mass shooting at massage parlors in Atlanta; the ongoing drama of missing and murdered Indigenous women in Canada and the United States; the unsolved femicides in Juarez, Mexico, and the global South; or the incessant murder of transgender women in the streets of every urban capital, at the moment of their death, so often the victims' relationship to puta life hovers around the circumstances of their violent ends. For some, any association to sex work becomes a way to discount the violations to which so many are routinely subjected, concluding that because the victims were engaged in intimate forms of labor, because they were on the street dressed a certain way, because they were out alone at night, because they were drug addicted or poor, because they knowingly stepped into a car or an alley to work, because they consented to sex with a stranger, the violence committed against them is to be expected, if not deserved.[29] For others wishing to solicit outrage for the crimes committed against them, any connection to sex work must be denied or dismissed in order to "humanize" the subject because as social outcasts, sex workers are too often perceived to be beyond the pale of human connection.[30] In these cases, suggesting that the victim's involvement in the sex trade might be connected to the violence committed against them is deemed as disrespect for the dead because even in death the indelible stain of sexual labor endures. Therefore, this book also harbors another guttural meaning for puta life. As a response to puta vida, a fucking life, a life defined by condemnation, violence, and contempt, I offer the possibility of puta life, an affirmation of the beauty, value, and spirit of putas everywhere.

If this introduction has been focused on the place of putas in the cultural imagination, including my own, part I of the book digs into the roots of that psychic implant, offering two chapters that explore the historical currents that bind sexual labor to visuality: in the first case, by diving deep into the archive of the Mexican state to witness the coming together of state regulation and biopolitical technologies of capture; and in the second, to trace the aesthetic motifs about racial and sexual deviance that coalesce to produce a visual representation of puta life. Part II then shifts to offer three distinct, more intimate, case studies that foreground first-person accounts of some of the many women who work sex—archival encounters with different women in different locations, representing decidedly different kinds of sexual labor. Here, readers might note an uncanny connection between this author and those I have elected to feature. Like myself, those I profile in these chapters are all well past their sexual prime. Like the brief stories I have shared in this introduction (as well as those I have kept to myself), their biographical accounts of puta life are narrated from the vantage point of advancing years, described and written from the security of having survived their pasts. As I engage the distinct and contradictory temporal dimension of both photography and biography, I insert the undertheorized dynamics of aging into discussions of gendered and racialized sexuality.

In these chapters, I rummage through these visual archives of puta life, not to offer any comprehensive account or representative sample of the different facets of sexual labor but because their faces and their words had something to say to me about my own relationship to puta life. In the first of these chapters, I look at the larger-than-life figure of Vanessa del Rio, a Cuban–Puerto Rican from the Bronx who went on to become an international porn sensation. I grew up watching her films at the XXX drive-in of my youth, so Vanessa has always been a Latina femme icon for me, but studying her life, taking seriously her theorizations of sex and violence, power and submission, allowed me greater access to my own understanding of the terror and thrill that these terms inspire. It was Vanessa del Rio—and the many ways I felt an affective kinship with her through her life narrative—who brought me to this project; it was Vanessa who inspired me to probe the cultural associations projected onto sexual labor, and my own associations with puta life.

The second archival case study considers the loose collective of women associated with Casa Xochiquetzal, a home for elderly sex workers in Mexico City. This chapter was motivated first and foremost by the visual surprise of seeing photographs of the naked bodies of older women, women who reminded me of the older women in my own life, and the older woman I am becoming. Shifting the lens from the purported glamour of pornography to aging streetwalkers in the Mexican metropolis foregrounds the harsh realities faced by sex workers who work the street, as it reveals how so often these women's lives had already been shaped by gendered stigma, discrimination, violence, and globalized politics that culminate in localized neglect. Charting their biographical recollections across the different registers of an archive of representation that seemed to multiply every few months, I became focused on exploring how narrative frames shape the affective relationship between those in front of and those behind the camera. Spending time with their faces and their stories and taking seriously the relationship between image makers and their subjects forced me to reflect on my own practices of representation, to mark those moments when I felt the gulf between the women I studied and the woman I am widen, as well as reflect on unexpected moments of identification and connection.

In the final chapter, I look at trans activist Adela Vázquez, who has been working sex all her life, even as, like most people engaged in sex work, she only exchanged sex for cash for a brief part of her life. Adela is my friend, my age mate, mí paisana, another Cuban immigrant and an inexhaustible storyteller, who is frequently given opportunities to represent her own puta life to whoever is interested in hearing. Despite our similarities, our lives have been defined by different structures of the possible, determined as much by history, desire, and the privileged particularities of our own embodied forms. In these final three chapters, even as I try to press the words of these women against the images and narratives that have circulated around them, I also try to expose the ways—as subjects and critics struggling to assign meaning to the myriad ways that sexuality shapes our lives—we remain trapped within webs of mediation. Our language, what we are able to say about ourselves and others, is always encumbered and enlivened by our horizon of possibilities, the worlds we can imagine. That all our attempts to represent ourselves and others will never fully satisfy all that we wish to share does not diminish the gesture of reaching out to open ourselves to another, the promise that touch offers to transform us. Who we are shapes how we tell stories but also impacts how we listen to them. Our understanding—experiential, affective, and academic—of the worlds in which actors move and actions transpire functions as our available resources for meaning making, each complicated and partial, each imbued with its own biases and assumptions. But this project also asks you, the reader, to sit alongside what lies outside meaning, to open to sensation and feeling, to join me in a femme practice of friendship and mutual care. In sharing my own erotic and ethical sensibilities, I invite you—the one reading, watching, listening alongside me—to think about the sexual messages and memories that have accompanied you to this page, a dialogic academic exercise in exploring the creation of sexual meaning and what might lie beyond it.

This book came looking for me, whispering the word *puta* as the word that cannot be named, to name the thing that we cannot be, to name that to which we have already been condemned. To this word I add life, the possibility of a life that will exceed the word and remake it. These encounters with the putas I have profiled, so like and unlike myself, have allowed me to grapple with my own messy feelings about violence, pleasure, and care; about my aging body and my ageless desires; as well as my own stubborn attachments to representation and recognition. My wish, full of utopian yearnings, is that in addressing the stigma that surrounds sexual labor, we might begin to redefine sexual politics in ways that tend to the harms of police violence, state surveillance, and the censure of sexual expression; that we might quell the murderous violence of everyday misogyny and nurture the sparks of carnal beauty and courage that are everywhere pouring out into the streets to demand the right to own our bodies; the right to live free from stigma, violence, and harm; the right to know care. Bold in its political aspirations, tender in its queer feelings, this book is my homage to those whose lives have been marked by the regulatory power of puta life, an opportunity to engage in the reparative potential of images and stories so that we might see ourselves, and each other, anew.

PART I

ARCHIVAL ENCOUNTERS AND AFFECTIVE TRACES

Visual Genealogies
of Puta Life

Every work of photographic art has its lurking, objectifying inverse in the archives of the police.

ALLAN SEKULA

The Photograph is a certain but fugitive testimony.

ROLAND BARTHES

WOMEN IN PUBLIC

Biopolitics, Portraiture, and Poetics

Guided by Allan Sekula's (1981) keen observation about photography's duplicitous past and Roland Barthes's (2010) insights into its beleaguered future, this chapter turns to one of the earliest archival records of sex work in the Americas to witness the convergence of empire, technology, and statecraft. As I ponder the affective traces that photographs leave behind, I probe the ways that archival encounters mark us as curious subjects capable of being touched by what we do and don't find in the faces and biographical accounts of others we will never know. The name of this singular tome of puta life gestures to the imperial authority of its provenance: *Registro de mujeres públicas de la Ciudad de México, de acuerdo con la Legislación de V. M. El Emperador* (Registry of public women in accordance with the regulations issued by V. M. the Emperor) (1865), the emperor being Maximilian I, archduke of Austria, the first and only monarch of the Second Mexican Empire. Initiated after the 1861 War of French Intervention, which saw France invading the Mexican Republic, and only one year after Maximilian arrived in Mexico in 1864 as the newly installed emperor, this text functioned as the state's official database of the women working sex in mid-nineteenth-century Mexico City. Modeled after a similar legislative practice begun in France, the *Registro de mujeres públicas* was designed as a program of public health and sanitation in a moment when syphilis was rampant and incurable. Of course, the mandate was less about the health or safety of the more than five hundred sex workers living in Mexico City at the time and more about keeping the occupying French soldiers, and by extension the body politic of the newly colonized settlement, free from disease and contamination. In fact, it was rumored that Maximilian had his own attachments to paid sexual labor and had contracted "the pox" while traveling in Brazil (Fregosa 2018).

The *Registro de mujeres públicas*, and the newly established state protocols that surrounded it, instantiated a new biopolitical project of sexual surveillance, control, and regulation; it marked the first time in Mexico's history that sex workers were required to pay the state in order to profit from their own sexual labor.[1] At its core, Michel Foucault (1978, 140) defines biopower, which he sees as foundational to the establishment of industrial capitalism, as "the administration of bodies and the calculated management of life." This new type of power, administered at the level of populations through a series of apparatuses or deployments that Foucault terms *dispositifs*, installed new institutionalized systems of exercising control intended to create a cohesive social body, one that could be subjected to an ever more centralized bureaucratic state authority. Begun in a moment of declining sovereign power and increasing investment in industrial capitalism, biopower functions through a series of various administrative, institutional, and discursive structures. In contrast to the forms of discipline enacted at the level of the individual, these new machinations of the state "had very different procedures, completely new instruments, and very different equipment" (Foucault 2003, 36). In imperial Mexico, the kinds of procedures and instruments imposed on those populations trying to extract a profit from their own sexual labor included a medical exam, an initial registration fee, and a monthly quota paid to the state. However, the new law required something else as well: each and every sex worker had to go to one of the dozens of different photographers that were already beginning to populate the city in order to have her photograph taken.

In mid-nineteenth-century Mexico, prostitution was considered a necessary evil, a corporeal release required to keep male sexuality, deemed "naturally" lascivious and at risk for perversions of all kind, safe enough for the mujeres decentes, the decent women of the new nation (Bailón Vásquez 2016). Mujeres decentes were those women under the protection and control of masculine authority, be it emperor, husband, father, or parish priest; those who could be entrusted to reproduce and care for the future citizens of the nation; those who needed to be kept free from both disease and moral contamination. In contrast, una mujer pública (a public woman) was decidedly not that. Like the legislation that inspired it, the phrase *una mujer pública* echoes the common nineteenth-century French term *fille publique* (a public girl). In that euphemistic designation, it produces sex workers as subject to the legal control and authority of the public, as biopolitical subjects in a state project that used legislative regulation to extract profits from sexual labor and categorize the women who performed it. In this moment of scripting sex work into the written record of the state, this once informal mode of address becomes a legal designation. This new juridical identity constructs the one who dares to occupy the space of the public absent the control and protection of a masculine authority as part of a newly formed social body under the control of the state. In doing so, we witness the state assuming control over the sex worker's body, her labor, and her morality. This thoroughly modern set of state regulations created a "meshed grid of material coercions" that combined emerging trends and technologies in medicine and law as part of the installation of its biopolitical administrative control over a newly constituted population, mujeres públicas (Foucault 1978, 35).[2]

In the 1865 *Registro*, each woman is assigned a number, marked sequentially "Patente No." throughout, a rhetorical gesture that establishes that these women are now wards of a nascent administrative accounting system. In *Listening to Images*, Tina Campt (2017, 81) describes what she sees as the grammar and temporal imprint of the archive and the arithmetic of biopolitical control: "The grammar of this archive is an anterior tense of present and future capture, and its first haptic temporality is this initial moment of capture: compelled to pose for a compulsory photo, confronting the unreturnable gaze of the camera, an individual is transformed into a number that will capture him for years to come." In the context of a public health registry, I initially thought *patente* might be an alternate spelling of *paciente*, or patient, rather than corresponding to the English-language word *patent*. However, a glance at the various definitions offered by the Real Academia Española affirms just how appropriate it is as a word choice to indicate the authority to make, use, or sell a product or invention. In requiring the women to establish a patent for their own sexual labor, the *Registro* turns these women into sexual commodities and establishes its own authority to regulate them.[3] Banning or eliminating sexual commerce was never the point. Instead, this early biopolitical apparatus, like those that would follow, establishes the state's jurisdiction over sexual labor in order to wrest profits away from individual workers and establish itself as the patent-granting authority, as the authority needed to authorize someone else's sexual labor.

In describing what would become the prevailing model for monetary extraction from sexual labor and sexual pleasure, a model later made more expedient through criminalization and commercial control, Foucault writes:

> Its function is to bring back to capital itself, to the normal circuits of capitalist profit, all the profits that can be extracted from sexual pleasure, on the triple condition, of course, that, first, this sexual pleasure is marginalized, deprecated, and prohibited, and so then becomes costly solely by virtue of being prohibited. Second, if one wants to make a profit from sexual pleasure, then it must not only be prohibited, but it must actually be tolerated. And, finally it must be supervised by a particular power, which is ensured by the coupling of criminals and police, through the procurer-informer. (2006, 111)

As a form of state bureaucracy, the regulatory system behind the *Registro* funneled the profits from sexual labor into the hands of the state and its business partners through a set of fees charged to individual workers and brothel owners. The result is that sex work is morally condemned to ensure its ongoing control, regulated for maximum financial gain, while still being available to satisfy men's "natural" lascivious tendencies. Whereas before women worked for themselves or perhaps shared their earnings with a single madam, now they formed part of a large state bureaucratic system, required to pay for photographs, medical exams, and the very right to be entered into the registry, "an exhibition of the links between legal science, medicine and visual technology, which will give birth to a new discourse called criminology" (Cortés Rocca 2005, 219). As part of the new legislation, sex workers were issued individual passbooks that they were required to carry and that indicated they were lawfully registered with the state, current on their monthly dues, and had fulfilled the required medical examinations. Therefore, clerks had to be employed to enter relevant data into the new state records, police had to be instructed to monitor and punish those that were noncompliant, and of course bribes of both the monetary and carnal variety had to be negotiated and paid in order to circumvent the authorial apparatuses of the state. What made the new bureaucracy particularly pernicious, however, was that now that the state had a way of identifying those attempting to defy its authority, it had a visual replica of a face to attach to a name and an identity: mujer pública.

In *La foto de identidad: Fragmentos para una estética* (The identity photo: Fragments for an aesthetic), Camilo Restrepo Zapata (2002, 50) not only questions just what the state performs through these processes of systematic identification but also asks, "What types of subjects are built with those photos that lack context and are born linked to the public?"[4] The subjects that emerged as mujeres públicas in 1865 Mexico were deemed not just immoral but potentially dangerous and in need of state control. But the *Registro* didn't just trap these women in the snare of the state's elaborate system of sexual surveillance—it tracked them. It was a living, pulsing text, an ongoing analog database of each woman's life and her activities; it was the arm of the state, and it pursued its subjects. The registry not only regulated these women's sexual labor; it also monitored their mobility as they navigated the burgeoning metropolis. As a form of administrative biography, it recorded their movements as they went from one location, one brothel, or one category to another; it followed them into the hospital, into jail, and into the lives they hoped to live outside the demands of sex work. Once their face appears on paper, "born linked to the public," fixed onto the pages of the state registry of criminalization and deviance, these women were held prisoner by an elaborate bureaucratic apparatus that aimed to document and preserve the details of their puta lives, forever more.

And what now? How might I recover more than the administrative details of a life weighted down by the archival intentions of a punishing state? In *Wayward Lives, Beautiful Experiments*, Saidiya Hartman (2019) weaves critical fabulation and empathic imagination into the archive of Black female life under white misogynist cruelty. Like Campt and Restrepo Zapata, Hartman points us to all that is kept out of these accountings of human life and instead invites us to search for the unimagined possibilities the archive might pry open and to sit with the heavy burdens of the secrets it refuses to reveal. Hartman (2019, xiv) writes, "The endeavor is to recover the insurgent ground of these lives; to exhume open rebellion from the case file, to untether waywardness, refusal, mutual aid, and free love from their identification as deviance, criminality, and pathology; to affirm motherhood (reproductive choice), intimacy outside the institution of marriage, and queer and outlaw passions; and to illuminate the radical imagination and everyday anarchy of ordinary colored girls, which has not only been overlooked, but is nearly unimaginable." Like Hartman's luminous text, as an imaginative project of documentation and interpretation, *Puta Life* reaches out in a gesture of solidarity and shared belonging across the deep spaces of unknowing and speculation. The women cataloged in the *Registro de mujeres públicas* are likewise ordinary colored girls, overlooked and unnoticed while practicing open rebellion, quiet refusals, and everyday anarchy to eke out whatever hidden moments of tenderness their fragile lives might afford. The juridical violence that occasioned the production of the *Registro* today makes my investigation and imaginative reflections possible. These images, arresting in their beauty, also carry the trace of this intended act of public shame as state punishment, where shame becomes another technique of biopolitical control.

Technologies of Capture

While the daguerreotype was first introduced in the 1830s, the advent of albumen prints, a thin paper photograph mounted onto thicker card stock, quickly overtook the daguerreotype by the mid-nineteenth century as the most widely used photographic technology owing to its less expensive production costs and its faster processing time. Popularized as cartes de visite (visiting cards) in France, these small, roughly two-by-five-inch photographs were readily adaptable to the interests of local state authorities. This period and the technological innovation it inaugurated see the increasing utility of photography, not only as a new tool in the state's arsenal of social control but as a new visual mode of racialized knowledge production.[5] In *La fotografía durante el imperio de Maximiliano* (Photography during the Maximilian empire), Arturo Aguilar Ochoa (1996) documents how during Maximilian's reign this new technology functioned as a form of political propaganda and statecraft; as a visual record of court dignitaries and celebrities; as a catalog of local monuments and landscapes; and as a way to visually render the national types, costumes, and traditions of Mexico. As a politician, appointed and anointed by Napoleon himself, Maximilian was an enthusiastic early adopter of the political potential of photography. Already quite attuned to the powers of this new image-making technology, before he arrived to Mexico in his new role as emperor, Maximilian circulated photographs of himself dressed in the finery of his Austrian admiral's uniform as a way to introduce himself to his new imperial subjects (Aguilar Ochoa 1996; Cortés Rocca 2005) (fig. 1.1). In fact, the photographs—celebrity postcards, if you will—of the newly appointed emperor went on sale in local bookstores just days after he accepted his post (Aguilar Ochoa 1996). Ironically, shortly after he was executed by firing squad in 1867, photographs of

FIG 1.1 ▸ Portrait of Maximilian I of Mexico, ca. 1864. Photograph by Andrew Burgess. Library of Congress digital ID cph.3a16880.

Maximilian's dead body laid out in a casket with knee-high military boots; of his bloody shirt and military jacket pierced by bullet holes; and of the firing squad itself, posed with their rifles, also went on sale by one of the leading photography studios in the city, as vistas históricas (historical vistas) (Aguilar Ochoa 1996, 46).[6]

The popularization of photography during the latter part of the nineteenth century enabled the growing circulation of photographs of Mexico and Mexican life throughout Europe and the United States, part of the genre of travel writing in which photographs came to replace lithographs of "popular types" as the visual referent of a far-away elsewhere that travelers could bring home. In his text, Aguilar Ochoa (1996) locates many of the contemporary stereotypes of Mexico and Mexicans in these early studio-staged portraits, where the quaint and picturesque are displayed alongside images of Mexico and its inhabitants as dirty, diseased, and primitive. The "tipos populares" (popular types) of Mexicans depicted included street vendors carrying oversized bundles of ceramic jarros; dark, barefoot men wearing traditional jorongos and sombreros; and dirty-faced young girls with babies wrapped in thread-bare rebozos peering suspiciously into the camera. In his book *Americans in the Treasure House: Travel to Porfirian Mexico and the Cultural Politics of Empire*, Jason Ruiz (2014, 45) notes that "the makers and users of photographic types thought they could make better sense of seemingly unknowable (and perhaps dangerous) populations by documenting exactly what someone of that type looked like." Photography as a project of knowledge production allowed unnamed individuals to stand in for national "types" and enabled the cataloging of raced, classed, and gendered types for both national and international audiences. As we will see as in the following chapter, photography proved an exceptional medium for teaching suspicious publics to identify sex workers as a "type" of human subject, identifying them through gestures like a raised skirt, locating them through an address or neighborhood or simply by the ways they occupied the space of the public. In much the same way that casta paintings had been used a century before, these photographs of tipos populares instructed viewers to identify and assign differential value to visual markers of racial and gendered difference. And while photography was extraordinarily effective at disseminating a generic "type" for the purpose of ethnographic categorization, the *Registro de mujeres públicas* used this technology to produce a much more precise correlation, indeed an indisputable correlation, between the image and the individual subject, at the level of the face.

In her pioneering work on this unique archive, "Subjectivities and Techniques of Control in Late Nineteenth-Century Mexico: Emperor Maximilian's 'Registro De Mujeres Públicas,'" Paola Cortés Rocca (2005, 214) credits the *Registro* with inaugurating "the relationship between photography and legal control in Latin America" and with providing one of the earliest glimpses into how the nascent technology of photographic capture was used as a system of surveillance intended to control racialized, classed, and gendered access to the space of the public. In thinking about how photography functioned in this early moment of institutionalization, she argues, "What the emergence of photography implies is a radical change in modes of production, reception and discursive circulation. Photography— as a practice, as a technique and as a mode of representation—is a new way to think of the relationship between the subject and the world, between subject and object, and between the thing and its representation" (221). Through photographic representation, the image indexes the name and the identity of the subject. This new photographic image is not just "any" body, however; this photograph attaches a name, a government name, to an image, and it fixes an identity—mujer pública—to that name. In the case of the *Registro*, the "thing" being represented by that identity is nothing less than aberrant female sexuality.

This indexical use of the photograph, and the individuation it performs, becomes foundational to the function of disciplinary power at the level of the "somatic singularity" of the body and to biopolitical power at the level of this newly constituted social category named mujer pública (Foucault 2006, 55). What we see happening at the level of the individual identity in the *Registro* demonstrates how the biopolitical does not displace disciplinary power but works alongside it, becoming increasingly more enmeshed through "concrete arrangements that would go to make up the great technology of power of the nineteenth century" (Foucault 1978, 140). But aside from becoming a visual modality of biopolitical state surveillance, these images also suggest so much of what photography was destined to become: a place to instantiate and mimic gendered conventions around portraiture and visual representation, a way to identify and codify racial categories through ethnographic documentation, a secure private medium for the salacious gazing upon those imagined as sexually available, and an aesthetic sphere intent on capturing the alluring appeal of female sexuality. As we will see in subsequent chapters, as photography developed as a medium, becoming increasingly more accessible to larger publics, each of these new visual modalities come to serve the biopolitical interests of sexual categorization, surveillance, regulation, and control. However, in this early moment of photographic reproduction, the aesthetic, the erotic, and the disciplinary gaze of biopolitical surveillance remained intertwined, destined to travel together.

While photographing criminals was starting to be used as part of policing practices elsewhere, the photographic conventions of the iconic mug shot, the visual pairing of the profile and the frontal closeup, was not yet established in 1865, having been introduced years later in France by Alphonse Bertillon in 1900. Therefore, neither Maximilian's new legislation nor the new technology offered specific guidelines for how these newly patented subjects were to appear in front of the lens of the Mexican state. Most of the photographs in the *Registro* are stylized as an expression of early photographic portraiture; they frequently deploy standing poses, generally with one hand resting on a pedestal or the back of a chair, or make use of painted backdrops in order to execute the desired aesthetic effect. In general, the expressions appear solemn and stiff, attesting to Victorian standards of propriety or the decided discomfort at being ordered to submit to the ordeal of being photographed for the state's archive of sexual deviance. But the photographs collected in the *Registro* are also quite diverse, emerging from a host of different photography studios operating in the city at that time. As a singular archival record, it depicts a wide range of poses, gestures, articulations of femininity, and silent acts of refusal.

Although photographs were starting to circulate in Mexico at this time, this nascent technology was still less than thirty years old and generally accessible to only the middle and upper classes. This steady stream of new state-mandated customers must have been seen as a boon for the photographers of the era, just learning to perfect their craft, even as it also occasioned the possibility for these working women to hold a photograph of their own likeness. Perhaps some of the sex workers of 1865 Mexico City had already seen a carte de visite of the beautifully styled Carlota, wife of Maximilian, and entered the photography studio wanting to be similarly exalted through this new technology of visual representation (fig. 1.2). However, I imagine more than a few of the women who registered their visage, who sat before these new boxes that seized light in order to render their likeness, had likely never even seen a photograph before, certainly not of themselves. Aside from the increasing flow of new customers, it is difficult to ascertain how these early photographers understood their role in facilitating the work of state surveillance. What we know is that at some point, each woman left the photography studio with a paper imprint of her image that would survive her, an image that would live in the archives of the newly forming Mexican state to finally end up here, under a new set of inquisitive eyes.

Aside from a photograph of her face, the other necessary component of this biopolitical *dispotif* was the production of state-authorized biography, truncated entries of what constituted a *puta* life, the scant details of a life lived under the watchful eye of the state. Like the photographic conventions of the period, slowly becoming established but unevenly executed, the requirements of state-authored criminal biography evidenced in this text were still in formation during this period. After assigning them a sequential patent number, the *Registro* recorded the name, age, address, place of origin, and profession in an embellished script, replete with misspellings and grammatical inconsistencies.[7] To each initial entry is added a record of each woman's movements, noting if she changed residences, joined or left a particular brothel, left the sex trade, took ill, died, or simply vanished. While these notations were intended to keep the women accountable and

FIG 1.2 ▸ Empress Carlota of Mexico, ca. 1864. Photograph by J. Malovich. Library of Congress digital ID cph.3a16881.

the registry current, these additional layers of biographical information are offered inconsistently. Most entries simply have the original biographical information recorded upon inscription in the *Registro*, while others have repeated lines of text indicating a change of residence or circumstance. In these penned biographical entries, the temporal markers that might indicate where one entry ends and another begins are often difficult to ascertain, only rarely offering dates. Mostly, an entry marking a new transition is perceived through textual clues or the visual suggestion of a slightly darker script on the page produced from a fresh dip of ink.

The image in figure 1.3 captures the layout of the *Registro* to illustrate how the individual entries appeared within the larger tome. As a page, it is as random as any others, filled with Dolores. Three of the six women are entered into the registry with a name that means sorrow, a name that appears almost as often as my own. Already in these images, we see that

Nº 289 Aislada **Dolores Barron** de Jalapa, 28 años sin [...]
en familia, vive en callejon de Sta. Clara casa [...]
tenece a la 3ª Clase. En 14 de M[...] devolvió el libro[...]
porque se retiró á vivir honradam.te con su familia [...]
fuente de Seguiano junto al Nº 1 y la Miseria

Abril 20 de 1865
Patente nº 38 expedida á **Ysabel Monrroy** que esta establecida en [...]
calle de Vanegas nº letra A con 2 mugeres de 2ª Clase. La sustituyó Ygn.ª [...]

1º **Dolores Martinez**, de Mexico, 24 años, [...]
ve en el callejon de los Mascarones ó del Bosque nº 4 por[...]
tenece á la 2ª Clase y Pat.te nº 38. En 11 de Mayo se paso á la[...]
Pat.te 15 f.º 20. En 27 de Mayo se separó y pasó á la 28. En 6 de Junio[...]
se fugó en el mismo día parió. En 14 de Junio se fué en el mismo[...]
día avuacion y Concepcion Moreno estaba encarga.ª de la casa. En[...]
[...] de Junio pasó á la Pat.te á la Martinez. En 16 de Ag.to avisó la[...]
Moreno q.e seguia con la casa. En 14 de Set.e entrego el librito[...]
por q.e se encargó de la casa de la Pat.te 2. En 6 de Oct.e se recogió[...]
la Pat.te 38 por su [...] muy [...] En 19 de Dic.e se le devolvió el libro á por[...]
que [...] la Pat.te 2. En 7 de En.º devuelve el librito p.r q.e es muy [...]
Abril volvió á la 28. pasó á la 21 En 27 de Oct.e pasó á la 39. En 11 de Marzo pasó á la 13. En 29 de [...]
en [...] marzo
Patente nº 39 expedida á **Jesus Miranda** que esta establecid[...]
la calle de Sta. Ysabel letra F. con una muger de 2ª Clase.
Nº 264 Se mudó á Orizes junto al 205. Devuelta la Pat.te p.r no tener muger. En 9/6

Rosa Mayer, de Puebla 18 años sin [...] vive[...]
dha. casa y pertenece á la 2ª Clase y dha. Patente 38
de Junio se separó y fué á la casa nº 5 de Lopez, ahora en los Pedil[...]
En 22 de Ag.to pasó á ser dilatada y vive en el C.º de la[...]
Nº 9 Se mudó á la 3ª calle Ancha nº 12 vivien.ª Nº 2.

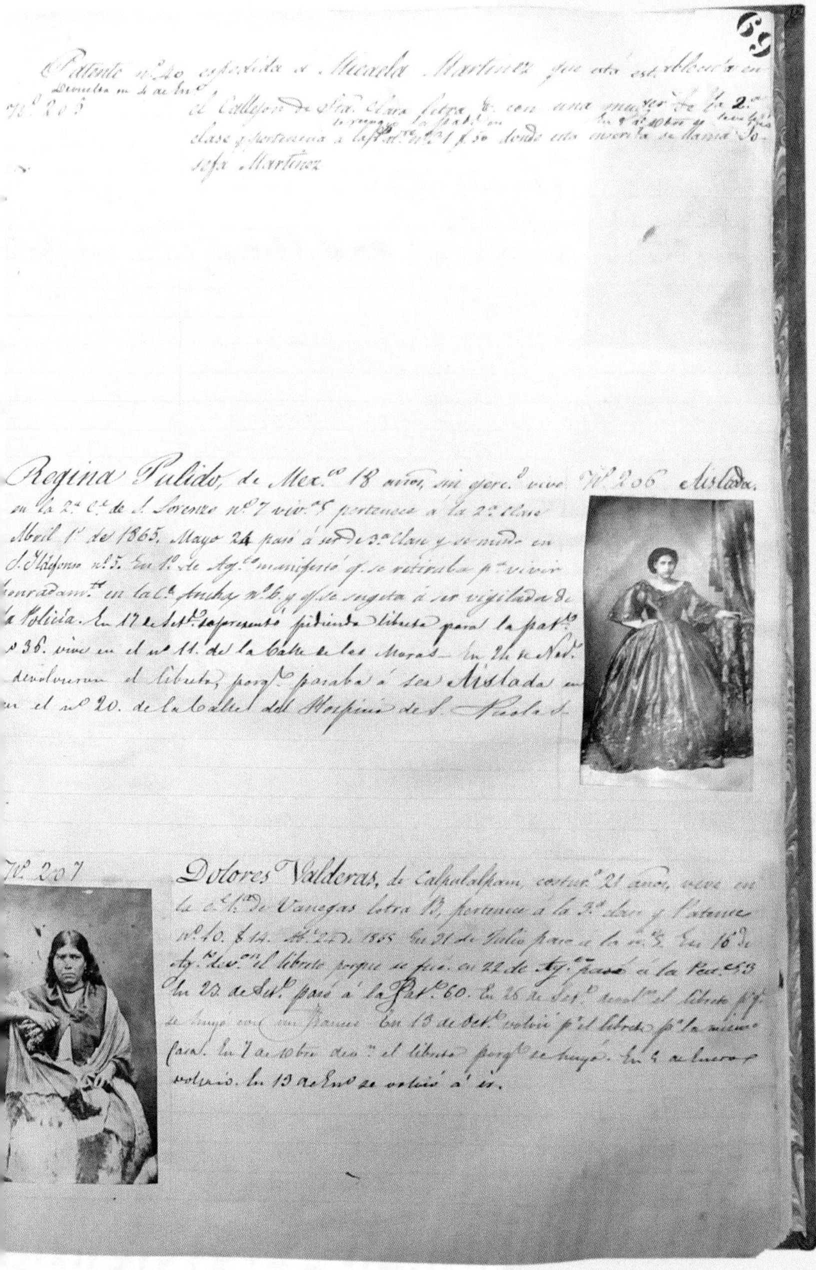

[handwritten manuscript entries in Spanish cursive, largely illegible]

Regina Pulido, de Mex.º 18 años...

No. 206

Dolores Valderas, de Cahualchpan, costur.ª 21 años...

No. 207

FIG 1.3 ▸ A spread from *Registro de mujeres públicas*, 1865.

Micaela Martinez, Patente No. 205, has disappeared. In the top-right corner, where her photograph should appear, we see the image lifted out of the archival record by whoever had the access, the audacity, or the means. The glue that had held the image in place has left a stain, and what was used to dissolve it has smeared the ink. The blank lines below the initial entry serve as the end of her visual imprisonment by the state. I imagine a public health worker or curious state official finding the *Registro* and recognizing the face of his wife, sister, mother, grandmother, or perhaps his treasured mistress, pressed within these pages. Curiously, while the photograph has been removed, her name and other identifying biographical markers are left undisturbed. Perhaps her liberator thought it was only the face of his beloved that needed rescue from the prison of criminal representation.

On the top left is Dolores Barron, twenty-five years old, Patente No. 202, a second-class worker "sin ejercicio, sin familia" (without a trade and without family); we learn that she has returned her passbook and retired to live honorably, "vivir honradamente." But deciphering the handwriting is maddening, and much of it appears riddled with spelling and grammatical errors. It appears to say that she will live "con un familia" (with a family), which, while grammatically awkward, could suggest simply "a family," not necessarily with *her* family. In either case, does living honorably become a euphemism for working as a live-in maid—honorable, because it is not public? How does the labor of the servant, the washerwoman, or the seamstress, the most common occupations described, function as honorable feminine labor precisely because it is invisible to the public? And how do we account for the unrecognized domestic labor of the daughter, the mother, the wife, or, more defenseless still, the widowed aunt, the orphaned niece, the cousin who has nowhere else to go? What kind of honor, or refuge from sexual or economic exploitation, did returning to family offer?

Below her is Dolores Martinez, twenty-four years old, Patente No. 203; this Dolores belongs to the third category of workers and has a much longer entry recorded in the *Registro*. Her story recounts her movements from one brothel to another, joining up with two other third-class women, and finally returning her passbook when she becomes responsible for her own house. But her narrative also recounts a series of departures; she leaves, she returns; she escapes, she reappears: "En 6 de junio, se fugó. En el mismo día pareció" (On the 6th of June she escaped. She appeared the same day). One of the details that stands out in this unusually long detailed entry, which describes the numerous ongoing series of movements between addresses and brothels, is that it makes mention of friends, twice. In fact, the entry ends with her living with "una amiga de la 2a clase" (a friend of the 2nd class). I wonder about the female friendships that must have developed among those women who worked sex in nineteenth-century Mexico, those who shared the space of a brothel, who lived and loved and worked within ear shot of each other's sexual labor.

As noted in these entries, in the *Registro* the women were divided into three categories. In some scholarly and journalistic accounts, it is reported that first-class sex workers, termed *mujeres de primera clase*, included those women who worked in residential districts and those associated with the era's elite as well as foreign women, including women from Germany, France, New Orleans, and Cuba, attesting to an already robust transnational flow of sexual migrants across the Americas. Second- and third-class women were those who worked in brothels and cantinas or worked on their own (Fregosa 2018). Upon encountering the *Registro*, this question of categoría was initially quite fascinating to me; I kept looking for ways visual or biographical characteristics associated with race, age, or class would map onto these categories of sexual laborers. As I peruse pages and pages of photographs, I pour over every detail of their outfits, looking for evidence of lace, buttons, jewelry, or ornate fabrics as evidence of class status. I stare at their noses, lips, and hair for racial markers. But the more I studied the actual images and biographies, the more these easy visual designations of category eluded me.

It turns out that many of the published versions attempting to account for categoría in the *Registro* were simply incorrect. In her essay "Burdeles modernos y mujeres públicas: El trabajo sexual en México," Mexican historian Guadalupe Ríos de la Torre (2008) disputes these more commonsense accounts of how categories were constructed. She determined that in this early moment, rather than being assigned a category, one had to pay for the privilege of a particular designation: ten pesos a month to be considered primera categoría (first category), four pesos a month for second class, and one peso a month for third-class status. The initial cost of registering also varied, costing twenty, ten, and four pesos.[8] In effect, selecting a category might have functioned as an aspirational claim, a strategy of selecting a category that might cost you more on a monthly basis but that might also allow you to charge more for your services. First-class workers were able to charge three pesos or more for a visit, second-class workers charged two pesos, and third-class workers charged even less. What remains unclear is how ideas of beauty, provenance, color, age, sexual experience, or sexual innocence might have been understood or remunerated in this early moment of sexual commodification.

FIG 1.4 ▸ Guadalupe Romero in *Registro de mujeres públicas*, 1865.

Let us look closer. Figure 1.4 is a photograph of Guadalupe Romero, Pat-ente No. 452, listed as belonging to the second class of sex workers, offering the camera just the slightest hint of a coquettish smile, posed lifting the hem of her elegantly voluminous dress just enough to offer a visual clue of her vocation. This demure gesture, so subtle as to perhaps be missed by contemporary conventions of coquetry, gets repeated several times across the photographs collected in the archive, but no one else does it with quite the same easy aplomb as Guadalupe. I imagine her getting dressed to visit the photographer's studio, selecting a preferred garment, ensuring that each ac-cessory—the droplet earrings, the beaded choker, the dark netted gloves— was perfectly presented. But surely, it was the photographer who suggested the three-quarter turn, the raised skirt, the gloved hand resting on her chin that makes her appear as if she is contemplating her options. Beautiful, youthful, and dressed to impress, what options did Guadalupe have to con-sider? Perhaps these studio photographers saw the portraits they produced as an early form of advertising—using the image to market and promote an available commodity. But just what kind of commodity did these images represent? Was Guadalupe's dulcet face the face of syphilis, of Mexico, of carnal delights, of sexual desire, or of errant female sexuality needing state regulation?

In another photograph (fig. 1.5) is Carlota Yengst, Patente No. 7. Originally from Germany, she seems quite at ease seated in front of the black box of capture. Carlota is positioned in front of a backdrop that manages to convey elements of both the cosmopolitan and the pastoral. Dressed in a hoop skirt of the period, she is staring directly into the camera, her arm resting gently on the back of a chair, posed wearing petite dangling earrings and what appears to be a cameo broach. There is little in the photograph suggesting that she is anything other than a proper Victorian woman or that this image is anything other than what would become a standard portrait photograph. Carlota Yengst's short biography tells us she is originally from Germany, a seamstress, and belongs to the second category of sex workers. It also reports that she has changed brothels at least three times and is now returning her passbook and headed off to France. In the *Registro*, her age is recorded as twenty-four. Curiously, this is one of numerous Carlotas, the name of Maximilian's wife, in the archive. Perhaps then, as now, sex workers took the names of celebrities to add a certain appeal or cache to their brand or as a way to rewrite their own biographical connections to family, the state, or tragedy. How might naming itself have implied a technique of evasion, fugitivity, and freedom from the vice grip of biopolitical capture?

In contrast, another second-class worker, Juana María de Jesús, Patente No. 435, appears more Indigenous and not particularly well heeled and is posed wrapped in a rebozo, that ubiquitous garment of traditional Mexican womanhood (fig. 1.6). Nothing in her outfit suggests any semblance of luxury, and the photographer seems to have expended little energy in constructing the image; there are no backdrops or props, and seemingly little direction about how to sit or engage the camera. As a photograph, it is poorly framed and haphazardly cut. Juana María, my tocaya, my namesake, looks sad, anxious, and unsure of the weaponized instrument of the colonial gaze pointed directly at her. Her right hand is pressed against her lap, long fingers spread wide, keeping her steady. While one foot is planted firmly on the ground below her, under the folds of her skirt we glimpse her other foot stretching out, ready to dart. Her short biography tells us that she is from Oaxaca, twenty-six years old, a washerwoman, and was originally registered as belonging to the second category of workers. On October 2, 1865, she went to the hospital, and she left five months later, on

FIG 1.5 ▸ Carlota Yengst in *Registro de mujeres públicas,* 1865.

FIG 1.6 ▸ Juana María de Jesús in *Registro de mujeres públicas,* 1865.

March 22. It is at this point, once the brothel she works at closes, that her status changes to third-class sex worker.

What do these details reveal and conceal about these women's lives? Initially Carlota's European provenance and stern composure resisted my curiosity, but the detail of her age and category returned my attention. What must have it been like to cross the Atlantic as a young woman, to travel from Germany to Mexico to work sex, only to cross back again to try another country closer to home? Did Carlota cross the Atlantic alone, and if so, what kinds of protection from casual lechery or moralistic judgment might the lavish details of her costume have offered her? Was she an immigrant to Mexico who stumbled into sex work, or did she board a boat—bound for adventure—and see sexual labor as the price of the ticket? What might have prompted her to change brothels three times, and how might that detail be connected to her categorization as second class? If Carlota's life seems ripe for intrigue, Juana María's seems heavy with the embodied burdens of history lived by poor Indigenous and mestiza women who migrated to urban centers hoping for more than what they left behind. The misfortunes of her life—a hospital stay, being cast out of the slim protection of a brothel to work the streets on her own—are summarized in a few short lines. What kinds of disappointments and tragedies constituted *her* life before her entry into the *Registro*? How does the mournfulness of her face, captured in this one moment in time, get projected back onto the arc of her life? Did Juana María also dream of adventure and freedom? Did my tocaya taste joy?

Archival Encounters

The truth is I didn't know what I was looking for when I visited the archive to linger on the faces of the women imprisoned there. What kind of meaning was I trying to craft from the snippets of their stories? What kinds of social, cultural, or sexual codes was I trying to decipher from the images collected there? The archive is a kind of puzzle in which any piece connects you to another but also directs your gaze in a particular direction. I begin to notice the gestures that were repeated for the camera, lifting the skirt, resting the chin on a delicately gloved fist, pulling on slender braids. And I take note of the women, like this other Carlota, who rebuffs the camera's gaze, women who refuse to look back (fig. 1.7). Carlota is not the only one who refuses. But as an author, what am I to do with these details of convention or defiance? What to make of the painterly beauty of her hands, cradling her fingers in the dark, shadowy recesses of her palm? Even if I dive deeper into the dead traces of each woman's life, rummage through the state-seized details of her existence in the fragmented interlocking historical records that might surround her, what would I learn about Carlota's wounds and wishes, and what secrets would remain out of sight?

As I read these short biographical accounts, stripped of social relations or other facets of their lives, I begin taking a special interest in how these women exit the archive, that moment that records the last known trace of them. Scattered across the entries, I find the phrases "se fugó," "se escapó" (she escaped), or simply "desapareció"—she disappeared. My favorite of these entries comes from the wayward refusal of Leonarda Almeida from Durango, whose biography reads: "devolvieron el libreto por insufrirle, y no quiere estar en ninguna parte" (she returned the booklet because she was insufferable and didn't want to be anywhere). Here, marked most clearly,

FIG 1.7 ▸ Carlota Trujillo in *Registro de mujeres públicas*, 1865.

is her desire to elude capture, to refuse the options available to her, to escape the archive, to be a fugitive from history. In the photograph in figure 1.8 is Juana Rivera, Patente No. 143, whose entry reads, "Juana Rivera, de Cordova, 20 years old, seamstress, lives on Callejon de Dolores, no. 7 and belongs to the second class." On April 22, it states that she returned her booklet because she was leaving the profession and the police department is advised to keep her under surveillance ("mandase vigilar"). Juana Rivera was being kept under surveillance to ensure that she was not continuing to profit from her own sexual labor while trying to evade these new systems of control. There is little in this photograph to suggest the motivation behind its production, except perhaps her look of resigned irritation at having to comply with the new labor practices of her profession, or her determined discomfort at having to live her sexual life within the public pages of the state's registry. Each exit in the *Registro* is a story waiting to be completed: Zenora Gonzales, Patente No. 299, "devolvieron el libreto por estar en la cárcel" (returned her passbook because she was in jail); Maria Camargo,

FIG 1.8 ▸ Juana Rivera in *Registro de mujeres públicas,* 1865.

FIG 1.9 ▸ Juana Portillo in *Registro de mujeres públicas,* 1865.

Patente No. 345, sixteen years old, was apprehended and then left again, owing ten pesos; Angela Sosa, Patente No. 262, simply died.

There is also Juana Portillo, Patente No. 326, twenty-five years old, from San Luis Potosí (fig. 1.9). She is registered in the book as belonging to the third class of sex workers. There is something both unperturbed and fully on guard in her posture as she leans against the column, almost gripping the corner. Her head rests on her hand and she stares directly at us. Her gaze is both unsmiling and unflinching, and there is something almost accusatory in her piercing eyes. I wonder about the exchange with the photographer that might have produced such a venomous stare. Her outfit is neither demure nor extravagant; her shoulders are bare. If she entered the studio with a rebozo, it has since been removed, perhaps thrown over the pedestal where she rests. The accompanying biographical entry notes considerable movement between addresses, but at one point, she leaves the brothel and becomes "Aislada." This word is written here and throughout the *Registro* with a more intentional precision. When it is written, it is always capitalized; the ink is darker and the letters are perfectly situated between the thin blue lines. *Aislada*, the translation of the word, means isolated. Within the context of this public health registry, *Aislada* was the term used for streetwalkers, those who worked outside the security of a brothel, who worked isolated from forms of social protection. As the entry continues, we learn that Juana finds another home and becomes a second-class sex worker before entering the hospital. She manages to go home after that initial stay, but on June 26, the date of the last entry, she goes back to the hospital, and that is all the state wrote. There is something uncanny about my encounters with these Juanas, a connection across time and place crafted around a name. In total, I find nineteen Juanas and two Juana Marías in a book with slightly more than four hundred names; mis tocayas, my namesakes, those who share my very common, very nineteenth-century name.[9] And as you have no doubt noticed, somehow, I can't help but linger on their faces and their stories just a little bit longer, an identification and affinity born not of the state but through my own queer form of affective attachment.

Feeling Fugitivity

In their introduction to *Feeling Photography*, Elspeth Brown and Thy Phu (2014, 19) acknowledge that studies of image making that have emphasized representation and the disciplinary construction of meaning have "generally been less instructive . . . in providing a full account of alterity." Instead, they suggest that a "focus on feeling allows photo scholars a rich theoretical terrain to reimagine the complex relationship between images, power, and subjects" (21). Unsurprisingly, this unique photographic archive, so thoroughly implicated in the forces of state surveillance and biopolitical control, inspires contradictory feelings. There is the ethical weight of searching for possibility and pleasure in a tome created through coercion and state violence, the haptic transmission that carries the trace of so much harm done in the name of state interests, but there is also the desire to know these subjects—to imagine the fullness of their lives, the sensuous details of their quotidian existence that exceeded their momentary presence in the archives of the state. I wonder if perhaps everything I don't know about the lives behind the faces depicted in the *Registro* is precisely what draws me to these images.

In describing the regulatory function of photo IDs, Campt (2017, 32–33) writes, "The fugitivity of these quiet images . . . lies in the creation of new possibilities for living lives that refused a regulatory regime from which they could not be removed." Here, Campt names my desire as a feminist Latina scholar to recover these women and their stories from the archive, but her words also convey my fugitive hopes as a contemporary puta, looking for vestiges of myself in the biopolitical archives of the state. My yearning to look for "the creation of new possibilities for living" in the names and faces of another era bears its own weight of futility, wrapped in the allure of promise. Within the pages of the *Registro*, I find another figure that sparks my queer imagination, a name and a face that appears just a bit different from the Juanas, Doloreses, and Carlotas we have seen so far. Their name is Félix (fig. 1.10).

Félix Rojas is seventeen years old and is from San Luis Potosí; they are identified as belonging to the third class of sex workers. Their deeply brown face with chiseled features is seen looking sternly forward, one hand on their hip, the other resting in the folds of their skirt. The presence of this masculine name and what appears to me as a masculine face within this volume presents a bit of a quandary. Having to account for what I think I see requires another more concerted kind of looking, reading gender norms and their departures through gestures, aesthetics, and modes of self-expression. How might Félix's Indigenous features influence how I might perceive their gender, or, equally relevant, how might indigeneity influence how gender is understood or signaled stylistically? Yet even this line of thinking is predicated on an unverifiable set of assumptions; even as I might "read" indigeneity in their face, there is nothing in the biographical account that suggests any identification with any of the numerous Indigenous groups in Mexico. Moreover, there are several women in the *Registro* who also "appear" quite Indigenous without exuding this kind of queer gender presentation. I stare more closely. I notice the way the hair is pulled straight back into a low netted bun, not parted like the other women, producing a more severe look that mimics more masculine fashions of the era. Similarly, the shirt appears almost military in its styling, the plain double velvet stripes devoid of adornment; the hand on the hip seems particularly assertive in this seated position. Although there is no evidence of earrings, they are wearing jewelry, a very plain white beaded necklace. And there is the name, Félix. Yet nothing in the short bio offers anything suggesting Félix is different from the other women in the book.

My imagination cycles through interpretive possibilities for the queer feelings this photograph and this name evince. I wonder who Félix might have been, how they might have lived, and how they might have loved.

FIG 1.10 ▸ Félix Rojas in *Registro de mujeres públicas*, 1865.

I wonder if they are simply one of numerous masculine women who work sex to avoid marriage, to live and labor alongside their female lovers, or to savor the economic independence that sex work might afford. As I continue to stare at this photograph of Félix, my eyes settle on the stain, the punctum, the open wound where the surface of the photograph has been scratched away. Their wide, dark hand rests gently next to that spot, touching it tenderly. I, too, wish to touch the open wounds these archives pry open, to lovingly tend for the lives held within these bounded pages. In the end, I am glad for everything the archive has omitted, all the details that are left out of the deadening paper trails of history. In their absence, the possibilities for puta life in mid-nineteenth-century Mexico City float off the page and into the haze of an imagined queer futurity that might allow Félix and all the faces in the *Registro* to escape the vice grip of representation, to become fugitive traces of the images left behind, to know care.

Biopolitical Publics, Puta Poetics

Engagement with the biopolitical returns us to bios, to life, puta life. Biopolitical power does not just enumerate existing publics; it produces them—publics that need to be named, contained, quantified, controlled, quarantined, kept under surveillance; publics that need to be authorized and authored. That the lives captured by the bureaucratic snare of state machinations were female and poor, that they had traveled to the city from the provinces at home and abroad, already excised from any shelter of family and community, suggests how biopolitical forms of public control are unevenly executed, wholly dependent on existing vulnerabilities predicated on race, class, gender, ability, age, and social status. While obvious, it bears noting that it was not the invading army of foreign soldiers who were required to be registered with the state; the sexual lives of the state functionaries, including the police, were not the ones being interrogated, surveilled, or recorded. Maximilian's own encounters with "the pox" were allowed to remain out of the official public record, consigned then, as now, to the ephemeral archives of rumor. It is always and only the perceived vices of the vulnerable that are punished. The *Registro* records when these women became sick, when they went to prison, when they became fugitives; it conveys all the ways they died young and tells us about the heartbreak of their lives, but it also normalizes the inequities of race, class, and gender, making these appear inevitable and preordained. We know their futures could have been different.

While the entries in this inaugural Mexico City registry ended a few short years later in 1867 after Maximilian was executed by the military forces of Benito Juárez, its impact continued to resonate throughout the region. Soon, similar registries started to appear elsewhere in Mexico and the rest of Latin America. These include fifteen volumes of *Registro de la Sección Suntuaria para el ejercicio de la prostitución* (Register of the Sumptuary Section for the practice of prostitution), held in the municipal archives of Puebla, Mexico, dated from 1872 to 1927 (Damián Guillén et al. 2010).[10] It seems that by 1872, local authorities in nearby Puebla had elected to skip the euphemisms and simply label these women as prostitutes, punishing them by using sumptuary laws designed "to restrict excessive personal expenditures in the interest of preventing extravagance and luxury."[11] Sumptuary laws were used to require sex workers to dress in accordance with their "social station" in order to prohibit them from wearing items associated with "respectable" women. A fashionable woman, not known to have a wealthy husband or father paying for her silks, satins, and pearls, served as a dangerous *visual* enticement to "decent" women and therefore had to be publicly punished. That the registries in Puebla were authorized through sumptuary laws rather than addressed through the discourse of public health makes apparent how maintaining social control and existing social hierarchies were behind the regulation of sexual labor all along. But it also provides further evidence of the role of the visual in the construction of stigma that surrounds puta life.

The photographs of the registry in Puebla are not that stylistically different; however, the biographical information recorded starts to be much more racially coded. The records start to specifically list not just name, age, country of origin, and current address but specific information under the term *filiaciones*, which evokes hereditary or filial relations—height, hair color, skin color, complexion, nose, eyes, mouth. Frequently used options for color include *moreno*, *claro*, and *rosado* (brown, light, pink); options for noses include *regular*, *grande*, and *aguileña* (regular, big, fine). These terms hint at race while appearing more descriptive than categorical, even as they also perform an insistence on assigning significance to phenotypical differences. It is important to note that the types of specifically racialized terms that had formed part of the racial logics of the seventeenth and eighteenth centuries—terms such as *mestiza*, *india*, *castizo*, *negra*, *mulata*, and *blanca*— are not used in this archive.[12] The official discourse of the new independent

Mexican state would reject the legal racial classifications of colonial Spain, even as they remained determined to reproduce the racial hierarchies that Spain's own anxieties around the purity of blood lines had installed. Because even as the details are recorded on the level of the individual, the effect is about amassing information on the level of the body politic. The team of contemporary Mexican researchers working on these fifteen volumes also noted something else; it seems that at some later historical moment, several of the images became vandalized. Words intended to belittle and insult start to appear scratched across the faces of those confined to the pages of this public record—"lo mama" (she sucks it); "mamadora" (sucker); "da el chiquito" ("gives the little one," i.e., anal); and, of course, the word *puta*.[13]

The inauguration of the *Registro de mujeres públicas* produced those who exchange sex for money as a social category available to regulate, control, profit from, and abuse. That these faces of youthful vulnerability, of hopeful promises and dashed dreams, of quiet resignation and bold stares of refusal would inspire this discursive venom is indicative of the public scorn leveled at those whose labor is sex. It is not that these phrases or insinuations are untrue—no doubt these women did suck it; no doubt many did perform anal sex, and indeed, they were putas, women who exchanged sexual services for money. The violence here is not about naming these sexual acts; the violence is in how these words get scratched across their faces, used to define the sum of their lives, intended to shame and ridicule them, intended to make them less than fully human.

Las Horizontales

In predictable Foucauldian fashion, the *Registro* and the other similar registries that followed constructed more than an archive of recorded state subjugation; it also served to produce these mujeres públicas as potential agents of collective social action. Bound together in these books of state capture, they became bound together as political subjects, sharing similar and different obstacles and challenges as they navigated the new regulations and social attitudes intended to control their lives and their labor. Therefore, let me end this chapter by offering a glimpse of the kind of puta potential that was emerging just a few years and a few miles away.

In 1888 in Havana, Cuba, there existed a briefly lived political party of sex workers, a party with an official newspaper titled *La Cebolla* (The onion); they called themselves las horizontales. As the century drew to a close,

Havana, like Mexico City, was a bustling metropolis, central to transnational empire and commerce and full of sex workers from Cuba's interior provinces but also from Spain, Venezuela, Mexico, Puerto Rico, and the Canary Islands.[14] Here, perhaps for the first time in the Americas, sex workers spoke with a collective voice to demand the right to work freely without extortion, violence, and state control; to demand that their personhood and their labor be respected. And in the pages of *La Cebolla*, these mujeres públicas made their grievances against the state public.[15]

The first editorial in the inaugural issue of *La Cebolla: Órgano Oficial del Partido de Su Nombre* (Official organ of the party of the same name), dated September 1888, declared:

> Ha llegado el momento de que no toleremos con nuestro silencio esas multas injustas que se nos impone, unas veces porque no queremos ceder a los caprichos lujurioso de un polizonte y otras porque no le aflojamos el dinero que nos pide. Ya los tiempos ominosos de aguanta y calla pasaron para no volver. (Quoted in Barcia Zequeira 1993, 12–13)

> [The time has come for us to not tolerate with our silence those unjust fines imposed on us, sometimes because we do not want to give in to the lustful whims of the police, other times because we do not loosen the money he asks us for. Already the ominous time of take it and shut up has passed, not to return.]

In Cuba, as in Mexico, sex workers had grown tired of having to pay the state's bureaucratic fees; they were fed up with unjust fines, and they refused to keep quiet about the forms of sexual and economic extortion and exploitation they had to endure at the hands of police and state officials.[16] Then, as now, sex workers refused the expectations that they just take it and shut up. Rather than seeing themselves as stigmatized criminals, las horizontales viewed themselves through the lens of the growing labor, anti-colonial, and antislavery movements on the island, understanding themselves as an exploited work force. They argued that they were already paying more to the state than what would be required of any eligible voter and yet remained disenfranchised. The editorial continues,

> Y sin embargo, aunque contribuímos más que las otras clases a nutrir los fondos del Erario con el sudor de nuestras . . . frentes, se nos trata como si fuéramos esclavas, como si estuviésemos fuera de la Ley. Es decir, se nos considera ciudadanas para cumplir deberes, pero no para gozar derechos. (Reineri Gimeno 1888)

[Nevertheless, even though we contribute more than other classes to nourish the funds of the Treasury with the sweat of our . . . brows, we are treated as if we were slaves, as if we were outside the Law. In other words, we are considered citizens in order to fulfill obligations, but not to enjoy rights.]

Framed within the circulating discourse of workers' rights, the anti-slavery movement, and a nascent female suffragette discourse, these audacious women were claiming for themselves the rights of citizenship, as an exploited and disenfranchised class of workers who contribute to the coffers of the state.[17]

There is another aspect of this short-lived newspaper that bears mentioning, about another vilified sexual public in formation: queers. Although only four short issues of La Cebolla were published, there are two references to homosexuality within its pages affirming the ways queerness and sex work have always been bound together through the regulation of sexuality. The first reference is in an article titled simply "Los maricones" (The faggots). There, the author, La Conga, describes the number of homosexuals working sex on the streets of Havana, saying, "No queremos . . . que se suprima a estos individuos; sí, que no se toleran sus vicios en asociación, ni menos en explotación" (We do not want these individuals to be suppressed; if their vices of association are not tolerated, neither should their exploitation) (quoted in Barcia Zequeira 1993, 14).[18] But it is the second reference, a poem written by La Madrileña, that warms my queer heart.

La gachí que yo camelo
si el Arcalde la multara
Le cortaba el tragadero
Aunque a Ceuta me mandaran (no. 2, p. 4)
(quoted in Calvo Peña 2005, 26)

[The girl that I desire
If the Mayor fines her
I will cut his throat
Even if they send me to Ceuta]

Written laced with the caló of the Roma of Andalusia (even as it was authored by someone nicknamed La Madrileña), this lesbian love poem makes clear that unjust fines and the extortion leveled against sex workers would not be tolerated, even if the price was deportation to Spain's noto-

FIG 1.11 ▸ "La Madrileña," *La Cebolla*, September 23, 1888. Unknown artist.

rious colonial prison in Ceuta. The sentiment—La Madrileña will cut you if you mess with her girl—is one that resonates across the long arc of queer lives, recounting both a history of lesbian relationships among sex workers and the ferocity that queer love inspires.

One more detail of this unique, short-lived, and queerly fanciful newspaper merits attention: each issue featured a drawing of one of the women, an image that would put a face onto this category of sexual labor that was meant to be ashamed and unseen. This is La Madrileña, lover of her gachí (fig. 1.11).

Through these registries, sex workers had been "born linked to the public," conjoined to both the market and the police, defined as mujeres públicas, condemned to live their sexual lives under the gaze of civic scrutiny. Now, these women were not just women who exchanged sex for wages; they were mujeres públicas—identified, categorized, and registered with the state for all to see. In the pages of *La Cebolla*, they refused to remain quiet and elected to stare back, becoming public through the vehicle of their published words and their images, becoming visible as mujeres públicas who demanded representation, respect, and so much more.

All museums are sex museums.
JENNIFER TYBURCZY

COLONIAL ECHOES AND AESTHETIC ALLURE

Tracking the Genres of Puta Life

Sex workers are everywhere in the archives of photography, implicated in almost every genre that would come to be associated with this new technology. We see them in the state archives of criminality, the urban landscapes of street photography, the ethnographic depictions of places near and far, the abstracted nudes of fine art, the edifying accounts of photojournalism, the tourist's postcard, the glamour shots of advertising, and the low-brow genre that would become pornography. The distinctions between these genres, blurry from the start, would twist together as this new technology became more popularized. If the previous chapter looked to the archives of the state for photographs of real sex workers trying to live their lives in the shadow of a burgeoning biopolitical machine, this chapter is concerned less with the real and more with the phantasmatic projections of puta life that photography circulated globally. It brings together an eclectic range of photographers who would come to be identified with this technology as it evolved from the nineteenth into the twenty-first century. In the process, it peers into the colonial motifs, gendered conventions, and ethnic stereotypes that cling to the figure of the puta as she travels across continents and centuries.

By taking our attention away from those in front of the camera, it asks us to contemplate the position of those who would produce the images of puta life that surround us, to consider the social relations that emerge between photographer and subject in the space between the lens and the light. It is the photographer who becomes entrusted to capture the sexual allure that attaches to the idea of puta, to crystallize the sexual magic they are rumored to possess or to document the tragedy that their sexual immorality is destined to ensure. In fine art, the sexual labor of the model is intentionally erased to create an image of ethereal and unsullied beauty. In street photography, the sex worker under a street lamp or peering out a door becomes just another ever-present part of an urban cosmopolitan landscape. Under the sign of ethnographic documentation or journalistic exposé, the photograph provides the visual evidence of the deviance that condemns the sex worker to her fate as stigmatized social outcast. This chapter uncovers the ways visual access and sexual access become collapsed through the anonymous erotic labor of the women who serve as the subjects of the photographer's intention. The circulation of these photographs of nameless women also introduces another element that would come to dominate the reception of photography: speculation.

Unlike fabulation, which actively infuses narrative with imagination and fantasy, speculation is founded in conjecture; we see something and suppose we know something. The etymological roots of spectator and speculation are conjoined in their emphasis on suppositive vision. The Latin root *spect*, meaning to see, forms the base of *spectator, spectacle, speculate*, and *spectacular* but is also buried in the words *inspect, suspect*, and *respect*, hinging vision to these processes of surveillance and the conferral of judgment. Speculation, suspicion, and the spectacular are core to how sex work enters the visual field. The figure of the puta is always already phantasmagoric; she enters any scene burdened and buoyed with the imaginative tropes that have constructed her person and her labor. It is the photograph that mediates our perception of both the real and the projections onto the real, a visual palimpsest, offering glimmers of all the previous impressions that have been cast onto puta life.

The traces of colonialism and slavery echo in circuitous ways across the visual archive of Latina sexuality, a haunting that moves from the Moors of northern Africa through Spain and Europe into the Americas, overlaying racial and sexual motifs that trace conquest and subjugation as the defining visual markers of both latinidad and sexual labor. Therefore, like sexuality, like photography itself, identifying latinidad similarly relies on speculation, ambiguity, and suspicion, revealing only "a desperate resistance to any reductive system" (Barthes 2010, 8). Rather than try to discern the identities of the nameless women unearthed in the archives of photography, rather than try to determine if they are Latina or indeed sex workers, this chapter explores the origins of the visual tropes that remain attached to the figure of the puta to consider how meaning becomes attached to "bodies, goods, ideas, and aesthetic practices in the visual sphere" (Fleetwood 2011, 20), to discover how puta gets yoked to latinidad.

Nude and Naked

The realism of photography must have been quite shocking to those who first glimpsed a flattening of the physical realm, a moment in time imprinted on paper that captured in exact detail the contours of a once small world. Visual claims of verisimilitude in painting were no match for the precise replication that photography offered. But photography's evidentiary claims to reality also complicated attempts to translate the aesthetic practices associated with painting onto this new mode of image making. Impacted most dramatically was painting's most revered subject, the female nude. In her essay "The Female Nude: Pornography, Art, and Sexuality," Lynda Nead (1990, 326) writes, "Within the history of art, the female nude is not simply one subject among others, one form among many, it is *the* subject, *the* form. It is a paradigm of Western high culture with its network of contingent values: civilization, edification, and aesthetic pleasure." Whereas in painting, models were able to performatively represent an aesthetic ideal, thereby masking any erotic motivation on the part of the artist or the spectator, in photography the veneer of lofty aesthetic intentions was set in crisis. The female nude, that figure of divine, unspoiled classical (i.e., European) feminine beauty so revered in painting, became immediately suspect. Even as artists' models have always been assumed to be women of ill repute, the realism of the photographic print becomes the material evidence that two bodies, not necessarily known to be bound by blood or marriage, shared a space in which one commanded a set of poses and positions and the other obliged. One, no doubt a young and beautiful female, took her clothes off and let another, no doubt male, not only stare but also document the shame that her nudity should have performed. What brought her to that space and that act—money, vanity, desire, or just

FIG 2.1 ▸ Félix Jacques Antoine Moulin, *Two Standing Female Nudes*, ca. 1850. Daguerreotype.

her willingness—functions as proof of her immorality. If before she could be imaged as nude, now she was simply revealed as naked.

The patriarchal "possession, power, and subordination" that Nead argues typifies the female nude was made evident in early photography but so too were the ways that both sexual and racial deviance were literally etched into the technology's emergence (Nead 1990, 326). Figure 2.1 is an 1850 daguerreotype by French photographer Félix Jacques Antoine Moulin (ca. 1800–1875), who opened a photography studio in Paris in 1849 and specialized in académies, or artists' studies, nudes deemed suitable for painting the human form. The image, *Two Standing Female Nudes*, would probably have been presented as one such pedagogically motivated study, intended to train aspiring painters how to reproduce the way light reflects off budding breasts, the ways pubic hair blends into the shadow between sturdy thighs, the delicate spacing between toes pressed solidly against the ground. We might imagine how a painter might transpose these two entwined, graceful female figures onto a scene of naked nymphs frolicking in a mythological past, their beauty, their sensuous contours, the loving tenderness of their bodies pressed together rendering them as otherworldly. Yet, as a photograph, the material presence of their bare bodies against the stark emptiness of the blank wall marks them as all too human. Standing naked before the photographer and before us, the spectators who have been invited into this private moment, we might be inspired not to speculate on the bounties of a prelapsarian past but to fantasize about the pleasures of the flesh, the rising heat of their lesbian caresses, moist with the scent of their youthful desires.

In his volume *Early Erotic Photography*, Serge Nazarieff (2002) documents that while intended to replicate the conventions of nudes in painting, these early photographs initially sparked outrage and alarm. Nazarieff tells the story of how the photographer Moulin earned a month in jail and a fine of 100 francs for producing "obscene images" like the one shown in figure 2.1. Yet what is most curious about this early moment of criminalization was that the person punished most severely was not the photographer but the collector: "Sieur Malacrida, optician by trade, and at whose home the police seized a great many images so obscene that even to pronounce the titles as listed in the order to remit the case would be to commit an indecency, is hereby sentenced to one year of prison and a fine of 200 francs" (quoted in Nazarieff 2002, 110). In this scenario, it is not only the sexual act depicted that becomes constructed as a lascivious sexual act, or even its production; rather, viewing itself is presented as an obscene act that must be regulated and controlled. During this time, when it cost more to purchase an erotic photograph than to secure the services of a sex worker, it was the one who wished to relish the all-too-human nature of these young bodies again and again who was labeled as the real deviant in need of public punishment and censure. Similar to the ways in which sex work will later become permitted only under conditions in which it can be controlled, in this early moment of pornographic production, visual representations of nudity needed to be policed in order to secure distinctions between the aesthetic values of high art and the corrupting depravity of pornography, to ensure that such images would remain available, not to collectors of smut but to collectors of art and more importantly to those authorized to determine that distinction. Such was the case with Moulin. Through a series of very concerted political actions, he was eventually able to redeem himself in the eyes of the law, able to successfully establish himself as an artist, not a pornographer, and receive legitimation for that designation. As an artist, he could vindicate himself and these images as bearing cultural value. The collector, on the other hand, could only be framed as lecherous and concupiscent.

Moulin's moral vindication was so successful that he would later be commissioned by the French government to produce images of colonial Algeria, eventually printing more than three hundred photographs, beginning ten years after the French occupation of Algeria in 1839 (Moulin 2014). Once there, in addition to photographing the landscape and architecture and producing a series of scènes et types, staged studio scenes documenting the queer cultural practices of France's new colonial acquisition, he found new opportunities for his interest in erotic photography. This time, however, his photographs of naked women in sexually suggestive poses were inoculated against moral censure not under the cover of art but under the colonial shield of modernist knowledge production. Moulin's carefully staged images of Bedouin dancing girls and harem life fueled the market for Orientalist fantasies of the colonial erotic. Now, his sexual desires could be projected onto Algerian Others, allowing his own deviance from purported French moral standards to be used as evidence of colonial supremacy.

Desires for visual depictions of the racialized sexual sumptuousness associated with the harem had already begun traveling in the world of painting under the sign odalisque, from the Turkish *odalik*, meaning chambermaid. By the eighteenth century, this term, and the visual conventions in which it trafficked, had become well established within the French and English art worlds as a way to name the outpouring of aesthetic depictions of erotic Orientalism. In her book *Multiple Wives, Multiple Pleasures: Representing the Harem, 1800–1875*, Joan DelPlato (2002, 182) traces British and French depictions of the harem to expose the visual and textual motifs undergirding Orientalist representations. The women represented in these images were certainly working sex, categorized and condemned as "immoral and oversexed," "exotic prostitutes," according to European logics. Since these women were already constructed as Other, and therefore deviant, the shift from painting to photography simply served to provide new irrefutable material evidence of the sexual depravity of colonial subjects, further justifying European occupation. The scopic availability of these women, evident in painting and now verified as "truth" through photography, performed her visual subjugation as a colonial subject, as it reinforced the dictate that colonial subjects were by definition also sexual subjects.

Malek Alloula's (1986) master work, *The Colonial Harem*, presents an extensive collection of early nineteenth-century erotic photographs of the

Muslim and Arab world that circulated as postcards, illustrating just how common and widespread this photographic genre would become. Alloula (1986, 4) elegantly articulates all the ways that the postcard becomes "a resounding defense of the colonial spirit in picture form," a genre of knowledge production that performs conquest and control through photographic capture. Alloula explains how the image of the Algerian woman depicted as trapped behind the veil, imprisoned within the harem, provided the visual evidence of the presumed sexual degeneracy and moral inferiority of these colonial subjects. Within these erotic images, intended for a male gaze, depictions suggesting lesbian sexuality appear all too frequently. Unlike images that depict a single female figure, photographs that show two conjoined female bodies simultaneously perform a presentation of "innocent" nonsexual female intimacy that the male viewer is allowed to surreptitiously glimpse and an invitation to fantasize about the perverse sexual acts that a male viewer might witness or join. In his book, Alloula devotes an entire chapter to what he terms Oriental Sapphism to underscore the harem's presumed polysexuality. The sex worker, the harem girl, the puta is imagined as devoid of her own sexual desires, constructed as always already polysexual and perverse, as available to perform whatever sexuality is desired of her, but always under patriarchal power and control.

Indeed, many of Moulin's erotically tinged photographs include the staged nonchalance of shared intimacy between women. An 1853 image, *L'odalisque et son esclave* (fig. 2.2), exemplifies many of the visual elements that would come to be associated with the aesthetic genre for which the image is named: a reclining nude positioned seductively to reveal herself to the viewer, an interior shot replete with opulent fabrics, here including a tiger skin that adds an additional element of primitive iconography, the odalisque's brazen and seductive gaze that performs her lascivious desires and makes clear her sexual availability, and a slave. The inclusion of the Black slave adds an additional and not unfamiliar element of both opulence and sexual excess to the image of the odalisque. Slavery had been officially abolished in France in 1794; therefore, the presence of the Black slave here serves as further evidence of French colonial moral superiority, allowing viewers to both linger on the perverse erotics of colonialism and slavery and use this as further evidence of French moral superiority.

Even as the odalisque is said to conjoin the category of the slave and the prostitute in the Western imaginary, in this photograph what is visually highlighted are the differences between these women and the categories of sexual labor they represent. While neither of these women is "white" in

FIG 2.2 ▸ Félix Jacques Antoine Moulin, *L'odalisque et son esclave,* ca. 1853. Daguerreotype. Courtesy of the Bibliothèque Nationale de France.

the European sense, the image reproduces a clear racial hierarchy that is immediately apparent, one that includes the unseen European man who is both the photographer and the imagined spectator. The figure on the right is visually positioned as the one we are intended to covet and desire. She appears relaxed, framed by the arc of white tulle-like fabric that wraps around her head and bare breasts, setting off the darkness of her nipples; her hand is raised to her face in a coquettish glance directed at the viewer. Unlike the fully clothed Black maid in Édouard Manet's 1863 painting *Olympia* seen standing in service, the Black woman in Moulin's photograph is also naked, hesitantly positioned on the divan, bracing herself for another kind of service.[1] The Black slave, naked except for a head covering and a simple beaded necklace, turns away from both the camera and her mistress; her shoulders are slumped, her body curved inward in a gesture that signals her subservience but also serves to register her shame. Even as the female slave might be imagined as secondary to the scene of seduction, her nakedness, her placement on the divan, her gesture of subservience, and the very fact of her status as a slave make clear that her services include her sexual labor. Here, the bare, intertwined, differently shaded legs of these two female figures add an additional layer of perverse possibilities through a visual performance of intimacy with blackness. In this scene, the Black woman's presence is sexualized *through* her subservience, reframing this as a scene of a queer, interracial, coerced, and therefore more titillating three-way erotic encounter with the unseen viewer.

Even as puta and slave are both about sexual availability and sexual labor, the erotics they inspire function on different registers of fantasy.[2] The puta needs to seduce, enchant, or trick her masculine client; she needs to be, if not beautiful, then charming and inviting. The status of the slave *as slave*, however, ensures her sexual availability, constructing any scene in which the slave appears as one available to sexual fantasies of coercion or rape. Viewers at this time might have already seen the spectacle of naked, Black flesh in the numerous daguerreotypes of US American slaves that would begin circulating in the 1850s as part of a campaign to establish Black inferiority through the visual language of scientific racism (Wallis 1996). The presence of the slave's mistress, another woman not white, not a slave, but also not quite free—and the visual absence of white masculinity function to both occlude and make possible the fantasy of Black female violation. This scene conjoins the visual tropes that will continue to be attached to putas in the decades to come: a visual availability that performs her sexual availability, her racialization as the exotic foreign Other desirous of colonial conquest, her sexual deviance from norms of monogamy and heterosexuality, and a perverse sexualization established through intimacy and proximity with blackness.

Storyville Stories

One of the most famous visual chroniclers dedicated to depicting sex workers in the spaces where they lived and worked died in relative obscurity; his photographic treasures were discovered decades later, locked in a forgotten desk. Ernest J. Bellocq (1873–1949), a commercial photographer of little distinction, is responsible for the visual archive of sex workers and their environs that would later be discovered by Lee Friedlander and come to be exhibited at the Museum of Modern Art (MOMA) in New York in the exhibit *E. J. Bellocq: Storyville Portraits*, Storyville being a legally established red-light district that existed in New Orleans from 1898 to 1917 (fig. 2.3). The

FIG 2.3 ▸ E. J. Bellocq, *Storyville Girl Posing Out of Doors*, ca. 1912.

history of this archive has its own peculiar narrative. Here we have a presumed private collection of low-brow erotic photographs that through the sepia-toned filter of time become reclassified as art worthy of the MOMA. The Storyville portraits, and the speculation that would develop around them, became an occasion for art patrons, historians, and concerned citizens of all political persuasions to linger on the spectacle of sexuality for sale in turn-of-the-century New Orleans. Here again, we see how attachments to the sexual exoticization of the foreign and a proximity to blackness wrap around the archive of sexual labor. In the process, these images and the conditions of their production and circulation reveal how categories of race and sexuality were fabricated in law, in memory, and on film.

Bellocq's photographs and Friedlander's exhibit inspired considerable attention and speculation when they were first made public.[3] We know that the glass plates that constituted Bellocq's private collection were probably produced around 1912, discovered by Lee Friedlander in 1958, purchased in 1966, and first exhibited in 1970 at MOMA. Most of the other photographs Bellocq is said to have taken, including those of New Orleans's Chinatown opium dens, have never surfaced. Part of the visual significance of the exhibit was that Friedlander, in his attempt to reproduce the kind of photographic image that might have circulated in 1912, reprinted the photographs using a practice popular during Bellocq's time, called the "printing out process," that exposed the plates to indirect sunlight for a period between three hours and seven days before being given a toning bath of gold chloride; it was these reprinted photographs that were eventually exhibited. The MOMA exhibit included thirty-four of the original eighty-nine eight-by-ten glass plates made by Bellocq and reprinted by Friedlander; in other words, the archive itself is incomplete, edited, and curated for public exhibition.

Little is known about Bellocq himself, save that he was born into a well-to-do French family in New Orleans and had an unusually large and pointed head, a physical characteristic that was commented on in almost every recorded account of his personhood. In assembling the MOMA exhibit and accompanying catalog, *Storyville Portraits: Photographs from the New Orleans Red-Light District, circa 1912*, edited by John Szarkowski, Friedlander included historical information about Storyville, interviews he conducted with people who had known the person of E. J. Bellocq, but very little about the women in the images. The impression that emerges from the scant bibliographical information we glean about Bellocq from these interviews is that he was a "funny looking little guy" who was "awfully hard to get to know. And of course nobody was that interested in knowing him" ("Johnny," quoted in Szarkowski 1970, 9).[4] It is perhaps unsurprising that Bellocq, teased and ridiculed throughout his childhood, came to find solace in the company of those who had likewise been judged harshly by society. Among those interviewed for the catalog was Adele, identified as "Adele, formerly of the District, subject of several Bellocq portraits" (8); she is the only person in the registry of informants interviewed listed without a last name. This is one of the rare moments in the archives of this period where sex workers are invited to talk about photographers, although sadly she doesn't really say much: "He always behaved nice. You know, polite" (quoted in Szarkowski 1970, 11). However, none of the photographs that Bellocq took and that Friedlander recovered, printed, and exhibited at MOMA identify any of the subjects; they all remain nameless, even Adele. In describing life in Storyville at the time, Adele comments that many other photographers, aside from Bellocq, were also taking "lots of, you know, dirty pictures" (quoted in Szarkowski 1970, 15). Pornographic images were often part of what was on display in brothels, exhibited to get a patron's blood flowing. But of Bellocq, Adele states, "I don't know if he ever wanted to do nothing but look" (quoted in Szarkowski 1970, 15).[5]

The Storyville portraits are quite stunning. While the vintage details of dress, environs, and styling create their own visual interest, the photo-

FIG 2.4 › E. J. Bellocq, *Storyville, New Orleans*, ca. 1912.

graphic printing process used by Friedlander—the frequently ragged edges of the photographic frame, the cracks and imperfections of the plates, the depth of detail produced by the long exposures—add their own captivating ethereal and haunting quality to the photographs (fig. 2.4). In describing the images, Friedlander states, "They did not involve new concepts, only an original sensibility" (quoted in Szarkowski 1970, 10). What is particularly unique about the Storyville collection is its stylistic range; not exactly pornographic, these portraits included a wide variety of poses of the women of Storyville. Many images featured relaxed or playful poses that were somewhat unusual for photographs produced with glass plates and long exposure times. These stylistic differences suggest two things. The first is that Bellocq seems to have spent quite a bit of time in the many brothels of Storyville, composing photographic images that would involve costume changes, elaborate props, and diverse poses. The second conclusion we might draw, given the stylistic variety, is that these were most likely collaborative productions in which the women were involved in how they would be captured on film, even as the original terms of each photograph's production remain unknown. Did the prints function as mementos for the women depicted or as advertising for potential clients? Were they produced in exchange for cash or copies of the images produced? Or was posing for Bellocq's camera just something fun to do between the demands of an otherwise routine day of work?

After the MOMA exhibit, Bellocq's photographs inspired countless popular and academic articles, books, films, and oral history projects intended to capture Storyville's storied past, a past that aligns with popular depictions of New Orleans as a place of sexual excess, racial ambiguity, corruption, and vice. In her book *Spectacular Wickedness: Sex, Race, and Memory in Storyville*, Emily Epstein Landau (2013) uses Storyville to investigate how racial ideologies informed understandings of sexual labor in turn-of-the-century New Orleans. Like Mexico City and Havana discussed in the previous chapter, at the beginning of the twentieth century, New Orleans, having already been both a French and a Spanish colony, became a cosmopolitan destination for immigrants from Europe, other regions of the southern United States, and the Caribbean basin, including those that would come to earn their money from selling sex.[6] Data from the 1910 census suggest that the foreign-born women in the tightly bound geographic space known as Storyville made up about 15 percent of the population and came from "places as exotic as Jamaica, Cuba, Algeria, and Arabia" (Foster 1990, 389).[7] Here, we also see the invocation of "Algeria and Arabia" functioning as racially ambiguous "foreign" categories that invigorate an associative relationship to the harem, positioned alongside and in relation to the foreign and colonial registers that the Caribbean locations of Jamaica and Cuba might inspire. But racial categories, then as now, are not always so clear, and latinidad has a long history of crossing, confusing, and circumventing the binary black and white categories that have come to define US racial logics. Far from home and with increased earnings at stake, for those that could, crafting ethnic origins that would register as exotic or racially risqué became a way to navigate, service, and perhaps even profit from the US racial caste system.

In her book, Landau recounts the life of Lulu White, one of Storyville's most storied madams, known as the "Diamond Queen," who specialized in "octoroon beauties" (fig. 2.5). At a time when miscegenation was still illegal and scandalous, part of what was being sold at her infamous Mahogany Hall brothel was an erotic journey across the color line. The marketing niche of Mahogany Hall was about "capitalizing on the transformation of 'octoroon' from a racial category to a sexual one," even as Landau (2013, 147) notes that all the women in Lulu White's booklet of available escorts "appear white."

In describing White's own life on the color line, Landau describes how even though White was born in Alabama to a "colored mother" and a white father, she told the 1900 census taker in New Orleans she was born in Ja-

FIG 2.5 ▸ Lulu White, also known as the "Diamond Queen,"
ca. 1890. Unknown photographer.

maica and was recorded as Black; she told the 1910 census taker she was
born in Alabama and was entered as "Mulatto"; and she convinced the 1920
census taker that she had been born in Cuba, had Spanish as a first language, and had emigrated just one year before and was subsequently recorded as being an Octoroon. As origin stories, different locations come to
correspond to different racial categories. However, in 1917 when the New
Orleans City Council moved to make the Storyville district all white, Lulu
White claimed in court that both of her parents "were Spanish people of
the Caucasian race" and had been, like herself, born in Cuba, arguing she
had only previously identified herself as an octoroon to increase her sexual
value. Lulu White's story and the ways in which she self-fashioned the racial identity of herself and her employees around the color line "allows us
to see that line for what it often was: blurry, ambiguous, false, and none-
theless, vigorously grasped and violently enforced" (Landau 2013, 134). In
this narrative, Cubanness functions as referencing both white "Spanish
people of the Caucasian race" and "not-white," sufficiently proximate to
blackness in order to benefit from an exoticism that relies precisely on racial ambiguity. For African American sex workers, claiming the foreign appeal of Cubanness became a way to distance themselves from a localized
past bound to narratives of slavery even as it ignored Cuba's own heinous
history of Black enslavement. But in exploiting the imagined racial uncertainty of Cuba as a means of navigating a racially segregated social order, it
also worked to further entrench a connection among latinidad, racial ambiguity, and sexual availability.

Al Rose's (1974) book *Storyville, New Orleans: Being an Authentic, Illustrated Account of the Notorious Red-Light District* includes several oral histories of the surviving women who worked in Storyville and provides a sense of how the exotic and erotic allure of "Cuba" formed part of the marketing of sex. In a recorded interview with Lola, a former resident of the district, she tells the interviewer that although born in the Dominican Republic, she was known to Storyville patrons and her madam as Cuban.[8] Lola describes having arrived in New Orleans in 1911 at the age of sixteen with her husband, who abandoned her within the year, and the interviewer reports that she still speaks English with a "very strong Latin-American accent" (Rose 1974, 163). Of her madam, May Spencer, Lola states, "She's Dago, you know. She's speak espanish, too. She's take me in her house in 1911. I coo'n't speak no Eenglish. She's treat me better that my mawther, May Spencer. People say she rooeen't me, May Spencer. She din' rooeen't me! I was puta at home before' I come dees country" (163). This interview, conducted in 1961 and published in 1974, attempts to reconstruct Lola's accent, textually performing her status as still "foreign" fifty years later, but it also reveals the way the Spanish term *puta* had already entered an English vernacular, needing no translation or italics; neither did the slur Dago, used against Italian immigrants. Selling sex is always about selling a fantasy. And the Storyville archive allows us to see how an imagined or real association with foreignness and blackness come to be comingled in the popular imaginary through the figure of the erotic, exotic, racially ambiguous puta.

Street Views

While Bellocq was experimenting with interior images and staged poses intended for his private consumption, others were using the advances in this new image technology to photograph foreign and forbidden worlds for public inspection, edification, and enjoyment. As the twentieth century inched forward, street photography, and its frequent companion travel photography, started to acquire greater prominence in visually shaping our perception of the world. And once again, images of sex workers were central to its proliferation. Street photography became the visual genre of the flaneur, the masculinist figure who strolls, seemingly detached from society yet able to serve as the acute observer, "as penetrator of the city's secrets" (Scott 2007, 119). Street photography presented distant people and places as queer and curious sights that could be consumed for pleasure, often quite directly, as picture postcards that could be sent home. But in documenting the very difference that makes them visually compelling for a particular audience, these images of intemperance also serve as a way to register the imagined cultural, social, and moral superiority of those visually positioned to render judgment.

Unlike images of female sexuality crafted in the studio or for private consumption, images of sex workers in street photography functioned to represent and visually extract something authentic and real. And unlike paid artists' models one might hire, photographing the women who worked the streets was "free"; their very presence in the space of the public made them visually available for capture. These supposedly candid images of women working the street position them as the natural inhabitants of cosmopolitan urban life, visually establishing the relationship between the sex worker and the street, making each constitutive of the other. Like empty cafés at dawn, spiraling smoke towers, and crowded markets, the image of the street walker in photography forms one of the recurring photographic motifs of urban life that would persist throughout the twentieth century and beyond. Assumed as part of the landscape of seedier neighborhoods that photographers could bring home to curious middle-class and elite publics, these images allowed viewers to take a visual walk on the wild side. In the process, these photographs produce a visual imprint of what a "public woman" might look like and offered viewing publics another socially acceptable way to ogle and speculate on images of aberrant female sexuality.

As the bon vivant traveler became transformed into the photojournalist, the witness, or the social reformer, the modernist project of social documentation in Moulin's era that equated the sexual availability, exoticism, and moral wickedness of "foreign" women with the French colonial occupation of the region was extended closer to home. Even as the occupants of destitute neighborhoods were not necessarily considered "foreign" to the mostly European, mostly male photographers who would become most closely associated with the genre known as street photography in the interwar era, the sights were intended to be—street urchins, drunkards, and women of the night; tenement homes, alleyways, and brothels. These were the parts of even familiar cities that remained outside the sight lines of the more respectable denizens who might come across these photographs in galleries, museums, books, and postcards. These "foreign" bodies, bodies made foreign in their contrast to standards of upper-crust European propriety, become rendered as curious and inviting even as they are judged inferior and disturbing—visually affirming certain bodies as sexually available for optical consumption, state intervention, and social condemnation.

One of the earliest photographers of urban life, Eùgene Atget (1857–1927), attempted to capture the sights of "old Paris" before they were lost to modernization. Along with the narrow alleys, the street carts, stairwells, and crumbling facades Atget photographed, he also used his large-format bellows camera to photograph sex workers.[9] His biographers report that he had been commissioned to photograph prostitutes for a book by the painter, illustrator, and collector of erotic art André Dignimont in 1921 (Musée d'Orsay, n.d.). That book was never completed, but its premise affirms the interest in using this emerging technology to visually document the presence of sex workers in the city, for purposes both erotic and ethnographic.[10] Atget, known primarily as a photographer of architecture and cityscapes, situates the presence of these women as an almost architectural feature of the urban landscape.

In the photograph in figure 2.6, the women themselves are not identified; instead, the photograph is named after the street on which it was taken, in this case, Rue Asselin, a street in the nineteenth arrondissement known for its brothels. Like Bellocq's seated figure in the window frame, these figures are positioned peering out from an interior blackness, a doorframe, a dark cavernous hole that symbolizes the mysteries of the flesh available within. Positioned at the door, at the threshold between the spaces of the domestic and the street, in these photographs sex workers both reproduce and transgress the fictional boundary between public and private sexuality. And similar to the Moulin photographs previously presented, in this image the women are seen touching each other, performing a gendered intimacy into which the male viewer (and potential client) is invited to enter. These figures stare directly at the viewer, boldly confronting the photographer's gaze and our own. Not intended to be pornographic per se, and not really "news," these photographs functioned as a form of "objective" social documentation, a visual means of showing an uninformed public what had previously been kept out of sight, even if eventually these images would be elevated to the status of art.[11]

A generation later, another French photographer, Henri Cartier-Bresson (1908–2004), would become emblematic of this new cadre of street photographers, one who set his sights on photographing the world and bringing home these images to an eager public. Technological advances in air travel meant that the lucky could now board a plane to see the streets of Paris, New York, Milan, or Havana, while photography allowed those less for-

FIG 2.6 ▸ Eugène Atget, *Rue Asselin*, 1924–25. Gelatin silver print. WikiCommons via the Getty Center.

tunate to partake in these adventures vicariously, from the safety of their homes.[12] The interwar period also coincides with "the visual turn of the news business," the rise of photojournalism, and large-format picture magazines in Europe, the United States, and Latin America (Wilson 2016; Brizuela and Roberts 2018).[13] While these publications frequently had a small cohort of staff photographers, they relied mostly on stringers, unnamed freelance photographers who worked on assignments and were sent out to supply images for the stories that editors deemed worthy. Therefore, Cartier-Bresson is significant for another reason as well: in 1947 he served as one of the original founding members of Magnum Photos, an independent cooperative of photographers who changed the game by insisting on retaining the copyright to the images they produced. This claim to ownership allowed photographers to repackage and resell the product of their labor to different magazines, thereby expanding their spheres of circulation along with their name recognition. But it also authorized their ability to exhibit and sell their photographs as fine art, helping inaugurate an era of celebrity photographers. Rather than work solely on assignments offered by newspapers and magazines, photographers now had greater ability to select and curate their own photographic subjects, using the medium not just to photograph what others wanted to document but to visually imprint their own image of the world and its significance.

Raised with considerable means that allowed him the freedom to travel, study, and explore unfettered by material obligations, by twenty-six, Henri Cartier-Bresson had already toured France, Spain, and Italy; spent time in colonial Côte d'Ivoire; and had his first photograph exhibited in a New York gallery. As a European man of privilege, he saw the world as his oyster, and his camera allowed him to slurp it up. Mexico City in the 1930s was a lively, bustling modern metropolis with enough cultural difference and mystique to attract tourists and adventurers from around the world. Cartier-Bresson arrived there having been commissioned to photograph the construction of the Pan-American Highway, but eventually his plans got side-tracked. The colorful story told by Magnum Photos is that after being robbed of his money, he met the African American poet and expatriot Langston Hughes, who declared that "Cartier-Bresson must move into his home and meet his artist friends . . . in la Candelaria de los Patos, a lawless hive of prostitutes, thieves and gangsters, a no-go area for the city police" (Magnum Photos 2017). These streets and their denizens would form the subjects of the photographs that would result in Cartier-Bresson's first major exhibit in 1935 in the Palacio de Bellas Artes in Mexico City, a joint exhibit alongside a contemporary artist, the Mexican photographer Manuel Álvarez Bravo.

Photography served as the perfect vocation for a well-to-do young man like Cartier-Bresson, a way to make the most of the sexual adventure, creative exploration, and opportunities that formed part of his coming-of-age narrative. In an interview that first appeared in the French newspaper *Le Monde* in 1991, he reflects back on that earlier period in Mexico, stating: "Mexico in 1934 was a great adventure. I had a woman friend in Mexico City and a girlfriend in Juchitan. The girlfriend was the girl we danced with. She was called Lupe Cervantes and spoke only Zapotec. The dancer's privilege was to be able to slide his arm under her blouse, that is to say onto her naked torso, and above all to be her only dance partner" (Guerrin 1993, 333). Here, the aging photographer looks back fondly on the sexual escapades of his youth, slumming it in exotic Mexico, where Zapotec is as common as Spanish. To declare that his money, his gender, and his European provenance shaped how he was able to live, travel, and work, that it allowed him the "dancer's privilege . . . to slide his arm under her blouse . . . onto her naked torso," would be to state the obvious. But the privilege that created that access also molded the images of women that he and others

FIG 2.7 ▸ Henri Cartier-Bresson, *Calle Cuauhtemoctzin, Mexico City*, 1934.
© Henri Cartier-Bresson | Magnum Photos. Image Reference PAR45838/W00003C.

would produce for an international audience hungry to consume the sensual delights of the foreign and the exotic, audiences eager to slide their eyes onto the naked flesh of a young Zapotec dancer.

Like Atget's image a generation earlier, the well-traveled image in figure 2.7 is titled not with the name of the women photographed but with the name of the street in Mexico City that remains synonymous with the flesh trade, Calle Cuauhtemoctzin.[14] This coded reference, known to people in the know, serves as a kind of analogue geo-tracking system, instructing viewers where exactly they could go to find these women, waiting by the window. When the photograph was first exhibited at the Palacio de Bellas Artes, the title and the image captured by this French bon vivant might have signaled something just a bit scandalous, a depiction of Mexican street life that brought the faces of these low-brow women into the palatial gallery of Mexico's most iconic cultural institution. Ensconced within the magisterial opulence of the Palacio de Bellas Artes, positioned in front of this image, the museum-going gentlemen and ladies of Mexico's cultural elite, both foreign and domestic, were given permission to stare. Bringing images of the street into the museum provided viewers the necessary context in which they could look, linger, study, judge, remember, fantasize, compare, identify, and indulge their fascination and curiosity with those women who promise sexual adventures worth paying for.

In making clear that this is a photograph of a certain class of urban denizens—prostitutes—it offers viewers visual and textual cues to anchor the meaning of the image. These photographs, and others like it, work to teach spectators how to "see" sex workers.[15] Jennifer Tyburczy (2016, 1) writes, "Sex has never been outside the scope of the museum's representational field, and the museum has always participated in the disciplining of sexuality that occurs in other sites (e.g., the prison, the school, the asylum), albeit differently." Positioned leaning out an open window, a window that is also a door, the women are framed by the wooden panels, which also frame the photograph itself. The women look out of the dark toward us, available to our scrutiny, while the photographer peers inside through the black hole of the photographic lens. The lens becomes a permeable membrane that allows these women to peer outside while remaining inside, offering a mysterious interiority intended to draw in and tempt the viewer's gaze.[16] While the woman on the right looks up in curious amusement, the one on the left seems to consciously refuse Cartier-Bresson's gaze, perhaps saving her coquettish expression for paying customers. More than the heavy powdered makeup, or the perfectly painted arched brows, what makes clear these women's profession, however, is something else altogether: it is their proximity to the gaze from the street, their availability to the photographer's probing eye, and the implied invitation, extended to us, the viewing public, to stare.

I wonder if these women ever got to see the painted faces of their *puta* lives gracing the walls of high culture at El Palacio de Bellas Artes. Might the young photographer have returned to Calle Cuauhtemoctzin where he found them to gift them a paper proof of their own faces? Perhaps these women, one or the other, stumbled onto this image years later in a book or article recounting the talent of the great photographer who once passed by. Were they incredulous, embarrassed, elated, or bemused that their faces, marked by the title that made their profession clear, would travel around the world? As the image circulates across histories and geographies, the significance of the street's name begins to lose its function as a referent for most of its viewers. Once the photograph leaves Mexico City, what the name of the photograph registers changes. Absent any biographical markers of race or origin, these women *could* perhaps be read as Spanish, Italian, perhaps even French, but they are not; the name of the location fixes them as existing outside a European imaginary. Now rather than a precise location with a storied history, the name signals an exotic foreignness through

FIG 2.8 ▸ Henri Cartier-Bresson, *Alicante, Spain*, 1933. © Henri Cartier-Bresson | Magnum Photos. Image Reference PAR45838/W00003C.

the use of the Spanish word *calle* but more so by the crush of consonants in the street's name, evoking an Indigenous otherness that exceeds European difference.

In contrast to images produced in the studio, the images "found" on the street remark on the theater of the everyday: the alleyways, street corners, and sidewalks serve as the stages where things happen—curious, unexpected, queer things, things worth photographing. However, the difference between the staged poses of the studio and the candid realism of urban life can sometimes prove deceiving. What would become another of Cartier-Bresson's widely circulated images, *Alicante, Spain*, produced in 1933 (fig. 2.8), suggests precisely the kind of visual serendipity that street photography seems to promise. Here, we see a jarring juxtaposition of differently raced, classed, and gendered bodies seemingly "caught in the act," all staring back at us from the space of the street. Although invested in his own narrative about "the decisive moment," in an interview Cartier-Bresson states that at times, he consciously intervened in the photographic composition, including in this photograph of "the madam, the maid and a homosexual" outside a brothel in southern Spain (Guerrin 1993, 334; Cartier-Bresson 2015).

In his response to a previous question about reconciling the surrealist aesthetic that he has long been associated with and the geometric elements that are also a frequent feature of his work, Cartier-Bresson states, "Geometry is recognition of a certain existing order. It is there, it's not something you impose" (Guerrin 1993, 333). As we linger on the composition of this image, the geometry of the existing order starts to become clear, an order that is marked most visibly through a reading of hair and style. The woman on the left not only wears a fashionable flowered dress; she is adorned with bracelets and earrings, and one perfect curl poised on the center of her forehead. The center male figure, dressed in a drab undershirt, nevertheless registers as impeccably groomed, his wavy hair elegantly streaked with gray and his eyebrows sculpted to perfection. Meanwhile, the Black female figure on the right wears a stained house apron covering a nondescript blouse, her hair an untamed dark mass. Identifying the maid, like the identification of the homosexual, is immediately apparent, and it becomes understood that the existing social order is one rooted in hierarchies of race, class, and sexuality.

That we might assume we can easily identify these three stock characters and the existing order they represent might be part of the visual trick Cartier-Bresson seems to be playing with in this photograph. The gestures and poses of the photograph converge in an odd kind of triangulation to queer the assumptions that we might bring to the image. Already established as the handmaiden of female style and aesthetics, the homosexual appears to be doing the Black woman's hair under the direction of the woman in the hat standing behind him who has one hand embedded in the waves of his hair as she hands over the tools of the hairdresser's trade. It is the seated Black woman who assumes the role of the one being served; her right hand rests in his palm, offering itself as it were, perhaps for a manicure. The graceful curve of her left hand on his shoulder performs the affected gesture of properly cultured femininity as it establishes the distance between them, intimate but still appropriate. The photograph confirms a hierarchy that is both about racialized sexuality and the ways that forms of public sexuality come to be associated with both sexual and racial difference. Here, too, the location performs its own queer gesture. The figure's blackness marks this scene of southern Spain with an additional layer of foreign exoticism, an exoticism entwined with Spain's centuries-long occupation by Moorish rule and its associations with New World colonialism. Furthermore, these intimate moments of grooming are taking place outdoors, in the bright outdoor light of the Alicante sun, against the concrete facade of a building, the bars on the window situating us, the viewer, outside in the street, even as the viewer is once again offered a glimpse of

FIG 2.9 ▸ Henri Cartier-Bresson, *Mexico City, Mexico*, 1934. © Henri Cartier-Bresson | Magnum Photos. Image Reference PAR45835/W0043DC.

the black interiority that awaits within. It is precisely their position within the space of the public, their public performance of private practices, and their willingness to stare back into the eye of the camera that make clear that these figures operate within their own understandings of public and private sexuality.[17]

A glance at Cartier-Bresson's early work in Mexico would not be complete without a brief mention of another widely circulated image, one that came to be known as the "Spider of Love" (fig. 2.9). Magnum Photos, which remains as invested in cultivating and preserving the stories that surround photographers as they are in marketing the images they produce, describes the "serendipity" surrounding the capture of this intimate scene of lesbian eroticism thusly: "Cartier-Bresson was at a local party with his new artist friends. The tequila flowed, but he remained sober. He left the party to explore the higher rooms of the building. In one room, the door ajar, he could hear two women making love" (Magnum Photos 2017). Here, the French traveler is described as fully embedded within the local bohemian culture of Mexico City, and while "the tequila flowed, . . . he remained sober," allowing him the First World wits and wherewithal to "explore" these unwitnessed scenes of Mexican cosmopolitan decadence. In an interview, Cartier-Bresson declares, "In 1934, in Mexico, I was very lucky. I just had to push a door and there were two lesbians making love. What pleasure, what sensuality! You couldn't see their faces. I shot. Having seen it was a miracle. . . . I never could have gotten them to pose" (quoted in Assouline 1998).[18]

The story told by Cartier-Bresson and Magnum is one of fortuitous luck in being able to capture this private scene of queer erotic heat, a miracle. Part of his brand as a travel photographer was to bring audiences sights previously unseen, and his class privilege and the cultural cache that being a Frenchman in Mexico provided had everything to do with his ability to enter into these intimate worlds. But this photograph demonstrates the ways that the lens of the cultural explorer, the one authorized to document the foreign and the unseen, is extended to not just the dramas taking place in the street, in public view, but an imagined cultural license to access a previously denied interiority, made all the more delicious and exotic when it was intended to be private.

Part of what makes this image so compelling is what viewers are refused: not only their faces, or the visual clarity of exactly what they are doing (lesbian sex can seem so ineffable), but the conventions of erotic photography that would suppose their sexual energy be directed toward us rather than at each other. Staring at the image, I reconcile my own attraction to this private scene of queer passion. This is a position I know well, a familiar embrace that knows where it's going—hands in frenzied motion with legs pressed together, thighs locked tight. Here, the image, blurred and in motion, seems to resist the photographer's intervention and refuse the spectator's gaze. Instead, the two female bodies are witnessed in their shared moment of rapture that the static photographic image has difficulty capturing. There is nothing identifiable in this image or the stories that surround it to suggest that these were sex workers, yet positioned at the door looking in, there is a sense that as viewers we have stumbled onto a scene of secret lesbian sex, performing a visual moment that will become re-created in pornographic films for decades to come. There, captured for our erotic pleasure, these figures are conscripted—against their will—to work sex for us, their spectators. Cartier-Bresson's curiosity, his sense of racialized masculine entitlement to steal a glimpse of their pleasure for himself, is the violation that makes my own fantasy of identification and desire possible. What is refused creates what is enabled: the blur of fantasy and erotic possibility. Might these two entwined soft feminine forms be the same two women he photographed peering out the door? Have they slipped away from the demands of labor to grind away their passions, only to be tracked down by his predatory lens? Made to work for us now?

Female Photographers

If Cartier-Bresson typifies the male gaze, the foreign stranger who was deemed as ideally positioned to capture the "miracle" of female sexuality, the few female photographers of that era might have disagreed. As women, as photojournalists, female photographers seemed uniquely positioned to document the inner worlds of the women who worked sex and who had captivated so much photographic attention and fascination. Eve Arnold (1912–2012) was the first woman to join Magnum Photos, joining as a stringer in 1951 and becoming a full member in 1957.[19] Unlike the privileged provenance of Cartier-Bresson, Arnold was born in a Philadelphia tenement to Russian Jews, one of nine children, her connection to photography beginning with her work in a photo-finishing lab in 1946. "Known as a photographer committed to showing women 'as they really are,' not in men's fantasies of them," Arnold eventually published a book of photographs in 1976 titled *The Unretouched Woman* (Dyer 2013, 1). Even as she would become famous for her "candid" images of Marilyn Monroe, Marlene Dietrich, Joan Crawford, Cicely Tyson, and many others, a concurrent theme of her work would center around depictions of everyday African Americans and marginalized populations from around the world, in her words, "recording social history" (quoted in di Giovanni 2015, 24).

Still working as a stringer for Magnum, in 1954 Arnold was sent off to Havana, Cuba, on assignment for a feature that would eventually be called "The Sexiest City in the World." The text of that feature by Helen Lawrenson that would eventually run in *Esquire* performs precisely the form of exoticism that remains attached to Latina sexuality, particularly in its Caribbean articulation, which fuses in Lawrenson's text as the "subtly prurient mixture of African jungle and Spanish boudoir" (1955, 81). Even though the article itself is not about sex work, the opening line begins with a reference to a "Cuban whore" who "saw nothing degrading in her work and tended to regard it as a significant contribution to national welfare" (31) and where the city itself is described as "the geographical counterpart of Zola's *Nana*" (81). Lawrenson writes, "The intrinsic, basic quality of Havana is a deadly magic which permeates the very air which flows through the city, inescapable and inseparable, and which can only be defined, in the last analysis, as Sex. It is, without any doubt, the sexiest city in the world" (31). Here, Havana itself is presented as a sexual commodity for foreign consumption. The article features several of the images one might expect, beginning with a street scene that includes a partially hidden female figure

FIG 2.10 ▸ Eve Arnold, *Bar Girl in a Brothel in the Red-Light District*, 1954.
© Eve Arnold | Magnum Photos. Image Reference LON47 (ARE1954006W00001/24).

peering out from the black interior of a door frame, a shirtless mulato man
flexing his bare muscles and pounding on a conga with the caption "Everywhere, the sensuous beat of the rumba in the air," a color photograph of a
young light-skinned woman with thick dark hair peering over a balcony
with a caption that tells us that "beauty-contest winner Beatríz Sánchez is
a typist studying TV acting" (84). But the final image of the photo shoot, a
black-and-white image sized at 1/16 of the full page and positioned at the
bottom right frame of the layout almost as a coda without a caption, seems
to offer a counter to the narrative's mood of Havana as a playground of
sensual and sexual delights (fig. 2.10). And while most of the other images
Arnold produced for that assignment would disappear into relative obscurity, this photograph is the one that would have the most enduring afterlife.

As the image escapes its narrative frame as evidence of "The Sexiest City
in the World," as it becomes Arnold's property to repurpose and rename, it
becomes titled *Bar Girl in a Brothel in the Red-Light District*. The captioning
seems quite precise; even as we are not given the woman's name or a specific geographic location, we are instructed how to read her and assign her
an identity. Rather than a name, or even an ethnic identity, she becomes
"Bar Girl," a species of woman to be sure, but if that were not quite enough

to make the context clear, we are given the details of location "in a brothel in the red-light district." All these defining textual details are missing from the *Esquire* piece that is intent on selling Cuban sexual exoticism and pleasure rather than solitude and sadness. Here, Arnold's framing positions the transparent promise of tulle in contrast to the dark solid weight of alcohol and empty glasses; a figure in the back stands at the ready, elements of tragedy strewn about the reflective surfaces of feminine despair. This image brings together two powerful tropes of feminine tragedy: the mulata and the whore. The message is clear: tragedy, rejection, isolation, despair, and loneliness are the social price of veering off the assigned roles of sexual propriety and racial respectability.[20] In the visual archives of putería, blackness almost always emerges alongside tragedy.

The truth is that sex workers appear and reappear in the camera rolls of almost every photographer of distinction, and female photographers have not been immune to the magnetic appeal of sex workers as compelling photographic subjects. Diane Arbus, Mary Ellen Mark, Malerie Marder, and Jane Hilton have all produced substantial portfolios devoted to photographing sex workers. In Latin America, Chilean photographer Paz Errázuriz documented many marginalized communities during the Chilean dictatorship, including transgender sex workers for a 1983 series called *La manzana de Adán* (Adam's apple) and the 2014 series *Muñecas* (Dolls), about the sex workers and clients of a brothel on the border between Peru and Chile. As the perspective changed, however, so too did the depictions of puta life. But it was Susan Meiselas's 1976 book, *Carnival Strippers*, that broke new ground in documenting puta life in several significant ways. Meiselas collected stories over three summers of traveling with these "girl shows"; in *Carnival Strippers* these women were given names and allowed to share their stories alongside their photographs. In its depiction of sexual labor, it also shifted the lens—turning it not only on the women who strip but on the men who pay money to see them, the managers, the crew, the "talkers" who bark at the crowd, and the "roughies" hired to keep that crowd in check (fig. 2.11).[21] And significantly, it included fragments of the transcribed testimonies of those photographed, culled from more than 150 hours of tape-recorded interviews.[22]

At the time, Meiselas's book highlighted the difference between working on journalistic assignments and self-assigned creative projects. In presenting a more immersive engagement with not just these women but also the social economies of relation in which their work exists, Meiselas's photographs in this series expose how spectatorship is structured to perform dif-

FIG 2.11 ▸ Susan Meiselas, *Lena on the Bally Box. Essex Junction, Vermont, USA,* 1973. © Susan Meiselas | Magnum Photos. Image Reference NYC15658.

FIG 2.12 › Fernell Franco, *Série Prostitutas*, 1970–72. © Fernell Franco. Courtesy of Fundación Fernell Franco Cali | Toluca Fine Art, Paris.

ferent perspectives on sexual labor. As image makers, Meiselas and others like her shifted the terms of the dialogue about the relationships between photographers and their subjects, the ethics of representation, and the significance of photographic archives. These female artists began asking the rich, perplexing questions about how gender structures the power dynamics of the gaze and how photographic images move in the world. However, even as the perspective, intention, and contact that underscore image making changed, the desire, curiosity, and fascination that sex workers inspire have remained constant. In 2002 Meiselas published another book devoted to sexual labor, *Pandora's Box*, a visual account of Pandora's Box, a Manhattan sex club that specializes in sexual fetishes and domination, and once again she chose to include the recorded voices of those depicted.[23]

Across the hemisphere and over time, across a gendered range of photographic lenses, the tragedy of puta life develops into its own photographic genre, poised between pity and prurient fascination. In 1972 Colombian photographer Fernell Franco mounted a show in Cali in the alternative art space Casa Cultural Cuidad Solar, titled simply *Prostitutas*. The advertising for that exhibit featured a dark-skinned woman posing atop an uncovered mattress, as another woman, similarly dressed in a bra and panties, is glimpsed at the very edge of the frame (fig. 2.12). While lighter-skinned Latinas frequently appear in media accounts associated with sexual exoticism, mystery, and intrigue, Black sex workers—when they appear—invariably surface in these visual accounts as destitute and sad. This becomes solidified into the image of the pitiable Black whore, the one condemned to the confined space of sexual commerce, her world defined by the parameters of her vilified profession, her gaze met by the photographer who has invited her into this spartan space to offer the recognition that photography is said to provide. The look she directs at us tells us that she understands the terms of this arrangement and her role within it; this is her job, and she is doing it.

The poster advertising the exhibit featured a poem written by Hernán Nichols (quoted in Cano 2011).

click las putas
click las vulvas abiertas
que click click clack claman justicia
click los penes castigando click clack
garrotes fascistas click
los chirridos click clack
click de los catres click
ganarás el pan con el sudor de tu coño click
click clack los chancros en las paredes
click la limpieza de la pieza falsa
click el agua vaciándose
vacua vagina click
el inodoro click
los pachulis click
la virgen del carmen click click
papel higiénico gonococo click
click de la putería de negocio
click click pague antes piche después

click viceversa o viceputa click
pichar pisar pitar click click
click la vida de las putas click
click la puta vida click clack

[click, las putas
click the gaping vulvas
that click click clack clamor for justice
click the punishing penises click clack
click the fascist clubs
the screeching click clack
click from the beds click
you will earn your bread with the sweat of your cunt click
click clack the sores on the wall
click the cleaning of the fake piece
click the water draining
empty vagina click
the toilet click
the patchouli click
the virgen del carmen click
gonococcal toilet paper click
click the fucking business
click click pay first fuck later
click vice versa or viceputa click
fuck step blow click click
click putas lives click
click la puta life click clack][24]

Even as the poem seems to chronicle "la vida de las putas" and "la puta vida," it is the "gaping vulvas / that click click clack clamor for justice." The putas in the poem, like the ones in the photographs that formed the exhibit, never speak; what is delivered is Nichols's account of what constitutes the contours of their puta lives. In his rendering, there is no space outside the room where he has come to know them. Like the photographs included in Franco's series that position these women within the bare spaces where they service their clients, his reporting of their bare lives reveals the limits of his imagination, even as it records and performs a concern for the punishing despair that seems to define their existence. Yet, trapped within the logic of the space where he has come to enact the exchange, the poem cannot imagine the caress offered to a child; it cannot conjure the easy laugh shared between these women as they go about their day outside the spaces where they have come to work. Instead, the poem dawdles in chronicles of misery, just as the "click click" of the photographer's gaze invites another kind of lingering over their prostrated lives. Recording the distance between the quotidian violence and poverty of these women's lives and those who come to view their bodies on display in a gallery, Franco, like so many other photographers before and after him, would view these women's gestures of everyday survival as art.

Back to the Street

Despite all the places where we see sex workers in the archives of photography, this chapter concludes by returning to street photography and the photographers who contribute to this visual mapping of sexual labor from a wholly different vantage point, one that performs the colonial masculinist gaze using the new digital tools of empire and globalization, one that enacts a wholly removed corporeal distance between the viewer and the viewed—Google. DoxySpotting.com is a crowdsourced website that uses the steady flow of images snapped from Google Street View and Bing Street Side to archive photographs of brothels, pickup spots, and red-light districts that the site describes as "an archive of spotted prostitutes" and the "hot zones" of the world (fig. 2.13). Based on the number of submissions, they offer a list of worldwide red-light cities, with Mexico City topping the list, followed by Madrid, Bogotá, Paris, and São Paulo, with seven Latin American countries in the top ten.[25] With more than thirty-five thousand "sightings," the site uses different kinds of data visualization tools to provide different kinds of maps—red-light districts, spottings, heat maps, and density maps— each of which allows you to zoom in to any one of these locations to search the images uploaded there.

The home page includes ads for Global Network of Sex Work Projects, a UK-based nonprofit that "amplifies the voices of sex worker-led organisations advocating for rights-based services, freedom from abuse and discrimination, freedom from punitive laws, policies and practices, and self-determination for sex workers"; and Used in Europe, an organization and website that collects information on labor exploitation and forced labor in Europe.[26] However, these are simply decorative; there are no other references on the site to either sex worker rights or forced exploitation,

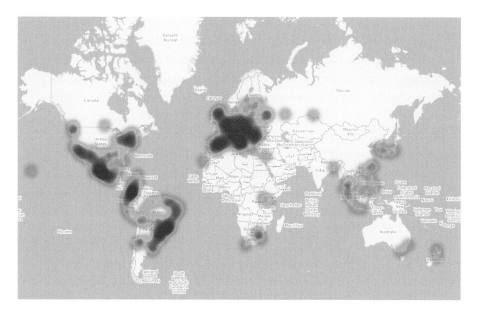

FIG 2.13 ▸ Screenshot from DoxySpotting.com showing the world's red-light cities, July 13, 2020.

and the intentions of the site are made abundantly clear in response to the question, "Why spot prostitutes on Google StreetView?"

> Google Maps Street View is the ideal voyeuristic tool. People are voyeuristic in nature—men especially. It is very easy to spot a girl with nice big boobs on Google Street View. Spotting prostitutes may seem a bit more difficult. But if you know what to look for, it actually becomes quite easy. . . .
>
> Doxy Spotting is almost a sport. It is the perfect and insuspicious [*sic*] way to kill some time at work or if you are bored. But be warned—doxy spotting is highly addictive. (Project DoxySpotting, n.d.)[27]

The language here is one of hunting—where "spotting prostitutes" is presented as sport, a way to "kill some time" if you "know what to look for," a particularly masculine sport premised on men's inherently voyeuristic "nature."

Like the photographers discussed in this chapter, the images captured and circulated on this site reveal as much about their authors as they do about puta life. While the administrator who created the site around 2010 posts from Germany, it relies on an army of DoxySpotters from all over the world to regularly submit to the site. The user names of some dedicated users are also quite telling: Cur_Monger has the highest number of

FIG 2.14 ▸ Screenshot of Google Street View of International Blvd. in Oakland, California, July 13, 2020.

postings with 17,990; other user names include SkankQuest, mrbadguy, BitchHunter, and Bitchhunter. The posts that tag and label the images are themselves frequently labeled with derogatory words and phrases, such as "Puta Vieja Esperando Clientes" (Old whore waiting for clients), "Crack Whore," "Heroin Addicted Skank," and "Fatty." Many of the locations tagged in this database are in fact quite isolated—truck stops, rural roads, abandoned buildings, and empty lots. Most terrifying is that the site encourages users to cross the line from digital representation to real-life encounter and offers geo-location data to facilitate those encounters.[28] That the women in these images might be engaged in criminalized behavior or might be undocumented migrants magnifies the risks they face, putting them in danger of extortion, deportation, and violence of all kinds.

When you click on any one of these dots, however, what you find is quite ordinary. Zooming into a location in nearby Oakland, California, what is revealed is a young dark-skinned woman walking down the street; the metadata that appear alongside the image provide the precise street address, map, and GPS coordinates (fig. 2.14). The link next to the image, "Legality in the United States," clicks through to a Wikipedia page about prostitution in the United States.[29] Nothing in the image suggests she is a sex worker; that designation is ascribed to her simply because of where the image was taken and the speculation of one of many dedicated DoxySpotters who chose to upload the image. But of course that is precisely the point. Any female-presenting person on the street is potentially a sex worker; her mere presence in the space of the public serves as all the evidence that is required. Like all the faces on Google Street View, the face is blurred—but somehow that does not really make her image less recognizable. For certain, if she saw this photograph, she would recognize herself. This is not just about fantasy: these are real streets with precise geo-location markers; this is a real young woman who was "hunted," "captured," and "pinned" to a location like a moth; this is another kind of colonial expedition.

This chapter has offered a decidedly haphazard and incomplete survey of some of the many ways photography constructs ways of viewing sexuality and the ways it makes visible and occludes the work of sexual labor. In providing a visual referent for what a sex worker "looks like," photography establishes the visual terms of recognition and identification. No matter that the women who appear in the visual archives of the photographers I have profiled are all just "ordinary colored girls," to borrow from Hartman's phrasing, visually not so different from other ordinary girls, or perhaps girls working hard to look not so ordinary. Through photography, they come to function as the visual referent for a sexuality that is marked as both deviant and desirable, visually and sexually available for consumption. In the process, these pictures also instruct viewers to associate sexual deviance with racial, ethnic, and national difference as they established the visual and discursive tropes that continue to be associated with all forms of sexual labor: criminality, foreignness, racial exoticism, polymorphous perversity, and immorality. But what all these photographic projects share is a visual fascination with the spectacle of puta life, a desire to peer into this private world that seems to be everywhere and yet is always presented as mysterious and out of sight, to step into the submerged spaces where sexuality lives and hides.

PART I

VISIONS, VOICES, AND IMPRESSIONS LEFT BEHIND

Representing

Puta Life

Now don't you ask yourself, who they are
Like everybody else, they wanna be a star
DONNA SUMMER, "BAD GIRLS"

CARNAL KNOWLEDGE, INTERPRETIVE PRACTICES

Authorizing Vanessa del Rio

Having picked through the scattered colonial vestiges that haunt the figure of the puta across archives of deviance and desire, in this chapter I
shift to another affective register born of memory and longing to linger
in the philosophical musings of one of my most cherished puta icons, Vanessa del Rio. Unlike the silent presence of the other women we have seen
captured on film rolls so far, now we have the vibrant voice of one of the
most celebrated Latina sex symbols in history providing a personal account
of her puta life in her as-told-to, multimedia life narrative, *Vanessa del Rio:
Fifty Years of Slightly Slutty Behavior* (del Rio 2010). Whether or not the name
Vanessa del Rio is familiar to you already signals a certain proximity to
the worlds in which puta aesthetics, race, and pornography intersect.[1] The
only child of a Puerto Rican mother and a philandering Afro-Cuban father, Vanessa del Rio was born Ana María Sánchez on March 31, 1952. She
grew up on IIIth Street in Harlem and attended Catholic school before
leaving home in her teens to venture out into the New York City of the
1970s, a world flavored with all the possibilities that sexual liberation, civil
rights, and drugs seemed to promise. Her memoir, made up of equal parts
hard-core pornographic images and titillating and terrifying life stories, is
unique in both form and content. In it, del Rio doesn't just provide a nar-

rative account of her life; here, through the documentary presence of the embodied speaking subject, we also hear her assert her own interpretive powers of meaning making. And what del Rio makes clear throughout this text is both the pleasure she takes in sex and her right to define the meaning of her own puta life.

As an adult film star, Vanessa del Rio was and is huge—legendary even—not because she starred in many films (the pervasive racism of the film industry meant she rarely received top billing) but because in the world of adult entertainment, during the golden age of pornography, Vanessa del Rio was a star.[2] While a few people of color passed through these early years of the porn industry, none developed the name recognition of Vanessa del Rio, and by the time she retired from adult films in 1985, her dreams of stardom had come true. Del Rio would appear in hundreds of films over the course of her career, and her face—and a whole lot more—graced the covers of international magazines the world over. During the end of her acting career, many of her previous performances simply began to be edited together and reissued as compilations with her image on the cover, while previous films were retitled to profit from her popularity.[3] When seen assembled together, it is clear that her name, her face, and her sexual enthusiasm became central to the marketing of films that might have otherwise been forgotten (fig. 3.1).

Today, del Rio's most frequent role is simply playing the celebrity diva she has become. As a public figure, she has long since moved from the underground scene of adult entertainment to the world of pop culture and has received shout-outs from Bernie Mac, Samuel L. Jackson, Junior M.A.F.I.A., Method Man, Chubb Rock, Snoop Dog, and Digital Underground as well as Lil' Kim, Rihanna, and Foxy Brown. A bio-pic film project about her life, *The Latin from Manhattan*, was released in June 2022. Focusing on her life hustling in Times Square during the 1970–1980s, the film is being described as *Boogie Nights* meets *Taxi Driver*.[4] Although Vanessa no longer turns tricks on Forty-Second Street or appears in pornographic films, there are many ways in which she is still a "working girl," hustling as one does to stay relevant in a business that does not view aging kindly. Today, in her role as a puta par excellence, she hosts her own X-rated adult film site, frequently appears at adult conventions to sign photos and books, on occasion appears in minor television roles and music videos, and even hosts one-on-one video performances. She also maintains an eBay site specializing in signed collectibles that arrive complete with a certificate of authenticity (fig. 3.2).[5] And thirty years after she last appeared in an adult feature film, Vanessa del

Rio remains a porn legend. As a representative of the racialized erotics and puta projections that attach to Latinas, Vanessa del Rio is iconic: racially ambiguous, stereotypically stylized, and unabashedly sexual.

Testimonio, Documentary, Porn

Like the person it profiles, the text at the center of this investigation, *Vanessa del Rio: Fifty Years of Slightly Slutty Behavior*, constitutes a genre of its own. As a book intended to represent the sizzle and the scandal of Vanessa del Rio's life, the text simultaneously intimates and distorts the conventions of autobiography, documentary, and pornography to unsettle assumptions about puta life as well as the interpretive practices we might bring to them. This massive tome, weighing in at more than six pounds, contains stills from adult magazines, movie posters, films, and photographs from her private collection; text transcribed from interviews conducted both on and off camera; and personal ephemera spanning her childhood to the present day. The 140-minute DVD includes an on-camera interview and a few "day-in-the-life" scenes that follow the contemporary Vanessa del Rio through the streets of *her* New York, all of which are intercut with numerous clips from her many pornographic films. These shifts between one kind of visual encounter (porn) and another (the speaking subject of documentary) require that viewers who might wish to revel unproblematically in the pornographic gaze bear witness to the stories of racism, violence, and state-authorized abuse that also form part of her life, even as these stories are often delivered with unflappable aplomb. Equally as important from a feminist studies perspective, it requires those interested in accessing the biographical details of this Latina icon to confront the explicit rawness of the pornographic image and del Rio's own accounts of herself.[6] This book is del Rio's representation of her own life, an articulation of her life and her work that she was centrally involved in crafting for our consumption. Throughout the text, in addition to commenting on her own sexual escapades, del Rio is quick to offer her own theoretical insights—variously contradictory, comical, and concerning—about the porn industry, the Catholic Church, blow jobs, race, Latinx culture, and feminism.

Thinking experience through puta life—through the life story of a legendary porn star; through the shifting textual, photographic, and cinematic traces of racialized sexuality—accentuates the buried tensions between lived experiences and the theories we might use to account for

FIG 3.1 ▸ Movie posters featuring Vanessa del Rio.

FIG 3.2 ▸ Vanessa del Rio signed memorabilia and pictures.

them. In some ways, her text calls to mind other forms of testimonial literature or testimonios that use an individual life story in order to make a larger public claim for the human rights of a marginalized or disenfranchised population.[7] Del Rio could be said to use her own biographical narrative to promote a fuller understanding of a community and a history that has been erased from public discourse, to make a claim for the human rights of sex workers. As a work of testimony, her text makes salient the racialized sexual politics and human rights issues that undergird del Rio's story, as it illuminates aspects of the text that complicate an already complicated genre. Like many working in the various sectors of the sex industry, in this text del Rio recounts the numerous times she was arrested and jailed and speaks with impassioned conviction of the hypocrisy, futility, and harm of laws that criminalize consensual adult sex work.[8]

Like other testimonial narratives, del Rio's life story is narrated in the familiar "as told to" format. However, rather than an anthropologist or an enlightened intellectual, the interviewer, editor, and transcriber in this case, Dian Hanson, is herself a longtime regular in the adult entertainment world and Vanessa's friend.[9] Hanson not only worked as an actress in adult films but also worked as the magazine editor of *Juggs* and *Leg Shows* before becoming the editor of Taschen's Sexy Books series. Taschen, a German publisher that specializes in art, architecture, and pop culture, is best known for producing oversized collector-edition volumes of notable photographers, such as Annie Leibovitz and Helmut Newton, and coffee-table standards of French Impressionists and midcentury design. Its Sexy Books catalog speaks to the mainstreaming of pornography and includes books on Tom of Finland (Hanson 2009) and Japanese bondage (Araki 2007), as well as *The Big Book of Breasts 3D* (Hanson 2011), which comes complete with 3D glasses. This framing within the world of publishing situates del Rio's text not as a testimonial life narrative but as art, as visual object, as living room adornment. The 140-minute DVD included with *Fifty Years*, more so than the 3D glasses, functions as its special marketing feature that augments the static photographic images of the text (fig. 3.3).

Like some other Taschen art books, *Vanessa del Rio: Fifty Years of Slightly Slutty Behavior* is available in multiple formats: a trade version that sells for $59.99 and two limited-edition formats, one that retails for $700 and another that goes for an astounding $1,800 and includes a signed print and a chance to spend an evening with the star herself.[10] All editions include more than three hundred glossy, image-rich pages documenting del Rio's life on and off screen. The book and the DVD cover much of the same ma-

FIG 3.3 ▸ Book cover,
*Vanessa del Rio: Fifty Years
of Slightly Slutty Behavior*,
2010.

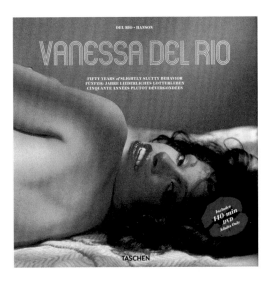

terial, and many of the taped interviews are unfaithfully transcribed in the book, revealing the seams of postproduction editing.[11] For example, there are entire sections that are recorded on camera, such as her describing the Santería practices of her Cuban father, a biographical similarity we share, that are not referenced in the book. There are also sections in the book that have no corresponding mention in the DVD—most notably her affair with S/M kinkster Reb Stout, discussed later in this chapter. To complicate matters further, there are passages in the book that *do* correspond to on-camera interviews but that appear to have edited del Rio's vernacular oral performances in postproduction for textual clarity. These shifts between one version of a story and another, between the oral and the written, between an omission and a revelation, perform and illuminate the vagrancies of biographical production that also form a core feature of this project— marking the gulf between depictions of puta and representations of life.

Today, publics are inundated with the visual packaging of life stories in social media platforms, reality television, tell-all biographies, fictionalized bio-pics, and biographical documentaries. Yet, whether presented as academic accounts, fictionalized depictions, journalistic truth, or TikTok confessionals, what we are offered for consumption about the lives of others, savvy audiences have learned, is never all there is to know; instead, we understand these biographical fabrications as cultural products mediated and designed to construct a narrative out of the "real," to give experience the shape of meaning. Nevertheless, the endless proliferation of these modes of self-representation and our hunger for consuming them suggest

that there is something about the human condition that remains captivating and compelling, an insatiable desire to access the interiority of another in an effort to better recognize ourselves. And when that interiority
is imagined to be shaped by sexual desire, that quest becomes all the more
irresistible. It is that insatiable desire to connect with the submerged parts
of ourselves for which we have no reasonable explanation, to account for
those parts of our psychic structures that seem to forever elude us, that
get activated when we linger on autobiographical accounts of sexual experience. Peering into the contours of another's sexual psyche, learning the
intimate details of someone else's erotic life, requires that we acknowledge
how our own archives of racialized gendered embodiment, our own erotic
aversions and attachments, might animate and unsettle not only our sexual
practices but our scholarly ones as well. But as we will witness, narrating
life experiences and the meanings we assign to them is always a messy affair,
particularly when what gets recounted across the gulf of memory are the
subjective senses that we bring to our understanding of desire, power, and
pleasure.

Racial Logics, Racialized "Spictacles"

In *Vanessa del Rio: Fifty Years of Slightly Slutty Behavior*, del Rio narrates her
childhood as a young Latina growing up in Harlem, her life in the white-
dominated adult film industry, and her current career as a pop culture diva.
Because del Rio is the first breakout nonwhite porn star, her racial identity
is central to her success, her story, and the subsequent persona she would
develop. Her biography also illustrates the ways US racial logic, born of the
one-drop rule, gets attached to certain corporeal signifiers and how the
racialization that attaches to latinidad has shifted over time. In her memoir, del Rio describes driving through the US American South with her
parents on their way to catch the Key West ferry to Cuba and having to
navigate the binary racial codes of the region. She states, "I think we were
just on the line, because we were Spanish, but it was summer, so we were
a little darker, tanned. My braids must've saved me, making my hair look
straighter, more like an Indian. . . . The signs either said blacks or colored
and we honestly didn't know if they meant us. Coming from New York,
it didn't make sense" (del Rio 2010, 261). Recounting this as a childhood
memory, del Rio describes both her color (a "little darker") and her hair
("straighter, more like an Indian") as the bodily markers that would deter-

mine her place "on the [color] line" and therefore her family's treatment in the segregated South. We also witness how within the polarized racial landscape of the 1960s and 1970s, "Spanish" as a linguistic designation was used to stand in for an ethno-racial identity, one that invokes a European heritage while eliding associations with histories of Caribbean slavery and blackness. During that time, particularly on the East Coast, "Spanish" became a way to mark people from the Spanish-speaking countries of the Caribbean and Latin America as something *other* than Black or white in a US context where those differences carried lingering juridical as well as social and cultural significance.[12] "Coming from New York," more specifically from the poor, working-class, multiracial, multiethnic space of 1960s Harlem, where the different hues, flavors, and colonial legacies of the African diaspora lived in intimate proximity to one another, the binary logic of the American South just "didn't make sense" to del Rio's New York racial sensibilities.

As porn historian Mireille Miller-Young (2014) documents in her field-defining book *A Taste for Brown Sugar: Black Women in Pornography*, at the time del Rio entered the world of adult films in the mid-seventies, the media landscape for adult films was similarly racially bifurcated into Black and white. While there was already an established market for Black porn that occasionally included Latinx and Asian actors, these films were still categorized as Black, and interracial porn still presumed Black-white sex. In a visual moment with only the most stereotypical images of latinidad, del Rio's racialized difference functioned to provide another kind of race play that didn't quite align with the Black-white binary, even as her films were marketed to Black, white, and Latinx audiences, in both Spanish and English.[13] Vanessa del Rio (2010, 194) states, "I never looked like the wife next-door. So I'd come in there 'chicka chicka boom,' the big red lips, the big hair, the long nails, and no matter how glamorous I looked I'd still be the maid or some smart-ass hoochie mama. . . . I never questioned why I didn't get the lead roles, why I played maids, until someone brought it to my attention. I was just happy for a part, and you know, it wasn't Hollywood." In this passage, del Rio describes walking in the door in her own stylized version of glamour, her own personal version of Latina femininity: "the big red lips, the big hair, the long nails." The maid and the "smart-ass hoochie-mama" are racialized and deeply classed caricatures that slide easily across the feminized categories of Latina and African American women. And in del Rio's rendering, as in the popular imagination, both are positioned in opposition to "the wife next-door," who is assumed to be middle class and white.

FIG 3.4 ▸ Vanessa del Rio in *The Dancers,* 1981.

In a cinematic genre not known for the originality of its plot structures, del Rio's Latina difference allowed her to simultaneously reference both a foreign exoticism and a domestic racialized subservience. In the film *The Dancers* (1981), for example, del Rio plays a waitress named Juanita with a thick Spanish accent who will do "anything" for a part. In a grotesque mash-up of pan-hemispheric Latinx visual and sonic tropes, in one scene she dances to the song "La Bamba," by Chicano crooner Ritchie Valens, dressed in an over-the-top Cuban rumbera outfit, complete with a Carmen Miranda–style, Bahian-inspired headpiece adorned with fruit (fig. 3.4).[14]

Similarly, in the film *The Filthy Rich* (1980), del Rio plays a Cuban cook, Chili Caliente, a recent immigrant whose character frequently reminds herself to "spic English" now that she is in America and whose over-the-top racial drag includes the detail of a straw suitcase (figs. 3.5–3.6). As Miller-Young (2014, 58) points out, casting "black men and women as domestic figures, rather than exotic characters" locates these interracial fantasies firmly within the "intimate and historically charged spaces of racial interaction like the white home." However, here, del Rio's Latinized difference is domesticated literally and figuratively, bringing the exotic but still racialized difference of the Latina maid to disrupt the scene of white domestic heterosexuality.

FIG 3.5 ▸ Vanessa del Rio in *The Filthy Rich*, 1980.

FIG 3.6 ▸ Vanessa de Rio in *The Filthy Rich*, 1980.

Yet how humor functions in porn during this era is quite a bit more nuanced than any surface analysis might suggest, and very often, the scripts insert their own comic jabs at the raced, classed, and gendered premise of the plots.[15] For example, in one scene, Ms. Caliente defines herself as a "muy grande supporter of women's rights, ERA," and when the "mistress" of the house asks her to use the back entrance, she threatens to quit, declaring, "I am a proud minority woman!" In other film sequences, her Latina difference is signaled by delivering lines like "Bailando me hace sentir muy sexual" (Dancing makes me feel very sexual) in perfect Spanish (DVD 00:06). In terms of national identity, del Rio is half Cuban and half Puerto Rican (even as she is fully a New Yorker), although that complexity frequently proves too much for US publics, and over the course of her career, she is often identified as simply Puerto Rican.[16] But within the binary logic of the US racial order, del Rio also comes to be frequently identified as Black, particularly early on in her career.

The line between Latina and Afro-Latina is frequently a nebulous one, rooted in very particular historical and geographic discourses of racial categorization, complicated further by the performative tensions between identification and self-identification, and always situated within larger colonial discourses of antiblackness.[17] Yet it is precisely this proximity to blackness, one that benefits from the hypersexualization of the Black body while managing to keep a safe distance from associations with African American blackness, that no doubt helped del Rio access different roles within the adult entertainment industry without being trapped into specifically "Black" roles or exclusively hired for Black-made films. Melissa Blanco Borelli (2015, 15) writes of the transfigurative power of the mulata body in a Cuban context, stating, "As a substitute, the *mulata* disguises the white male desire for black women; the fetish for blackness seems less of a vice when that same blackness pixilates around the *mulata* and her hips." As seen in the previous chapter, within a US and European context, these racialized associations with blackness also get enveloped within the scientia sexualis of the foreign, projecting onto the figure of the Latina the irresistible magnetism of the dark, mysterious, and exotic Other that is always already available for white masculine conquest.

Throughout her many films and photo shoots, and throughout *Vanessa del Rio: Fifty Years of Slightly Slutty Behavior*, we get numerous images where del Rio's skin color appears variously lighter or darker, depending on lighting, mood, and the skin tones of the actors around her, and her hair appears straightened to various degrees. But very often it is simply the contrast between her stylized aesthetic and the drab whiteness of actors with whom she is paired that serves to accentuate her racialized difference. While skin color and hair texture might function as the more obvious markers of her racial identification (along with frequent references to the fullness of her lips), audiences also routinely attach racialized and classed significance to the swing in her hips, the blood-red self-stylings of her three-inch nails, and her penchant for animal prints, or what Jillian Hernandez (2020, 52) calls "aesthetic excess, a discourse and constellation of practices that visually racializes and genders . . . as a form of class politics." It bears stating the obvious: the racialized classed markers that cling most fervently to Black and Latina bodies—skin-tight clothes, animal prints, red everything, bold lipstick and nails, high heels, visible cleavage, short skirts, and the performative attitude to pull it off—are also the visual signifiers that come to be attached to sex workers of all colors, mapping the visual iconography of puta aesthetics onto all racially stylized feminine bodies. In a scene from *Viva Vanessa* (1984), in which del Rio plays the star she has already become, we see her ample curves wrapped in shiny red latex (which covers a red lace bra, panties, and hose), sporting brash gold accessories and offering her tongue and manicured nails as suggestive enticements to two young hapless fans who cannot believe their luck (fig. 3.7). Even as she is performing "successful porn star" in this scene, this wasn't a "hoochie-mama" outfit; this was her own latinized "aesthetic of excess," one born from her own wardrobe and her own puta life.

In response to a question about her strong fan base with Black women, she replies, "Yes, I've been in black women's magazines, and to a lesser extent Latin. My own Latin culture has not been as accepting of my chosen career; it's a Catholic thing. Black women have a higher sexual confidence" (del Rio 2010, 197). Here, del Rio seems to differentiate between her "own Latin culture" and that of Black women on the basis of culture, not of race, even as her comments seem to ignore the overlap between the terms *Black* and *Latina*. She then goes on to describe how when she was asked to appear for a feature in *Latina* magazine, the editors "cleaned up her image" for their more conservative audience, dressing her in a pantsuit and having her remove her jewelry, while the Black magazine *Urban Belle* put her on the cover and styled her "smoking a cigar in sexy poses" (197).[18] In other moments, del Rio seems to temper her previous statements about Latina sexual attitudes to view the terms *Black* and *Latin* in tandem—as existing in opposition to whiteness: "Black and Latin women like to strut their stuff . . . they're more comfortable with their bodies. . . . If you grow up held down, the one thing

FIG 3.7 ▸ Vanessa del Rio and her fans in *Viva Vanessa*, 1984.

they can't take from you is your inner soul, your body and sexuality. It comes from survival. These women are less afraid to get down and dirty when it comes to sex" (200). Here, del Rio attributes to "these women" the qualities that she herself has become known for—an uncensored, unfiltered attitude toward sexual expression. Yet her memoir also makes evident the ways Black audiences, including the Afro-Latinx audiences from the Harlem she grew up in, saw Vanessa del Rio as one of their own—dubbing her their "Black Marilyn," writing her into the archives of African American popular culture, and honoring her with a Lifetime Achievement Award at the first Black Adult Entertainment Awards in 1997 (Body-Rockin, n.d.). Having emerged from a social and historical context of overlapping forms of cultural solidarity and community, this identification with blackness is one that del Rio readily embraces.[19]

Although in her own text racialized terms like nonwhite, woman of color, Latin, and Black are frequently blurred, what her narrative makes clear is that as a racialized actor in a white-dominated industry, Vanessa del Rio was continually being typecast as something other than the lead. Although she worked steadily in pornographic films from 1974 until 1985, appearing in more than one hundred films, she was rarely offered starring roles, playing instead the maid, the hooker, or the Latina spitfire, her racialized difference representing the forbidden fruit that fed endless appetites fueled by jungle fever even as her Latina spiciness offered a slightly different flavor from what African American blackness was intended to register.[20] Yet, despite having to continually play the racialized sidekick to the white female lead, del Rio would invariably make every role a starring role, working sex for the camera and an American consumer market that had already started to develop a taste for what performance artist and cultural theorist Xandra Ibarra terms "spictacles" of South American exoticism, Latina spiciness, and West Side stories of puta life.[21]

Sexual Scripts, Authorizing Subjects

As with many of us, the formative seeds for del Rio's sexual scripts of puta life were delivered through the power of mass media. If Vanessa del Rio served as an early role model for my teenage version of a sexual life, Isabel Sarli served that function for the young Ana María, the girl who would become a future porn legend. Several times throughout the book, del Rio credits Isabel "Coca" Sarli, the Argentinean actress of the 1950s and 1960s, as being an early influence.[22] Sarli was another kind of silver-screen puta, successfully navigating the imagined border between sex work and working sex. A former Miss Argentina, Sarli became wildly famous for appearing naked in feature-length movies made by her lover Armando Bó, who served as writer, director, and producer, helping inaugurate the genre of Latin American sexploitation films: soft-porn films that circulated widely in the Spanish-speaking world, including the Spanish-language movie theaters of 1960s Times Square that Ana María would frequent with her mother (fig. 3.8).

In these films, sensuously directed by Bó, a married man forbidden from divorcing his cuckold wife by the Catholic Church, Sarli frequently plays a nymphomaniac or sex worker in features with titles like *Insaciable* (Insatiable), *Intimidades de una cualquiera* (Intimacies of a common girl), *Éxtasis tropical* (Tropical ecstasy), *Mariposas de la noche* (Butterflies of the night), or *El demonio creó a los hombres* (The devil made man). One critic describes the plot of one of her most famous films, *Fuego*, as follows: "*Fuego* . . . where the poor Coca suffers a uterine fever, or is a nymphomaniac, or is simply *putísima*; a condition or illness that the Alba Mujica character takes advantage

FIG 3.8 ▸ Isabel Sarli, ca. 1969. Photographer unknown.

of to establish a lesbian relationship with the young woman" (Brackes 2012) (fig. 3.9).[23] Being putísima became Sarli's signature role in every film, a role after which del Rio modeled her own burgeoning sexuality as a young person and, years later, as an adult film star.

In describing the impact of these films on her developing teenage psyche, del Rio insinuates that rather than Latina sexuality being shrouded in Catholic propriety and sexual repression, her mother's sanctioning of this kind of entertainment suggested the ways these films also functioned as culturally authorized performances of a Latina *hyper*sexuality. And for the young Vanessa, Sarli's gendered performances of puta life proved foundational to del Rio's own self-fashioning. She writes,

> Watching *Fuego*, a movie I originally saw when I was 16, I thought how most people don't want to accept all aspects of woman, they just want to praise the Madonna, the mother, and not explore the slut. . . . I like the word *slut*. It is a strong word for women who embrace their sexuality and refuse to be sexually controlled. . . . Sarli's films sometimes ended tragically, but I think I consciously didn't pay too much attention to the ends of the film, I was

FIG 3.9 ▸ Isabel Sarli and Alba Mujica in *Fuego*, directed by Armando Bó, 1969.

admiring the sin. . . . I was liking her power and daring, the life that that represented, her confidence in her sexuality, and to be able to use it, to be that type of woman, to be *all* woman. (del Rio 2010, 28)

Del Rio claims that she learned how to be "a wanton woman" from Sarli, and this passage hints at del Rio's early innate understanding of sexualized gender as performative, as a self-styled instrument of "power and daring" that one could use (28). In her reclaiming of the word *slut*, another common English translation for *puta*, del Rio rewrites the female narrative of the sexual tragedy that is intended to define puta life, cheekily subtitling her memoir *Fifty Years of Slightly Slutty Behavior*.

In refusing to be sexually controlled by the promise of respectability, del Rio's narrative counters the standard formula of victimhood, salvation, and redemption that is so prevalent in tell-all biographies of retired white American adult stars like Linda Lovelace, Jenna Jameson, Traci Lorde, and Jennie Ketcham.[24] As a literary genre, the (auto)biographies of porn stars tend to traffic in sad stories of teenage sexual abuse and addiction, intermingled with sufficient doses of sex and scandal to feed prurient curiosity, and generally end with the triumph of true love. The very title of Jenna Jameson's *New York Times* best-seller *How to Make Love like a Porn Star: A Cautionary Tale* perfectly exemplifies the redemption narrative that allows readers to soak up all the titillating details of a porn star's life while still promoting narratives of sexual respectability through the moral filter of a "cautionary tale." The *Publishers Weekly* review of that book reads, "Beneath Jameson's monstrous diva exterior, however, was a girl who just wanted to become a loving mother and wife. After many failures, she finally succeeded, and her X-rated book ends on an uplifting family-values note" (Strauss 2004).[25] Here, we see how whiteness, particularly when paired with motherhood, works to authenticate narratives of redemption and romance even as it facilitates the mainstreaming of pornography. Keenly aware of how others have been able to profit by fulfilling narrative desires for erotic confessions that end with moral redemption, del Rio seems to hold those who claim they "only did it for the money" in particular disdain.

In contrast, in her text, del Rio refuses to cast herself as a victim of the porn industry or of life and reiterates her sense of control and sexual agency throughout the book. But she is invested in asserting more than her agency; what del Rio seems most intent on describing is her pleasure, the sheer joy and satisfaction of her many sexual escapades, a direct challenge to prevailing claims that those who labor in the sex industries are always and only victims of economic desperation. She clearly avows: "I like sex, I have always liked sex; and I will never deny liking sex" (del Rio 2010, 28), and throughout the text, she narrates an almost insatiable appetite for sexual adventure. A story that seems emblematic of this attitude takes place early on in the DVD when responding to a question from the interviewer Dian Hanson. In narrating her first performance in an adult film, del Rio describes her nervousness, not about having sex on camera but about saying her lines correctly. Partway through the on-camera interview, she interrupts herself, turns to us, her viewers, and blurts out—"And I blew the cameraman! During a break!" At this point in the interview, she begins to laugh uncontrollably, finally adding, "In those days everybody just had a good ol' time" (DVD, 00:31). Blowing the cameraman, in this story as in others, becomes a way for her to assert that sex was not just something she did for money; it was something she did for fun.

The structure of the book, with chapters that are not quite chronological and not quite thematic, suggests that Hanson tried as best she could to group hours of filmed interview material into some sort of narrative shape. For example, the chapter titled "I Want to Be a Whore" discusses aspects of her childhood; "Chicka Chicka Boom" is devoted to del Rio's discussion of how racial politics informed her career in the adult film industry; and "Gym Rat" highlights the brief period where del Rio left porn, took steroids, and began a career as a bodybuilder.[26] Even as this project with Dian Hanson and Taschen is another attempt to reinvigorate her brand—the book is dedicated "To My Fans, May I Always Be Your Mistress of Masturbatory Memories"—and turn a profit doing it, it is also an opportunity to author her own public image, to control how she will be remembered. The addition of a DVD with on-screen interviews, not found in most print memoirs, allows the consumer of these narratives to actually see the protagonist speaking on camera, offering her many fans a glimpse of her contemporary life alongside sexually explicit clips from the numerous pornographic films that made Vanessa del Rio famous. As in the scene described earlier in this section, in the DVD, we get not just her story but the performance of her story. We are able to see her laugh and gesture and several times turn away from Hanson to address us, her viewing audience, directly. Not only does she insist on telling her story *her* way, she also insists on interpreting it within her own frame of understanding. And it is this element that I ultimately found most provocative about the text and most challenging as a critic.

Throughout the recorded interview and repeated throughout the text, del Rio continually insists that she never really had any "bad" experiences sexually, stating, "I really enjoyed my life. I never did anything that I didn't want to do where I wasn't in on it, even if I felt it was something that I had to do. I would always find some way to be in on it. I would never let myself become the victim or feel victimized" (DVD, 00:13). The book does not shy away from describing the many forms of violation and victimization that impact the lives of women, people of color, and sex workers, and del Rio acknowledges she is grateful she never got "sucked in" and "spit out," but she also distinguishes that from feeling like a victim (DVD, 00:23). Theoretically, del Rio's refusal of the term *victim* marks an important interpretive intervention into dominant narratives that cast sex workers, as always and only perpetual, de facto, ahistorical victims of sexual violence and patriarchal oppression.

In juridical discourse, the term *victim* operates within the binary poles of guilt and innocence, victim and victimizer, setting the foundation for reparations and punishment. But the term also contains other meanings that surface in its deployment, a religious reference to sacrifice that is linked to salvation and another that defines it as "one who is reduced or destined to suffer some oppressive or destructive agency."[27] In contrast, the Anishinaabe scholar Gerald Vizenor's term *survivance* offers an apt corrective to help elucidate del Rio's discomfort with the term *victim*. Writing in a Native American context, he explains how the word intervenes in dominant depictions of Indigenous life: "Survivance is an active sense of presence, the continuance of native stories, not a mere reaction, or a survivable name. Native survivance stories are renunciations of dominance, tragedy and victimry" (1994, iii). Like the Indigenous populations of North America and elsewhere, when sex workers are not being romanticized as sexual goddesses, or vilified as morally bankrupt, they are most often depicted as the perpetual victims of patriarchal power, damaged beyond repair, even as liberal politics plot their salvation. Del Rio's repeated insistence on not wanting to be cast as a victim functions to repudiate dominant feminist critiques of those who work in the porn industry while refusing salvation or redemption. In contrast, Vizenor's term *survivance* brings together the resilience of survival *as* resistance, as it insists on acknowledging presence in the face of societal demands for disappearance.

Survival and resistance, however, have also come to function as familiar and expected narrative tropes in feminist scholarship on sexuality, eliding the more complicated and vexed question of how pleasure might endure in the shadow of violence and abjection. Nicole Fleetwood (2012, 422) makes this point most powerfully in her essay "The Case of Rihanna: Erotic Violence and Black Female Desire" when she asserts that "black women are brought into dominant narrative folds as victims of unbearable suffering" and urges cultural critics to probe "possibilities for black sexual practices that are not framed through dominant frameworks of suffering, resistance, or exploitation." In her work on race and pornography, Jennifer Nash (2014, 25–26) similarly argues against what she terms the "twin logics of injury and recovery which make theorizing black female pleasure from within the parameters of the [pornographic] archive a kind of impossibility." These African American feminist scholars echo del Rio in their refusal to elide questions of racialized female pleasure, and it is this resolute determination to assert possibilities for sexual pleasure within a landscape saturated with sexual violence that functions as del Rio's ongoing retort to her imagined feminist critics. She declares, "Some feminists have said, 'Wasn't that exploitation?' And I'd say, 'No, that was my pleasure'" (del Rio 2010, 84). But del Rio's insistence on not being perceived as a victim can also be read as her demand that she be recognized as an authorial agent, capable of not only narrating her own version of puta life but determining its significance.

Many of the stories in the book are those you might expect from a porn star: her on-screen accomplishments (she claims the distinction of having filmed the first double penetration in porn), her frustration at being continually typecast as the ethnic Other to the blondes who received top billing and top salaries, and her early days in an industry that was just starting to explode with crossover films like *Deep Throat* (1972) and *The Devil in Miss Jones* (1973). But del Río's book also recounts stories that are considerably more disturbing, if also equally commonplace, stories that too often constitute the sad stuff of the everyday for many women of color forced to bear the projections of puta life on their flesh. In del Río's narrative, the lecherous uncle, the manipulative boyfriend, the abusive police officer all make routine appearances. The familiarity of these tales is itself unsettling. However, rather than recount these stories through the language of victimhood and trauma, del Río narrates them with comic nonchalance, as another obstacle to overcome, another futile attempt to make her feel less than whole, another testament of survivance. As a theoretical intervention, del Río's repeated insistence on narrating everyday forms of violence without recourse to "fixing," in the Fanonian sense, subjects as traumatized victims reorients feminist sexual politics away from gendered norms of protected white womanhood, positioning those of us who have been violated, abused, harmed, and exploited at the very heart of feminist politics, as the norm of what constitutes a gendered experience.[28] For so many racialized feminized subjects, these everyday violations include the nefarious modes through which our sexuality is used to define and discipline the possibilities of our social worlds and sexual pleasures, social codes that would render the presence of our colorful, stylized, hybridized, exoticized bodies as wholly excessive yet always lacking. And very often what we are said to lack is simply shame.

In Spanish, the word *sinvergüenza* (shameless) is frequently used to discipline the possibilities of puta life. Like many Latinas, I often heard this word growing up, shame being that boundless resource that every immigrant daughter cannot afford to not have. Here, the sexual shame about how female bodies look and smell and feel is compounded by the immigrant shame of how our families eat and work and live. Frances Negrón-Muntaner (2004, xviii) situates this trope of shame as foundational to the ethnic, racial, and gendered identities of Puerto Ricans, declaring, "*Boricua* bodies are persistently negotiating their shameful constitution, refashioning the looks that aim to humiliate or take joy away from them. At the same time, it is impossible to deny that our most vital cultural production as *boricuas* has sprung not from the denial of shame, but from its acknowledgment into wounds that we can be touched by." Because Latinas come to sexuality through the multifarious forms of violence brought about through colonization, enslavement, migration, and the wounds of public and private patriarchy, scenes of violence, violation, and shame are core to our understanding of sexual subjectivity, even as these might inspire diverse and divergent reactions. Our Latina bodies and tongues bear the imprint of our histories of sexual violation and all the ways our sex, our desires, and our refusals have been used to define us. But shame can function as more than just a cultural asset for our creative production or something to speak out against; shame and abjection can also function as a resource for pleasure, a way to attach erotic significance to the paradox of desire and disgust that so often defines racialized sexuality. Living with shame is also an insistence on living, a refusal to disappear, an acknowledgment that some semblance of self-love might outlive the harms.[29]

Frequently in her narrative, del Rio asks readers to dwell in the complicated erotic registers that violence can sometimes instantiate, even as she actively describes how the lines between fantasy, reality, the narrative scripts of porn, and her own intimate sexual play melt into one another. Early on in the book, she recalls being around twelve years old and hearing her mother warn her of the dangers of the streets by reading her newspaper articles about young girls getting raped. Rather than instilling terror or inspiring caution, although perhaps this was also their impact, those stories were used by the young girl who grew up to become Vanessa del Rio as the narrative building blocks for her sexual fantasies. She states, "There was a popular Spanish wrestler . . . El Santo. . . . [He] was the masked good guy, but he became tangled up in my fantasies. I developed scenarios about being overpowered by masked rapists based on his image, which I later played out with my lover, Reb" (del Rio 2010, 32) (fig. 3.10). Already in this moment of recounting her childhood, we witness how a childhood image of masculine mystery and power gets mined for its erotic potential as she manages to hold in tension the threat of violence and possibility of pleasure.

Returning to Nicole Fleetwood's pointed insights proves invaluable here. Fleetwood (2012, 422) challenges what she terms "a coercive agenda" of "black recuperative heterosexuality" to offer alternative forms of understanding erotic attachments to violence "that do not conform to dominant frameworks of exploitation, of racial uplift and respectability" and that are not predicated on narratives of victimization or pathology. She writes, "How do cultural critics account for highly eroticized attachments in black heterosexual intimacies that are hinged on the force of masculinized vio-

FIG 3.10 ▸ Ediciones José G. Cruz, comics cover for *Santo,
El Enmascarado de Plata*, no. 316 (January 1, 1955).

lence? In moving the analysis of sexual subjugation beyond the framework
of fantasy, we need to fashion analytic tools to examine black women's
sexual practices where pleasure and attachment are interwoven with the
threat or reality of physical harm" (421). As Fleetwood suggests, moving
the analysis beyond the framework of fantasy complicates our ability to
come to terms with all the ways that, as women of color, violence, domination, and abjection get multiply coded into our sexual psyche. In Vanessa
del Rio's retelling of her life, we see not just the eroticization of narrative
violence and even terror; we also witness the possibility that some forms
of corporeal and psychic violence might come to function as self-defined
forms of sexual pleasure.

Let me present another biographical scene, a decidedly disturbing one,
that pushes the boundaries of understanding even further, well beyond fan-

tasy. Del Rio shares another episode that happened before she entered the world of adult entertainment. As a young person first experimenting with freedom, she hit the road with her then boyfriend and lived in a Volkswagen van. At one point, in a situation involving a stolen motorcycle and a pending warrant, she describes having to have sex with a state trooper in order to get her boyfriend out of jail. She begins telling the story by explaining, "It was like the movies, where you have to put out to get your boyfriend out of jail. And to the extent that it was like the movies, there was something exciting about it—plus he was handsome, blond, and ruggedly studly" (del Rio 2010, 107).[30] Once again del Rio returns to the representations of sexual exchange that have been projected on the silver screen as a narrative filter through which to make sense of what is happening in her real life. And while the trope of a good girl forced to do something immoral to save the man she loves might be a familiar one in Hollywood, in real life, it is easy to define what she narrates as an instance of state-authorized rape, coerced sex at the hands of the police, an all-too-frequent reality for sex workers and other women deemed not worthy of respect or protection. As the story continues, it takes a decidedly twisted turn when she reveals that over the course of the exchange with the officer, she had an orgasm. She goes on to exclaim, "It was so theatrical, such a humiliating adventure, that I have an orgasm but I don't let him know because I don't want to give him the satisfaction. I don't think he would have believed it if he'd known, since this was supposed to be his power game. . . . Ooh, I felt like such a dirty girl for enjoying it!" (107).[31] In the filmed interview, she ends her account laughing, as if she is keenly aware of the ironic perversity of the juxtaposition of state coercion and her own sexual gratification. At this point, the DVD cuts to a clip of one of her porn performances in which she is playing an inmate being forced to sexually accommodate her prison guard, and we witness another, much campier, representation of state sexual violence. In the scene, she is brought into the office, and the white actor who plays the warden states, "Now you are going to get a real taste of the whip," inadvertently or not performing a direct association between slave patrols, sexual violence, and the prison industrial complex.[32]

On one level, this story seems ripped from the headlines about Oklahoma police officer Daniel Holtzclaw, who was convicted of raping and sexually assaulting more than a dozen Black women, some of whom were street-level sex workers, because he felt they were unlikely to report his rape and abuse (Trombadore 2016). Both stories affirm studies that document the relationship between the criminalization of sex work, police en-

FIG 3.11 ▸ Vanessa del Rio in the DVD included with *Vanessa del Rio: Fifty Years of Slightly Slutty Behavior*, 2010.

forcement practices, and violence against those suspected of selling sex. One study goes as far as suggesting that "prior assault by police had the strongest correlation with both sexual and client perpetrated violence against female sex workers" (Shannon et al. 2009, 5). In fact, in her written account of this incident, del Rio (2010, 107) mentions that she "thought he must have done this before because he just nodded at the motel clerk and drove straight to the room." Sadly, the sexual violation of women imagined to be sex workers by police is a common occurrence, a direct result of laws that criminalize sex work. Daring to occupy the public sphere as a woman of color, Vanessa del Rio fit the racially gendered profile for a puta, even when she was not engaged in paid sex work. However, even if the events that del Rio describes on camera and the news accounts of the Holtzclaw case are strikingly similar and equally horrific, watching del Rio tell her story on-screen *feels* different to me as a spectator because of *how* it is told. As she sits in her living room, surrounded by leopard prints ("leopard" is her favorite color), drinking wine and telling story after story, her smiling, jovial on-screen image assures the viewer that she is just fine, that she not only endured the violence of her youth but managed to thrive (fig. 3.11).[33]

In recounting the story through the lens of mainstream cinema, del Rio uses the narrative familiarity as a way to normalize the violence, "where you have to put out to get your boyfriend out of jail." But as the scene continues, she uses this event to offer her rendering of how she was able to assimilate this violation within the interpretative framework of her own puta world-view: "This is the kind of thing I mean, where I take away but they don't take anything from me, I take from it" (DVD, 1:14). Del Rio regards this experience not as evidence of trauma but as an act of revenge that is made available to her through her ability to access pleasure, a pleasure that includes both her orgasm and her delight in hiding that fact from her assailant. In making sense of her experience, as one that is defined by coercion but that also includes her ability to experience orgasm, she attempts to rewrite the terms under which sexual violence, resistance, and revenge are understood. Moreover, as an interpretive intervention, del Rio's response to the extravagant and quotidian harms that surround racialized sexual subjectivity ruptures any semblance of an appropriate, rational response to the logic of sexual and racial subjugation that is intent on defining our position in the world.

As a critic, I return again and again to the axiom from Joan Scott's (1993, 412) essay "The Evidence of Experience": "Experience is at once always already an interpretation and something that needs to be interpreted." In that piece, Scott asks us to do more than just include other voices in our feminist formulations of experience; she compels us to think about the available frameworks of intelligibility that experience enters as it comes into language. Read through Scott, we can understand that del Rio's account of her experience already implies a level of interpretation; it has already been framed by the interpretive possibilities of puta life available to her, including those offered by both mainstream cinema and mainstream feminism. Following Fleetwood (2012) and Nash (2014), we also see how race functions to censor the sexual narratives of certain subjects, making some accounts unspeakable. Yet for both the young Latina who was stopped and assaulted by the police for no apparent reason and present-day del Rio, the seasoned sex worker and porn star who has lived in intimate proximity to sexual violence and is now looking back on that moment, the interpretive possibilities include her ability to access her own sexual pleasure and script it as an act of sexual subversion, even in the midst of a coercive encounter. Furthermore, del Rio's account of herself exposes the ways the experiences of racialized female subjects that are not white, middle-class, or "respectable" are made illegible within feminist frameworks that fail to account for the possibility of pleasure in the sexual lives of those who are constituted by violence. As a critic, I might be able to argue with her analysis of these events, but in order to do justice to Vanessa del Rio's version of her puta life, I also have to find a way to make sense of the trace of the real, of her laughter, of the materiality of her orgasm, and of her desire to control the terms under which intelligibility functions. Even in the face of police violence that aims to subjugate and dehumanize her, Vanessa del Rio rebuffs efforts to reduce her experience to the narrative tropes of normative hetero-femininity or redemptive victimhood; she refuses to vanish and instead shamelessly relishes the dirty, sensory, and performative excesses associated with her puta life.

The Reb Stout Affair

In a book that repeatedly asserts del Rio's sense of control and sexual agency, the inclusion of one particular chapter stands out for the ways it complicates narratives of how sexual empowerment and sexual representation might be understood. It also shifts the emphasis from Vanessa del Rio's spectacular public life as a porn star to her private life as a sexual rebel eager to explore the boundaries of her own erotic limits. Titled "The Reb Stout Affair," the chapter is devoted to a seven-month affair with Reb Stout, a Los Angeles native and s/m aficionado. Stout claimed to have seven distinct personalities with male, female, and genderqueer manifestations, each with a distinct name, wardrobe, and sexual proclivities, some quite dominant and indeed sadistic, some wholly submissive. In the introduction to this chapter, Hanson states, "Every sexual encounter was captured on film, including all the ecstasy, terror and tears. It was love 1970s style and not for the faint of heart" (del Rio 2010, 163). And while the rest of the book is full of glossy movie posters and professional stills from her films and colorful magazine spreads, the photographs in this chapter are taken from the extensive amateur photographic archive Stout and del Rio produced during their time as lovers, pictures that often include costumes, wigs, ropes, whips, and assorted sexual paraphernalia. Del Rio describes her initial coming together with Stout: "It was, 'Oh, you like to wear makeup and women's clothing and stick dildos up your ass? And jerk off and take pictures? Ok!'" (167). This too is puta life, a moment where the everyday pressures associated with living your sexuality in public are transformed into private experiments with the sensorial possibilities found at the limits of pleasure.

Many of the images in this chapter are quite playful and queer and depict the spirit of endless sexual experimentation that their brief affair was founded upon. In the photograph in figure 3.12, we see Stout in a platinum blond wig, spike heels, and pearls, bound and bent over while del Rio stares at the camera coquettishly with her mouth agape as she yanks her lover's penis back between his legs. Like other photos in this series, here we see the couple posing against the makeshift background of a rather ordinary domestic space with the electric clock about to strike two o'clock. In other photos, we are able to piece together a room decorated with a fish tank, assorted six-inch high heels, potted plants, erotic art, a fishing net with starfish, scattered sex toys, and lots and lots of mirrors. "Whenever we got together we had a scene, every day. Sometimes other people would be there . . . and we'd always take photos" (del Rio 2010, 167). In a few of the photographs, Vanessa is seen wearing her lover's exaggerated blond wig, the only images of her as a blonde that we see in a book that is replete with images of physical transformation.[34] If in her professional career her dark tresses were central to her Latina vixen persona, here she is free to play with racial self-fashioning. Twenty-one photographs are included in this chapter—nine black-and-white images and twelve color images—but we can imagine that many more were produced during their brief period together. The inclusion of this chapter also performs something else: it demonstrates Vanessa seizing control of the means of production (and the viewfinder) to craft images of her own puta life. Staring straight into the camera, in this image as in many of the others in this chapter, del Rio seems engaged with the framing of the shot, producing a photographic record intended for personal arousal rather than as a commodity to satisfy the sexual desires of others.

Part of what we see documented in the amateur photographs included in this chapter is an enactment of the sadomasochistic fantasies that Stout and del Rio explored and performed together. These included several photographs that featured Stout's "Ripper" persona, which del Rio describes as being rooted in "an extreme male fantasy of rape and force," one she associated with her earlier fantasies about El Santo (del Rio 2010, 167). It should be noted that del Rio has appeared in several s/m-themed films, or "roughies," as they were called, and describes enjoying the emotional potency, stamina, and physicality that they require. For example, in a scene from the 1982 film *Top Secret*, del Rio plays a secret agent, once again named Juanita, who is being tortured, yet somehow her makeup remains impeccable (fig. 3.13). It is not that these scenes of her having "rough" sex are not real—or do not depict real pleasure; they might. However, because they were also work, because she was performing for an audience, she seems to maintain a certain composure, even glamour, even in the midst of scenes of sexual submission, that suggest her control of the scene. In contrast, the amateur quality of the sex scenes with Stout exudes a different kind of intensity and intimacy.

In several of the photographs in this chapter, we glimpse something ineffable—a sexual vulnerability that exposes her willingness to experience something beyond the carnal pleasures of sex, outside the structures of ra-

FIG 3.12 ▸ Vanessa del Rio and Reb Stout, ca. 1979. Photograph by Reb Stout. Courtesy of Vanessa del Rio.

FIG 3.13 ▸ Vanessa del Rio in *Top Secret*, 1982.

tionality. Reflecting back on that time, she remarks, "As I got deeper into the relationship with Reb I pushed all the limits of his personalities and found I liked being really frightened. I wanted to push them until I believed their threats, not just submit because someone said to submit. . . . 'Make me,' I always said. Reb told me I was a SAM, a Smart-Ass-Masochist, always egging on the dominant" (del Rio 2010, 171). In these scenes, del Rio is not just asking to be dominating; she is demanding it, goading her top into seizing greater control. Here, the romanticized kernel of a childhood sexual fantasy about El Santo is transformed into an affective encounter with terror in adult sexual play, an opportunity to use sex to explore the psychic residue that her experiences have imparted and make of them something else. In these photographs, del Rio, the porn star, seems to disappear into her own interior psychic landscape, holding in tension violence and pleasure, submission and agency. She continues, "Every scene was about trying to break me, but I didn't know how to be broken. Breaking would have meant tears, I think, tears of total submission. There was sobbing, from pain and discomfort and sexual pleasure, but the pleasure always won out, which I guess meant that I stayed strong" (171–72). Curiously, while del Rio is frequently photographed staring into the camera, Stout's face never appears in any of the images included in this chapter, his face either covered with flowing long hair or concealed behind the black mask of his "Ripper" persona. And although the book devotes an entire chapter to her affair with Stout, there is no mention of this period in the on-camera interviews recorded for the DVD. Nevertheless, in a Taschen promotional video for the book, del Rio holds up the book and points to the series of photographs that depict this particular sexual encounter with "Ripper" as being her favorite images in the entire book (Taschen 2008).

These are also *my* favorite images in the book, as a scholar *and* as a sexual subject. These are the photographs that are the most erotically charged for me, the ones that speak to me most forcefully about the irrational delights of sexual submission, of erotic subjugation, of what it might mean to fully abandon yourself to puta life. The final image in this series is striking. Stout's shaved pubis appears almost feminine, queerly juxtaposed against the hairiness of his arms. Here, Vanessa's usually flawless makeup is smeared from sweat and tears; her eyes, thick with smudged mascara, are closed; her mouth ajar; her teeth showing slightly as the head of his penis rests between her lips (fig. 3.14). Even as we might read this as an image of physical and emotional intensity, the silence of the photograph invites other erotic projections. I recognize a tenderness in the position of his fingers on her

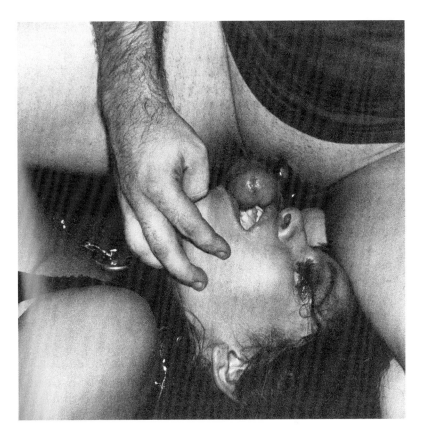

FIG 3.14 ▸ Vanessa del Rio and Reb Stout, ca. 1979. Photograph by Reb Stout. Courtesy of Vanessa del Rio.

face, a calmness that defines the quiet release into the terror of submission. She writes, "I think the only time I truly submitted is in these pictures where Reb's in his Ripper personality and his balls are in my mouth and you see the sweat and mascara running because I was choking on them" (del Rio 2010, 172). Even as it is *her* pain, *her* submission that is evident in these photographs, the absence of his face in these images, like his testicles in her mouth, serves to evidence *his* vulnerability—to exposure, to memory, to revealing the contours of his own carnal and psychic desires. And while Stout's face never appears in this chapter, his words do.[35] And in reference to these images, he states, "She had tears in her eyes while she was cumming— a series of concentrated orgasms like I'd never seen before . . . and it was marvelous to see!" (176). It bears emphasizing that this was consensual sex, it was desired submission, and in del Rio's mind, this scene and these images capture an emotional intensity beyond agency, a corporeal desire to be free from the rational demands of self-control and composure.

In her eloquent treatise *Sensational Flesh: Race, Power, and Masochism*, Amber Jamilla Musser (2014, 6) declares, "Reading [masochism] as exceptional reifies norms of whiteness and masculinity and suppresses other modes of reading power, agency, and experience." For racialized subjects, for feminine subjects, for all of us who are always imagined as the victims of someone else's cruel deployment of power, masochism functions as a way to both claim an intrinsic power that can then be surrendered and to actively inhabit the social and sexual roles to which we have been assigned on our own terms. Violence permeates this text, just as it infused so many aspects of del Rio's life, yet her reaction to it—whether to news reports of neighborhood rapes, her own violation at the hands of a state trooper, or her desire for sexual submission with her lover Reb—at times seems to call her account of herself into question, making her very personhood unintelligible. Yet that unintelligibility is precisely what offers a critical perspective on the very structures of meaning that would suggest that an adequate, rational, and recognizable response to puta life is possible. As a scholar, I think this is a lesson that bears repeating—not everything makes sense. Furthermore, the stories that del Rio shares expose how feminist frameworks sculpted through the life experiences of those for whom the privileges of race, class, or social position have provided shelter fail to account for the sexual experiences of racialized feminine subjects whose lives have been formed through abjection, violence, and terror.

For a porn star like Vanessa, whose sexualized body has been captured, reproduced, and circulated a million different ways, the photographic memorialization of an intimate affair offers something beyond autobiographical documentation; it memorializes a moment of profound interiority, a psychic space that disrupts the coherence of sexual subjectivity. Del Rio describes this desire for release and her inability to allow herself to exceed the limits of reason when she states: "I didn't know how to be broken." Of this series of images, she writes, "It wasn't horrible in any way, but it was total submission, and that was a strange feeling for me. It felt freeing; I didn't feel any responsibility in any way. It was also very rough" (del Rio 2010, 172). We can imagine that "very rough" might refer to being bound and nearly gagged by her lover's testicles, but I have seen enough of del Rio's on-screen performances to know that the physical demands of this scene were not unfamiliar to her as an actor. Instead, perhaps what was "very rough" was the freedom, the freedom to submit completely, to give herself over to another and to herself and to dwell in the space beyond rationality and reason.

In the book, the caption for this final photograph reads as follows: "I will refer you to the Spanish saying, 'Sin palabras,' without words" (176). In this moment, without words, del Rio resorts to Spanish to mark something beyond the logocentrism demanded of rational subjects. Like the other narratives collected in this book, Vanessa del Rio's account of herself presents complicated psychic realities that require us to question how we engage with the stories of puta life that are too painful, too twisted, too raw to fully process in language. Yet, this image and these words speak to me; they legitimate something about my own perverse desires for the self-shattering that submission seems to promise. I have known the edges of this feeling; it is a feeling I chase with the urgency of advancing years, a release from the limits of my own psychic interiority that always seems out of reach. Even as I concede the ways nostalgia for the pleasures of youth might dull the pain of decidedly less pleasant memories, I recognize something deeply familiar in del Rio's quest for the thrill of erotic adventure. That an aging Latina porn star might offer us alternative understandings of the workings of female sexual survivance and pleasure requires that we wrestle with the ability of speaking subjects to narrate their own complex realities, even and especially when their interpretations unsettle the preexisting logics we might wish to impose. But while we need to listen to these alternate forms of meaning making, we also need to leave room for those moments that resist meaning, that refuse transparency, that remain sheltered in the space of unknowing. Those moments beyond reason and intelligibility also have the power to touch us so deeply. As a young person, del Rio modeled for me a way of being sexually adventurous in the world, of transforming experiences of pain and violation and making of them something else. Now, as we both advance in years, she was again teaching me something about the uses of the erotic, what to do with memory, how to understand submission, and how to represent what exists beyond words. In a world where so many of us who are condemned to puta life are defined as always already irrational and outside structures of sexual and social legibility, those moments of carnal pleasure, liberated from the constraints of language, and reason, might burst open to create possibilities for something akin to freedom.

Vende caro tu amor, aventurera
Dale el precio del dolor, a tu pasado
Y aquel, que de tu boca, la miel quiera
Que pague con brillantes tu pecado.
AGUSTÍN LARA

TOUCHING ALTERITY

The Women of Casa Xochiquetzal

This chapter begins with two books of photography, *Las amorosas más bravas* (Desrus and Gómez Ramos 2014) and *The Women of Casa X* (Venville and de la Rosa 2013), to think about the different ways we see and feel the vicissitudes of puta life. Both of these books pair European photographers with local Mexican journalists, and both combine photography and biography to document the same unique subjects: the female residents of Casa Xochiquetzal, a shelter in Mexico City for elderly sex workers, some retired, some not. As my work on this project continued, the visual archive around this house and its colorful residents started to multiply. Soon other photographers, journalists, and filmmakers started to report on the women of Casa Xochiquetzal, many of whom appear across these differently authored projects, attesting to a fascination in visually depicting these unlikely subjects of Latina sexual labor. As a corrective to other forms of visual documentation such as pornography, street photography, or the images housed in the archives of criminality, these texts all share an intentional investment in augmenting images of sex workers with first-person accounts of these women's lives even as they reveal significant differences in tone, visual conventions, narrative framings, and the negotiated terms of their production. Positioned alongside one another, these variegated forms of constructing knowledge about puta life occasion an opportunity to probe the relationship between the ways we tell stories and the feelings they leave behind.

Drawing our gaze to these viejas, these putas, these aging Latina sex workers, this chapter asks us not just to look into their faces and onto their lives but to linger in that sensory encounter, to sit with the memories and associations that are ignited in our gaze. For image makers, a focus on the face becomes a visual strategy for humanizing subjects, for creating a visual encounter that might inspire an ethical engagement with alterity. Emmanuel Levinas (1997, 294) writes, "In front of the face, I always demand more of myself." Yet looking at a face in a photograph or hearing a voice in a documentary is a vexed form of social engagement, an elusive kind of haptic connection; we know that the recognition of humanity is not universally conferred. Who we are invariably shapes what we witness within these frames. Judith Butler (2005, 30) asks, "After all, under what conditions do some individuals acquire a face, a legible and visible face, and others do not?" Focusing on these aging sex workers, these unimaginable sexual subjects of contemporary urban Mexico, this chapter asks: How does the narrative voice of the speaking subject transform our engagement with the aesthetic representations of their lives? How does the juxtaposition of image and voice impact how we see, hear, and sense puta life?

Casa Xochiquetzal

Situated between the neighborhoods La Merced and Tepito in Mexico City, in front of la Plaza San Sebastian, Casa Xochiquetzal was founded in 2006. This is un barrio bravo, a rough neighborhood known primarily for its open-air markets, pirated merchandise, street crime, and sexual commerce. The person credited with the idea behind the house, the only one of its kind in the Americas, is Carmen Muñoz, herself an aging sex worker. Muñoz tells the story of working one night and encountering three older women she had known as fellow sex workers who were now homeless and living under a tarp on the corner where they had once all worked. That night, Muñoz committed herself to finding a solution, stating: "I'm going to do whatever it takes to at least put a roof over their heads" (Venville and de la Rosa 2013, 10). Herself the daughter of a pimp, she explains, "Who's to say that these women that are now 80 or 90 years old weren't extorted by my father so that I could eat? That's why I'm here" (10). Muñoz describes reaching out first to Maya Goded, a feminist artist and photographer she had previously known. Soon afterward, several other iconic Mexican feminist names started to get involved with the project, including the anthropologist Martha Lamas, the journalist and author Elena Poniatowska, and the performance artist and former Mexican senator Jesusa Rodríguez.[1] These women set the gears in motion and were pivotal in moving this from idea to edifice, eventually writing the proposal that was subsequently approved by then mayor and future president of the Republic Andrés Manuel López Obrador. After acquiring financing and support from various Mexican social service organizations, they eventually secured a building that they began renovating in 2005. They named it Casa Xochiquetzal, after the Aztec goddess of female sexual power, beauty, and feminine crafts.

The first of these two books that document the stories and the faces of these women is *Las amorosas más bravas* (fig. 4.1).[2] Published in 2014 in Mexico, this book is the result of a collaboration between two women, Bénédicte Desrus, a French photographer, and Celia Gómez Ramos, an independent Mexican journalist and novelist.[3] Drawn by local publicity surrounding the founding of Casa Xochiquetzal, Desrus had begun taking photographs of the residents of this house and eventually sought Gómez Ramos to help her publicize the story and the images she had produced. Before being compiled into a book, Desrus published her photographs in numerous magazines and newspapers in Mexico and internationally in order to raise awareness and funds for the house. The final imprint, published by Conaculta in Mexico, was funded in part by several national grants.[4] In total, this book took six years to complete—during which time Desrus and Gómez Ramos visited with these women for extended periods, documenting their lives through interviews and photographs. It is written as a kind of long-form journalism, interspersing extended quotes from the residents about their past lives and present circumstances with expository description and analysis. The book's title, which might be translated literally as "Lovers Most Fierce," appears in the English-language translation insert that accompanies the book as *Tough Love*. This emphasis on strength, toughness, and resilience is evident in one of the opening sections: "Living together and getting along hasn't been easy. Though several Casa Xochiquetzal residents knew one another, they weren't friends since they always competed for johns. They may not even be friends now. Survival made them tough. They're wise, fun, good storytellers with strong imaginations. They tend to distrust, don't build lasting relationships; they like analyzing everyone else's weaknesses and strong suits. They're born observers and practical psychologists. They eat life with a spoon, or they bite as may be required"

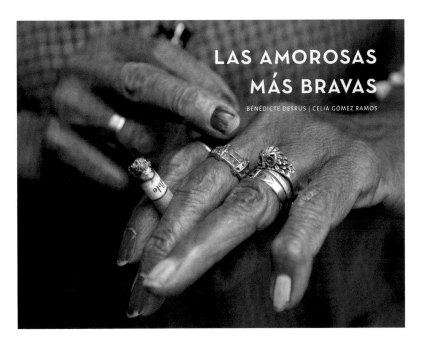

FIG 4.1 ▸ Book cover, Bénédicte Desrus and Celia Gómez Ramos, *Las amorosas más bravas / Tough Love*, 2014. Photograph by Bénédicte Desrus.

(Desrus and Gómez Ramos 2014, 4).[5] This opening text captures the collective complexity of the house's residents, presenting them as neither hapless victims nor empowered heroines, subverting the two dominant narratives that revolve around sex workers. The protagonist that emerges at the center of the narrative is the house itself—the space of the collective—and as in the quote here, the women are often referred to in the plural, as if they share a single personality.

Painted in the vibrant hues so often associated with Mexico, the house —a restored eighteenth-century structure with an open courtyard and a fountain—imparts its own visual appeal as a backdrop for these colorful lives.[6] As a photographic subject, the structure's bright-yellow walls and terra-cotta floors provide a vibrant backdrop for the bright-blue metal bed frames, the startling pink details of stuffed animals and hair ribbons, and the glossy white of so many plastic chairs. Many of the images depict the intimate spaces of the residents' private rooms, the bags and boxes strewn about serving as the visual evidence of the chaos of their mobile lives; photographs of faces, feet, and hands sit alongside images of plates of food and decorated altars. The individual residents are named in the quoted passages, frequently using nicknames; however, they and their possessions are left unidentified in the photographs, playing down an emphasis on individual residents. Importantly, on the Sipa USA website that secures photo permissions, Desrus makes a point to identify each of the residents by name in her descriptions, names that I have included in my own captions. However, within the context of the book, there is no attempt at establishing a concordance between the narratives and the images; they all belong together within the narrative frame of Casa Xochiquetzal.[7]

Photojournalism as a genre provides visual documentation as evidence in the production of news. A state-subsidized house for elderly sex workers certainly constitutes news, but the particular circumstances or life stories of any one resident only acquire value relative to their ability to illuminate the larger narrative. Unlike the singularity of a porn star like Vanessa del Rio, here, the one, any one, is intended to stand for the whole, to depict the story that is Casa Xochiquetzal. Photojournalism thrives on narratives of the unknown and unseen, and frequently aims to make knowable a segment of society that has been constructed as hidden from view. As a genre, it is concerned with "the faithful and comprehensive depiction of the subject" (National Press Photographers Association, n.d.). Even as *Las amorosas más bravas* is about documenting this house and its residents, it is also a pedagogical project, intended to educate and advocate for the rights of these stigmatized and forgotten members of society. It even includes a link to a website that provides information on how you can contribute to its ongoing solvency. Drawing on the seemingly odd, dare I say queer, juxtaposition of aging bodies and overt sexuality, the authors of *Las amorosas más bravas* frame the story of Casa Xochiquetzal for an intended audience that supposedly has no knowledge of how these women live, not because they are foreign but because they are invisible. In the process, it constructs an insider/outsider binary wherein the photographer/reader/viewer is never imagined to already know the subject, let alone to *be* the subject.

Most of these photographs situate these women within the visual registers of the everyday, sharing a life together. We see them sweeping, sleeping, eating, napping, even showering, but the authors also make a point of showing us images of these women applying makeup, putting on high heels, and taking to the streets dressed in their finest attire, in other words, carrying out the rituals of gender so often associated with their profession. As part of the imperative of photojournalism, these images confirm the fact that these really are sex workers; they provide visual evidence of the

FIG 4.2 ▸ Amalia, a resident of Casa Xochiquetzal, puts on makeup before going out to work, 2010. Photograph by Bénédicte Desrus. Courtesy of Bénédicte Desrus and Sipa USA.

deviance from social norms and expectations that makes this a newsworthy project in the first place. It is important to note that many of these women continue to work the street, servicing clients, some of whom they have known for more than half a century. And this is a freedom that is understood as a foundational premise of the house. If the women presented are being rescued, it is not from the imagined exploitation of sex work but from the poverty, violence, misogyny, and stigma that define their lives as poor, aging, female inhabitants of a decaying Third World metropolis.

In the image in figure 4.2, we see a resident applying what appears as another layer of rouge to an already heavily made-up face. In this close-up, each detail of her appearance is presented in sharp relief: the pores on her chin, the deep creases of her brow, the chipped gold and red nail polish of her stubby nail. She wears an ill-fitting wig that reveals wisps of gray beneath; the darkened eyebrows and blue eyeshadow against her deeply wrinkled face scream the feminine excesses so often associated with puta aesthetics. As my gaze scrutinizes every inch of the image, I wonder if, as viewers, we are supposed to be charmed, bemused, or horrified at these attempts at femme vanity. The truth is I am ashamed of how sad this photograph makes me feel, how far away from this image of puta life I want to situate my own attachments to performances of feminine beauty imagined to be past their prime. In her hand, she holds a small mirror with a blurry image of a bikini blonde, a seemingly universal image of sexy that is far away from both of us.[8] This is femme aging and it is terrifying.

Categorical markers of age are always both historical and cultural, assigned meaning within very particular local contexts. In Mexico and other parts of the Spanish-speaking world, the term *la tercera edad* (the third age) is a popular euphemism for the aged, a social-cultural term predicated on divisions intended to divide one's life into childhood, one's "productive" and "reproductive" years, and the imagined decline that follows; a sequential categorization that situates normative sexuality squarely in the middle. Yet while almost all the residents at Casa Xochiquetzal have borne children, and more than a few have been married, their sexual lives fall outside the temporal logics of reproductive sexuality and heteronormativity. This chronology of "straight time" has little meaning for these women, many of whom were molested as children and continue to be sexually active well behind the temporal horizon deemed socially appropriate. Age here is marked not by stages of life but by the ways homelessness, social stigma, and violence wear on the body across time; the ways the cruel marks of neglect are etched into the skin, teeth, and soles of those who have lived unprotected from so much harm.

Often in these photographs, we are positioned at the door frame, at a safe distance, as outsiders peering into this private sphere where these unknown subjects dwell, poised to venture assumptions or cast judgment. In most of these images, there is no direct engagement with the camera; instead, the presence of the photographer seems to disappear, and we, the audience, function as reluctant but willing voyeurs who gain access into these intimate scenes of puta life. If, in depictions of sex workers in street photography, the door frame teases the viewer with the promise of what might lie inside, in these images we are ushered into their interior spaces, allowed to let our gaze roam across these private quarters and by extension the interiority of these seemingly public lives of these twenty-first-century mujeres públicas.

In figure 4.3, two women comfort one another, their plump bodies pressed together. There is nothing in the image to suggest that they are sex workers; instead, they seem to defy any visual expectation of what that designation might suggest. There is no narrative depiction of what occasioned

FIG 4.3 ▸ Canela and Norma, both residents of Casa Xochiquetzal, 2013. Photograph by Bénédicte Desrus. Courtesy of Bénédicte Desrus and Sipa USA.

this embrace that registers a moment of shared comfort. Their dark clothes and gray hair seem to merge together into a single mass of sorrow and solace in the center of the frame. Seated on a shiny blue tarp that covers their bed, they seem as oblivious to the camera as they are to the mess that surrounds them. Panties hang drying on the bed post, and a white plastic bag heavy with unseen weight is slung over the ear of a pale turquoise chair piled high with clothes.

In his essay "The 'Stuff' of Archives: Mess, Migration, and Queer Lives," Martin Manalansan (2014, 94) develops a notion of the archive that locates "the quotidian within the messy physical, symbolic, and emotional arrangements of objects, bodies, and spaces in queer immigrant lives." Read this way, each of these items, each pile of scattered objects, forms an archive of the disarray of these residents' lives, making material the unruliness of puta life. But Manalansan's text also reminds us that a mess can represent elements of a life and a kind of order that are simply not visible to someone else, emphasizing that sometimes a mess "is not always about misery, complete desolation, and abandonment but can also gesture to moments of vitality, pleasure, and fabulousness" (100). I look again and no-

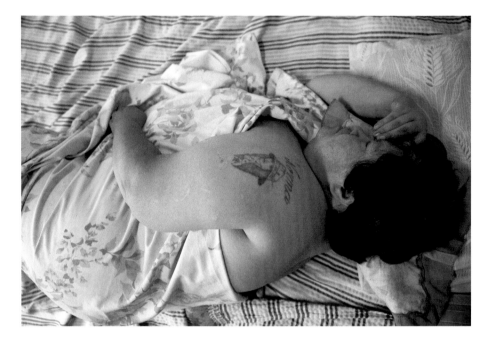

FIG 4.4 ▸ Norma, a resident of Casa Xochiquetzal, rests in her bedroom, 2013. Photograph by Bénédicte Desrus. Courtesy of Bénédicte Desrus and Sipa USA.

tice the neatly folded blankets, how carefully the tarp is stretched across the bed, the objects on the wall that seem more intentionally positioned: a photograph of a couple, a blond Jesus, and childlike toys; material memories of happier times. I am reminded to look more carefully, to look beyond despair, to fabulate other possibilities for the pasts that these women have carried with them into this frame.

In only a scant few of these photographs are the subjects consciously posing for the camera. Instead, very often, the camera seems to sneak up on its prey, capturing a moment that might never have been intended for prying eyes. In the image in figure 4.4, we see a sleeping figure, her stout naked body barely covered by a thin flowered sheet, hinting at the sticky heat of Mexico City. Her eyes are shut, her fingers cinched together at her brow. I imagine she is dreaming, and I wonder about the horizons of her dreamscapes. As viewers, we hover directly above her dormant body, peering down, lingering over each detail of her reposed form. The photographer has brought us so close that we are able to see the pale remains of the scars on her upper arm, the white roots of her short brown hair, the pink ruffle of her pillow. The proximity of the shot confirms Desrus's seemingly unrestricted access to the residents. Pages later, we stumble upon a story, under the heading "Normota, with more lives than a cat." It reads, "Tattoos, yeah, I've got one on either arm. I did the first one when I was sixteen; it's a Panther's head and the other one is a woman's torso with her breasts exposed and up above, my name: Norma. Other markings on my body are the scar that the screwdriver left on my brow; three knife wounds, from muggings; a pair of nasty bites on my left arm, a souvenir from Rosa; a slash in my right arm, from an argument; and that first cut from when I was a girl" (Desrus and Gómez Ramos 2014, 15).[9]

The image of a sleeping tattooed form glimpsed pages before unfolds here in Norma's response to a question that doesn't appear in the text but that prompts her to narrate her life story through a recounting of the marks left behind. Even as her illustrated and scarred body is separated from the biographical story that describes it, her tattoo serves as proof of identification that attaches the story to the image. Each element of Norma's narrative does its own work of documentation, affirming precisely the kind of "toughness" that the title of the book suggests, producing the kind of journalistic knowledge that attests to the truth of the image and the story, the faithful depiction of the subject. But the narrative also oozes other random biographical elements that do and don't fill in the details that the image provides. As the passage continues, Norma tells us that she is a mujeriega (womanizer) and that the father of her first born was a travesti named Arturo who was also known as Erika. She rattles off a long list of female lovers, including Rosa, a taxi dancer and occasional sex worker who was her girlfriend for thirteen years, whom she would sometimes pimp and protect; the same Rosa who left bite marks as souvenirs. But Norma says she is too tired for women these days.

The story moves forward and back in time; in these pages, Norma talks about her children and her childhood. We learn that at fourteen she crossed the border, went to San Francisco, and worked as a babysitter and that she spent five years as a lucha libre wrestler under the pseudonym La Sombra. But she also offers up her other nicknames: la Güera, la Jefa, el Gordo, la Sinaloense, Cachetes de Gatito, Maria Machetes, Normota, and la Juguitos, a nickname she earned in jail after stealing a juice pop (Desrus and Gómez Ramos 2014, 16).[10] She tells us that the fight with the screwdriver destroyed her optic nerve and caused her to lose an eye, and that for a while she hated mirrors. A few paragraphs later, we read: "One day I slit my left wrist twenty-some times with a razor blade because I didn't think life made a lot of sense" (15).[11] Even as these residents are presented as "tough," and Norma's queer masculinity might make her appear tougher than most, as readers we become witnesses to the psychic and corporeal scars left behind, the extracted wages of survival. Norma tells us that today she has heart problems and a few extra pounds. She ends her narrative by saying, "I've got my regular customers. I may be old at this point, I am what I am, but you never forget your old tricks" (16).[12] The portrait that emerges of the sleeping tattooed figure slides out of the dingy confines of her mismatched sheets and reappears in my imagination on a lucha libre stage, in a posh apartment in San Francisco tending to crying babies, sitting in jail, or fighting with her lover Rosa, who wants more money than Norma can provide. The images and the stories, each partial and incomplete, resist any kind of narrative closure. Even as her stories are filled with violence and hardship, there is also a sense of transnational adventure, queer lovers—loved and lost—and the longing for the boundless futurity that youth promises. These narratives hover around the image, offering an opaque screen onto which we can project our own anxieties and desires—about violence, desperation, and the slow decay of time but perhaps also about youthful escapades and the things we did for love.

Within the visual register of photojournalism, the precarity of these women's lives functions as the necessary precondition for our visual access. Because they are also residents in a shelter that provides them certain protection and security, they are also exposed to the glare of publicity, curious foreigners, and well-intentioned helpers who use the very compelling story of Casa Xochiquetzal, and the mixed emotions of pity, empathy, and perhaps identification that its residents might inspire, as the lure that will secure its ongoing financial solvency. Maybe documentation is the price of the bed.

In their introduction to *Feeling Photography*, Elspeth Brown and Thy Phu outline what they see as the difference between discursive modes of representation with their emphases on the disciplinary construction of meaning versus an approach that emphasizes feeling. They write, "Whereas discursive approaches to the archive have focused on presence and memory, by contrast, affective approaches attend to the nuances of absence and forgetting, precisely those qualities that would appear to scatter irrevocably beyond the archive" (Brown and Phu 2014, 19). Reading and seeing for feeling, for absence and forgetting, opens an interpretive space that challenges the evidentiary logics of knowledge production. Following José Esteban Muñoz (2019, 65), as a methodological mode of interpretation, lingering in the affective spaces the sensorial pries open registers a queer form of evidence, "an evidence that has been queered in relation to the laws of what counts as proof." Reading for feeling, however, also raises new questions: If the intent of the authors of this project is to inspire feelings that will raise awareness and money, I wonder, precisely what affects are called upon to create care for another? Is it pity or compassion, identification or the affirmation of a safe distance?

The Puta and the Portrait

Let me turn to my second object of analysis, the book *The Women of Casa X*, to witness the difference that genres of documentation inspire and to delve deeper into the affective possibilities that the juxtaposition of biography and photography instantiate. Published in 2013 in Amsterdam, by London-based filmmaker and photographer Malcolm Venville and with text by Amanda de la Rosa, this book features color portraits of many of the same residents glimpsed in *Las amorosas más bravas*.[13] However, while *Las amorosas más bravas* emerged as an extended form of photojournalism and took six years to complete, the short testimonial accounts and studio portraits of *The Women of Casa X* were collected over the course of a single month. Within the pages of the book, Venville's portraits sit alongside the subject's name, age, and brief first-person accounts of these women's lives composed by de la Rosa. The title of this book, *The Women of Casa X*, keeps the Spanish word *casa* to maintain the referent to a Spanish-speaking domestic elsewhere even as all the biographical accounts de la Rosa compiled are presented in English. And it shortens the longer Nahuatl name Xochiquetzal to the letter *X*, to signal the *X* of X-rated, imagined as the universal linguistic signifier for sexualized content.

The brief introduction to the book offers remarkably little information about how this creative collaboration between photographer, interviewer, and models occurred, or how the stories or the portraits were solicited or compensated. And it provides no additional biographical information about Amanda de la Rosa, the Mexican journalist Venville hired to interview, translate, and edit these brief testimonial fragments from Spanish into English. What we are told is that the interviews consisted of two prompts: "tell me about your life and talk to me about men" (Venville and de la Rosa 2013, 5). The text does not mention how these women might have felt about having their portraits taken; we are only told that "Genoveva was happy when viewing a polaroid because it was the first time she had seen herself portrayed in a photograph" (4). In contrast to the visual presentation of quotidian life and domesticity in the book by Desrus and Gómez Ramos, Venville's studio portraits bring to these unlikely subjects the classic conventions of studio portraiture.

Portraits are intended to elevate the subject, to signal their singularity and significance as subjects of our gaze, to capture the individual spirit we each possess and that the artist is entrusted to portray. Unlike the visually cluttered images of Desrus, Venville's portraits attempt to extract these women's bodies from the visual context so essential to photojournalism, to brush away the mess of these women's lives to reveal something else. Gone are the colorful backdrops, the dirty dishes, and the crumpled sheets—instead, we get exposed flesh and a face peering back at us. A hearing child of deaf parents, Venville credits growing up surrounded by silence and deaf culture as being central to his work as a photographer and filmmaker.[14] In an interview, Venville states how for him "photography is about looking at the body, about attitude, gesture, and feeling as communicated through the body" (RLJE Films 2010). Even as the accompanying narratives collected over a brief span of time fill in details about the subjects of these photographs, these portraits are intended to function as works of art rather than photojournalism, and aesthetics rather than representation or advocacy function as the primary consideration.

The stories these women tell in *The Women of Casa X*—of abusive husbands, fathers, and clients; of the risks and rewards of sex work—are not that different from the stories recorded in *Las amorosas más bravas*, but their juxtaposition alongside these formal portraits unsettles the visual encounter with the aesthetic object. In attaching a singular name and face to each individual life narrative, we are instructed to project a sexual history and affective attitude onto the faces of those staring back at us. Rather than visual access to their everyday lives or the action shots made possible by the portability of Desrus's digital camera, these photographs, shot using a large-format Ebony 4×5 camera against a muted blue-gray background, emphasize the staged distance between photographer and subject.[15] Another significant difference is that in Venville's photographs, many of these women, who are all between forty-nine and ninety years old, are nude or in various stages of undress, radically altering the conventions of both portraiture and erotic image making organized around youthful beauty. In the introduction, de la Rosa states, "The original plan was that they would pose dressed so it took me by surprise that they agreed to the photographer's suggestion that they can undress in front of the camera, except for Aurelia who does not remove her clothes, not even for bathing" (Venville and de la Rosa 2013, 5). While their nudity might affirm a distance for some viewers, a distance accentuated by age, class, and race, it can also register an unsettling intimacy for others—as I flip through these pages, I realize that the only other older naked bodies that I have seen are of people very close to me. In their nakedness, Venville's photographs call to mind the soft, rotund contours of my own tías and abuelas, even as they also stage an uncomfortable confrontation with my own aging body.

The woman on the book cover is Raquel López Moreno (fig. 4.5). In her narrative, she describes working as a maid and as a seamstress after her mother died and nostalgically recounts learning to make stuffed animals and dolls. But early on in her life, her sexual history had already colored her social possibilities. She states, "I had already had my *fracaso* [downfall] and once you are not a virgin, men don't treat you right, and they don't respect you" (Venville and de la Rosa 2013, 64). Of her first time selling sex for money, she states, "I watched the women that worked the plaza and it looked like they were doing all right . . . and I said, 'it's nothing I couldn't do,'" and so began her life as a sex worker (64). In many ways, Raquel's story is a classic one, the tragic consequences of a poor girl who having already lost her virginity—the only value she is imagined to have and the necessary condition for future love and marriage—found sex work as a way to make ends meet. The reader is presented with a few paragraphs of first-person narrative that recounts this brief moment of biographical history, meant to explain so much. Raquel tells us that today she lives in Casa Xochiquetzal with her pet chameleon, Lirio, explaining, "I keep her in a plastic bag so she won't scare people and give them diabetes" (Venville and de la Rosa 2013, 64). But the juxtaposition of name, image, and story also enacts a reckoning with the singularity of the subject. In this case, that singularity presents a bit of a dilemma: this face already appears familiar, I have already seen this face, this wig before. Perhaps you did too, a few pages ago in my own text, applying makeup. There is already more to this story that we do not know.

The portrait of Raquel that graces the cover of the book has her standing in profile, her arms by her side, her face turned to look at us. She is only partially naked, topless with pantyhose covering a pair of red underwear. Hers is a serious expression—not angry, not joyful, but determined and focused, her body fully erect—and she looks stiff, as if she is unaccustomed to having her picture taken, yet adept at following the directions of the photographer who has directed her gaze. The look on her face is one

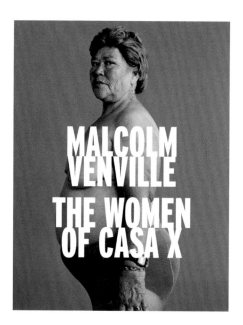

FIG 4.5 ▸ Book cover, Malcolm Venville and Amanda de la Rosa, *The Women of Casa X*, 2013. Photograph of Raquel López Moreno by Malcolm Venville. Courtesy of Malcolm Venville and Schilt Publishing.

of neither shame nor seduction. In fact, the photograph resembles a mug shot more than a portrait, certainly not erotica. Her expression seems to be one of quiet defiance—of judgment and of pity. Her age is not stated; the deep lines in her face and hands are contrasted with the smoothness of the skin that covers her breasts and belly. We see, even here, partially nude, the marks of her own self-styling, the material objects that she has used to decorate her body, the beaded bracelets wrapped around a digital watch, the hint of lipstick, and a wig. Partially hidden by the bold white letters of Venville's name on the cover, there is also the mark of the state, the circle left behind from a small pox vaccination, a mark I also share.

In contrast to most studio portraits in which the subject contracts the photographer to render a flattering portrayal of how they might wish to be seen, this image captures a performance for Venville, the photographer—a performance that also functions as a kind of sexual labor. There is an honesty in the exchange that I appreciate. The blue-eyed gentleman from London has contracted her to pose, he has suggested that she might undress, the Mexican woman that accompanies him has asked her a series of questions in Spanish, and to all of this Raquel López Moreno has dutifully complied. I assume that Venville, a professional photographer, compensated these women, his models, for their time and their labor. They are, after all, sex workers, accustomed to exchanging access to their body for a negotiated amount of coin. Part of what we witness in these images, therefore, is

 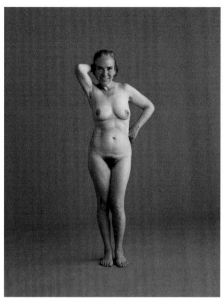

FIG 4.6 ▸ Sofía Priscila Aparición, "la Rubia," in *The Women of Casa X*, 2013.
Photograph by Malcolm Venville. Courtesy of Malcolm Venville and Schilt Publishing.

FIG 4.7 ▸ Sofía Priscila Aparición, "la Rubia," in *The Women of Casa X*, 2013.
Photograph by Malcolm Venville. Courtesy of Malcolm Venville and Schilt Publishing.

the visual trace of their sexual labor. Even as these images depict a consensual exchange performed across variegated forms of power difference, it is Venville's rendition of that exchange that circulates in what Deborah Poole (1997, 8) terms the "visual economy," the circuits of exchange in which "visual images move across national and cultural boundaries." These circuits of exchange hover around each possible interpretive encounter within this archive, emphasizing the variegated points of contact and the different affective registers they might instantiate.

The pair of images shown in figures 4.6 and 4.7 are of Sofía Priscila Aparición, "la Rubia." At forty-nine, she is one of the youngest residents, younger than I am today. Even as this book includes women in their seventies, eighties, and nineties, it is often the women closer to my own age who captivate my attention. While many of the women at Casa Xochiquetzal are already quite aged, most are not—not yet anyway. Sofía's narrative begins, "Falling in love is horrible. I tell you honestly, it is awful and I hope it never happens to me again. How can you fall in love with something as worthless as a man?" (Venville and de la Rosa 2013, 54). Sofía describes turning to sex work later in life: "No one told me how you do it, I learned on my own. . . . I was forty then. I'd go out to sell my candy in pants and sneakers, the miniskirt and high-heels girls don't steal clients from me . . . men come without me having to chase them." She goes on: "It's a job like any other and there's nothing to it. They are looking to satisfy their instincts, they give you your money and everybody's happy" (54). In the first photograph, we see her as she might dress to sell candy in the market, demure yet smiling, dressed for comfort and utility as she navigates the uneven streets of Mexico City, and in the second, we are presented with another view.

As a pair, these photographs work to reveal what is underneath, revealing not just her body but the sexuality that lives beneath the surface. To live in public, to be una mujer pública, is also about knowing how to conceal in public, how to keep parts of yourself hidden from public view, to assign value to your own sense of interiority. Yet, presented with the juxtaposition of these two different portraits, we might ask: What does la Rubia want us to see, and what are we, as viewers, invested in seeing? The differences between these poses are quite startling. In the first, her hands are folded, clasped together, resting over her sex in a familiar gesture of ladylike reserve. Even as her body appears closed unto itself, her wide toothy smile radiates joy. In contrast, the second image is reminiscent of a pin-up magazine, a classic pose of sexualized femininity, one hand on her hip, one hand raised behind her head, lifting her breasts ever so slightly. Her legs are positioned so that one hip juts out, creating a more curvaceous silhouette. Whereas in the first photograph, her head is pulled back, in the second it is pushed forward and skewed slightly to the side; her smile, while more subdued, is also more inviting, her eyes looking up just a bit seductively. We sense la Rubia is enjoying this interaction with the photographer whose camera and attention are focused only on her. From her face, and the easy demeanor of her story, I imagine she is a generally happy person. In her narrative, one of the longest in the book, she tells us that one of her clients hired her to clean and take his children to school. She tells us that they are friends now, and he and his new wife visit her on occasion. Her narrative ends with her saying, "I have no regrets. . . . This is the life I was given" (Venville and de la Rosa 2013, 56).

I realize that standing naked before this foreign masculine stranger, following his direction to stand here, or look there, might in fact be a rather familiar experience for these women. Nowhere in the text do we learn what these women thought about the strangers who came to photograph them and ask them questions. However, in the introduction, Venville describes *his* sense of the exchange, stating, "It is a feeling difficult to describe but the women were at once heartbreaking, funny, indifferent and emotionally cold" (Venville and de la Rosa 2013, 5). I am struck by how these words echo the ways many clients might describe the affective trace of sexual labor, how they might make sense of the women who have opened their bodies to them. Left with the photograph, the evidence of their exchange together, we might discern in their poses and gestures these women's own attitudes about the sex work they perform and the men they service. Venville was simply one of many men who have paid for access to their bodies, their stories, their time. Looking at the photographs, the trace of their labor left behind, I ask: Were they compliant workers doing a job, or did they search for the possibility of joy in their random liaisons with their clients? Or perhaps, more cynically, I wonder if these images simply demonstrate the skills of their vocation, their rehearsed ability to perform pleasure, interest, or submission for the satisfaction of others.

In the photograph in figure 4.8 is Paola Pacheco Juárez, sixty years old. Her story details how she came to Casa Xochiquetzal after being arrested. She describes how ever since coming to her house, "life is different, and I feel like another person" (Venville and de la Rosa 2013, 62). She tells us that she has been sober for ten months. She is in rehab now and sees a psychiatrist and psychologist, services provided by Casa Xochiquetzal. The eldest child of adult alcoholics, Paola describes being raped by her older stepbrother at age eight and working the cantinas at age thirteen. She remembers: "I'd drink and let any old ugly cologne-drenched asshole grab me but only as long as that money was right on the table. So I ended up in a dive cantina, drinking rot-gut from a jug until things would go blank" (61). In the photograph, she is completely naked. The five children she bore and abandoned have left their traces on her body, and she dreams of one day finding them. She declares, "I hope things can be different" (62).

I notice her toes, their curves and callouses, the pink where her shoes chafed the more delicate surfaces of her feet. I take in the fluorescent fuchsia of her short, manicured nails, the tattooed arch of her eyebrows. I fixate on what appears like a sore on her thigh. To appear naked is to leave yourself vulnerable and exposed, yet in this image Paola is covered in forms of protection. On her arm is a tattoo of la Santa Muerte, who Paola says "is always present, like God's secretary" (Venville and de la Rosa 2013, 62). An incarnation of death, an unofficial Mexican saint repudiated by the Vatican, Santa Muerta remains a favorite figure among thieves, sex workers, queers, and drug lords, and a shrine to her exists in the center of Tepito.[16] Paola

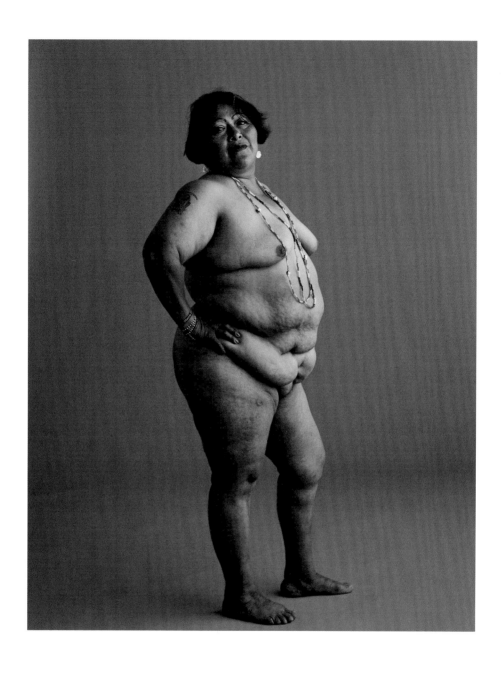

FIG 4.8 ▸ Paola Pacheco Juárez, in *The Women of Casa X*, 2013. Photograph by Malcolm Venville. Courtesy of Malcolm Venville and Schilt Publishing.

also describes how the necklaces she is wearing are related to Santería and that these, too, offer her protection. She does not tell us their significance or her relationship to this Afro-Cuban religious practice, but I recognize the yellow of Ochún, my own patron saint, and the colors of Las Siete Potencias Africanas around her neck, the bracelets for Orula y Elegua. As she stands before us, I try to imagine the other moments in Paola's life when she might have needed protection, when she might have been called upon to strike this pose, at once sexually provocative and fiercely combative. I try to imagine her at forty, at thirteen, at eight, the affective haunting of her narrative projected back onto the image. I want to offer her protection too.

Moving Accounts

As news of Casa Xochiquetzal started to circulate, other journalists, photographers, and image makers—amused, concerned, or inspired by these women—also began making the journey to this barrio bravo to make "visible" these women's stories and faces in an effort to bring them greater compassion and perhaps greater resources to the house and its residents. News of the house has appeared in newspapers all around the world, including Brazil, Macedonia, Germany, and the United Kingdom. And every story I have found included images, as if only by seeing these women's faces might we truly believe their stories or care about their lives. After publishing a story on Casa Xochiquetzal, *Stern*, a German weekly news magazine, raised ten thousand euros to donate to the house (Wiechmann 2019).[17] The *New York Times* sent its own photographer, Adriana Zehbrauskas, to Mexico City to file a photo essay titled with the misleading headline "Retired from the Brutal Streets of Mexico, Sex Workers Find a Haven" (many of these women are far from retired) (Zehbrauskas 2018). The word *dignity* appears frequently in all these accounts.

Mexican sociologist Nancy Flores Castillo, who has led an investigation into the house, describes how in these numerous accounts these women parrot a learned discourse that they deploy repeatedly (Flores Castillo, Cabello, and Cavalli 2017, 11).[18] For example, in most of these interviews, the women generally refer to themselves as "sexo servidoras," literally sexual service providers, a term, like the English-language term *sex worker*, that is intended to highlight the productive function of their labor as providing a service.[19] But in one interview, Sonia declares, "I don't care much for the term *sexoservidora*, «sex worker»—I think *puta* or *chica del tacón dorado*, or *mariposilla*, *cusca*, or *mujer de cascos ligeros* works better for me" (Desrus and Gómez Ramos 2014, 34). Sonia seems to be rebelling against forms of instruction, media training if you will, that would have her use more palatable or politically correct terms instead of these colorful local colloquialisms.[20] As these women became media celebrities of a sort, speaking into cameras, answering the queries of reporters from around the world, they seem particularly aware that they are also serving as public ambassadors for the mission of the house and as public advocates for the human, civil, and labor rights of sex workers.

In addition to these numerous magazine articles, photo essays, and these two books, there are at least three different documentaries that present stories about this house and these women. Rather than still images and transcribed texts, in these audiovisual accounts we now get to see and hear many of the same residents narrating the same biographical details of their lives. As we see their moving, breathing bodies and hear the tone and timbre of their voices, these narratives become imbued with new sensorial and affective elements. The first video documentary to emerge is a short three-part web series directed by Santiago Stelley titled *House of the Setting Sun*, produced in 2008 as part of the *Vice Guide to Sex*, a joint production of *Vice* magazine's video site in partnership with CNN.[21] As a journalistic accounting of their lives, each five-minute segment tries to balance the tears and tragedy of their stories of being pushed into the sex trade by families and husbands with moments of ribald levity and humor. As part of what makes this news worthy of a *Vice Guide to Sex* episode, considerable attention is paid to the fact that several of the residents still sell sex, and we hear questions asked and answered about how much and how many. Paola, discussed previously, is one of four women who is interviewed for this short series. In an appeal to the political and pedagogical impulse of documentary, she talks about the impunity with which sex workers are murdered and shows off her Santa Muerte tattoo. But she also mentions that she "still gets some young ones," and when the unseen masculine voice of the interviewer asks, "¿Qué tal?" she answers "Bien rico," and she smiles like she means it (Stelley 2008, part 1, 2:57). Later, she says, "I'll keep working into my old age, as long as I can" (part 3, 3:23). As an audience, viewers are supposed to be surprised that she is still able to seduce young clients and perhaps a bit scandalized that she might enjoy it. I am not amused.

La muñeca fea (*The Ugly Doll*), directed by Claudia Lopez and George Reyes (2016), shares many similarities in terms of journalistic tone with both the Desrus / Gómez Ramos collaboration and with Stelley's video documentary, even as several significant visual and narrative elements make it stand out.[22] Once again, we have a collaboration between a local reporter and photographer, Claudia Lopez, a native of Mexico City, and a foreign image maker, George Reyes, the son of Colombian immigrants raised in the United States. Like *Las amorosas más bravas*, the story it constructs from impressionistic fragments tracks a few of these women over time. The film opens with a combination of location shots and bilingual intertitles that situate us first in Mexico City, then in the neighborhood of La Merced, before introducing us to the premise of the film, "Casa Xochiquetzal, a shelter for elderly sex workers." However, instead of a story of collective survival and resilience, much of the narrative arc in *La muñeca fea* revolves around previously undisclosed seeds of discord about the overall management of the house, adding an element of nonprofit drama, exchanged accusations, and institutional cracks in this utopian story of feminist mutual aid.[23] And unlike the Stelley video, which appears to have been shot in a single day and offers just a few standard exterior shots of the neighborhood, *La muñeca fea* makes a point of following these women into the other spaces of their lives—the parks and street corners where they work, the hotel rooms where they meet their clients, the market where many work to sell candy and other goods, the road trips organized by the house administrators, and into some of the rural spaces that some once called home.

Despite the fact that more than three hundred residents have passed through Casa Xochiquetzal, several of the same faces make multiple appearances across these visual formats.[24] The movie poster advertising *La muñeca fea* features Reyna, one of the oldest residents of the house, and has us staring directly into her soulful eyes (fig. 4.9). A compelling visual subject, Reyna, with her tiny fragile frame and deeply lined sepia-tinged face, appears in both Desrus's and Venville's books of photography, and she also makes a short appearance in the Stelley video documentary, mostly singing. In *Las amorosas más bravas*, she is photographed shuffling around in her walker and being attended to in her bed, her hair dyed black, her white roots showing. In *The Women of Casa X*, we are only presented with a closeup of Reyna's face and her brief testimony where she vehemently denies having ever been a sex worker (Venville and de la Rosa 2013, 28).[25] Although she is somewhat coy about her age, at one point claiming to be forty, she serves as the perfect visual embodiment of the surprising juxtaposition of the precarity of advanced age with narrative accounts of open sexuality that forms the underlying appeal of these projects of documentation. The film was submitted as an official selection in porn festivals in Toronto, Berlin, and Rome, and I suspect that within this context, the film poster

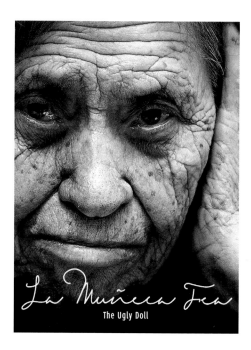

FIG 4.9 ▸ Movie poster, *La muñeca fea*, 2016. Photograph of Reyna by Claudia Lopez.

alone would have stood out from the other entries of the young buxom beauties that form the bread and butter of the porn industry.

Another resident who also appears frequently in these accounts is Canela. In the Stelley documentary, Canela is asked about how she started as a sex worker, and she tells us that she turned to sex work at sixteen because her family needed the money. In that film, we see her breaking down in tears on camera describing what it has meant for her to have Casa Xochiquetzal as a refuge, "to sleep with a blanket or something" (Stelley 2008, part 3, 4:23). Canela also appears frequently in Desrus's photographs, including one that has her sitting on the bed with Norma (fig. 4.3). But we also see her in her room next to a shopping cart loaded with personal belongings, napping under a portrait of the sacred heart of Christ, and dolled up in a body-contoured animal print, tugging at a small dog on a leash about to head out the door (fig. 4.10).

When we are introduced to Canela's story in *Las amorosas más bravas*, the journalist Celia Gómez Ramos reveals that "she's a little slow, but the girls never talk about that," and we are told that she has just returned to Casa Xochiquetzal "after trying to give love a chance one more time, at 72, although she prefers not to feel" (Desrus and Gómez Ramos 2014, 42).[26] In *La muñeca*

FIG 4.10 ▸ Canela, a resident at Casa Xochiquetzal, takes a visiting dog on a walk at the shelter, 2013. Photograph by Bénédicte Desrus. Courtesy of Bénédicte Desrus and Sipa USA.

fea, she is featured quite prominently, seen first using a digital camera to snap a picture of another resident and in numerous other scenes that capture the women of the house eating, cooking, chatting together, and doing chores. Later the resident psychologist reveals that Canela has Down syndrome along with a host of physical ailments. Hearing the psychologist discuss the details of Canela's various mental and physical diagnoses, I cringe at the ease with which she discloses details about this resident's personal history and my own complicity in repeating them even as I have no idea what kinds of permissions were requested or received. Rather than the more impressionistic sense we get from the juxtaposition of photographs and texts in the Desrus / Gómez Ramos collaboration, or the singular story of comic-tragedy we get in Stelley's more sensationalized account, in *La muñeca fea* we are given explicative narratives, and we see and hear Canela navigating the market stalls, calling out to sell her candy to the throngs of passing pedestrians. The scenes of her in the street deliver not the tragedy of Canela's past or the uncertainty of her future but the realities of her day-to-day present (fig. 4.11).

FIG 4.11 ▸ Canela in the market. Film still from *La muñeca fea*, 2016.

Like her age, Canela's cognitive difference is supposed to make her an unimaginable subject of love, sex, or indeed of any future worth desiring. Alison Kafer (2013, 2) writes, "If disability is conceptualized as a terrible unending tragedy, then any future that includes disability can only be a future to avoid." But where exactly might we locate the tragedy that is represented as surrounding Canela's life? In her lifelong disability, in the innumerable ways the precarity brought about by poverty has informed her life choices, or in her efforts to give love one more chance at seventy-two? Moreover, how might the narrative emphasis on tragedy obscure the moments of pleasure—sexual, romantic, and otherwise—that might also constitute Canela's life? What are the affective impacts of these different sorts of details and whose interests do they serve?

There is one figure highlighted in the documentary *La muñeca fea* whose face also appears in both Desrus's and Venville's photographs, wearing a wig: the same Raquel whose face and figure grace the cover of Venville's book and who is referenced in Desrus / Gómez Ramos's text as Amalia, the figure seen in the close-up applying makeup (fig. 4.2). In these varied texts, we see how her exceptional wit, facility with language, and lively presence make her a riveting biographical subject. In *Las amorosas más bravas / Tough Love*, Amalia is quoted more than any other single resident, and we are told that "Amalia is beside herself with happiness, imagining that she could be in a film" (Desrus and Gómez Ramos 2014, 44).[27] We also learn that she "has been hearing voices for twenty-two years": "Voices speak to Amalia at night. She struggles not to lose touch with reality, but she hears whispering that keeps her from sleeping; she feels like they throw mud and liquid filth at her from the holes in the wall; sometimes it's like they're out to kill her. That's why she always wears her wig and protects herself beneath the covers" (5).[28] In comparing the static visual images presented in these two books, I had suspected these were the same person, even as the detail of her name, Amalia/Raquel, was initially confusing. It is her biographical narrative that makes clear that these two accounts, and two different names, refer to the same person.

Early on in *La muñeca fea*, we hear Raquel describing how she wanted to study saxophone, and soon she is breaking into a classic Javier Solis bolero, "Loco," singing, "If they call me crazy, / because the world is like this. / The truth is I'm crazy, / crazy for you" (Lopez and Reyes 2016, 6:50).[29] Later, we see an animated Raquel telling us that "sex is very nice but you have to know what you are doing, the positions," and she proceeds to describe in exacting detail and with lively gestures and suggestive hip rolls just how she gets her clients in the mood, to the amusement of the house staff and the unseen film crew who serve as her audience for this erotic cinematic performance (0:29).[30] In one scene, we see her struggling somewhat comically with a stationary bicycle, to "matar la grasa" (kill the fat), demonstrating the kinds of exercises she does to stay in shape, and the scene is presented against a sonic backdrop of a lively staccato piano melody. However, soon the sound and scene shift, and Carmen, the house founder, tells us that Raquel is quite lovely and convivial but that when she "enters into crisis," she "refuses to speak to anyone and gets mad for no reason" (0:42). A few seconds later, the camera moves to Raquel's room, where we see her bunk bed covered in a black tarp held down by plastic water bottles (fig. 4.12). The background music enters again slowly, with a low ominous resonance that creeps into the scene, followed by measured piano notes that provide an eerie aural backdrop for Raquel's long continuous monologue chronicling her nighttime hallucinations. Now, instead of reading Amalia's description of these persecution fantasies, we hear the same account spoken by the person identified as Raquel, who tells us she covers her bed to "keep it free of dust, dirt, and dirty water, animal pee, drunk man's urine. That's what they throw down at me" (43:05).[31] Hearing these visions described in an almost breathless monologue, we witness how her hallucinations make

FIG 4.12 ▸ Raquel, posing in front of her bed. Film still from *La muñeca fea*, 2016.

literal the forms of filth, abjection, and abuse that are routinely thrust onto the figure of the sex worker. Once again, it is the house psychologist who tells us on camera that Raquel suffers from schizophrenia. Later in the film, Raquel declares, "The truth is, I am not crazy. I don't feel that I am crazy to those extremes" (1:07:02). Even as the documentary *La muñeca fea* features her quite prominently, and follows her into several scenes where we hear articulated her elaborate descriptions of the ongoing hallucinations that torment her, it balances those moments with on-screen instances of her singing, dancing, and telling jokes.

Like the song "Loco" that introduces Raquel in the documentary, the other musical moments associated with her in the film prove quite telling. At another point, we hear her singing to Agustín Lara's timeless bolero "Aventurera."[32] Boleros are slow-tempo compositions that frequently evince forms of romantic tragedy and melancholic attachment.[33] This particular song, whose original Spanish lyrics appear as the epigraph to this chapter, serves as a masculine homage to a sex worker, aventurera, even as it also calls to mind the ways these women's stories of pain and tragedy circulate as forms of commodities in the media marketplace. The English translation reads:

Sell your love dearly, adventurer
Give the price of pain, to your past
And the one who wants honey from your mouth
Let them pay with diamonds for your sin.

These two musical selections, "Loco" and "Aventurera," both perceived as timeless classics of the Latin American songbook, reflect Raquel's repertoire, *her* musical selections, even as the director puts her a cappella renditions of these familiar boleros to effective narrative ends. But I realize that before we hear Raquel speak or sing on camera, we have already seen her dancing with another one of the house's residents in the courtyard. The opening scene of *La muñeca fea* has Raquel dancing salsa to Afro-Colombian Joe Arroyo's rendition of Sonora Matancera's classic "Mala mujer"; she is leading.[34] This is a song I have danced to frequently. It is a spirited arrangement that has the blaring horns so familiar to salsa punctuating the chorus—"Mala mujer, no tiene corazón" (bad woman, you are heartless). However, as the translated lyrics scroll across my screen, I stop to realize what I have been dancing to for so many years—after this repeated phrasing that calls out this heartless "bad woman," we get another punctuated refrain, this time with vocals singing, "mátala, mátala, mátala, mátala" (kill her, kill her, kill her, kill her). By mimicking the tempo of the horns' blasting notes, the meaning-making function of the words becomes obscured, receding into the sonic backdrop, yet the price for feminine misbehavior becomes terrifyingly clear. That femicide is normalized, that it has become the soundtrack to so many nights on so many dance floors—that it is a song from which both Raquel and I have extracted pleasure—reveals another moment of how deeply rooted the embodied hatred of female sexual deviance is engrained, how puta life is continually being threatened with death and annihilation.

The stigma that conditions the life and death of sex workers is part of what these projects of representation, including my own, are intended to address. Yet even as *Las amorosas más bravas* and *La muñeca fea* use different modes to create a cohesive narrative arc, they offer surprisingly similar conclusions. At the end of both texts, we are presented with two possible future outcomes awaiting these women, equally sad and inevitable: death and a return to the streets. In *Las amorosas más bravas*, on the penultimate page of text under the heading "Mujeres Bravas, Mujeres Amorosas," we read, "One Sunday afternoon Carmelita died" (Desrus and Gómez Ramos 2014, 44).[35] And as we flip through the last few pages of photographs, we see an altar to la Santa Muerte, a close-up of hands with gold glitter nails holding a Bible opened to the Book of Psalms, and a photograph of a resident standing over an open casket. A few pages before, we also learn that Paola, who had lived at the house until January 2011, who wrapped herself in symbols of spiritual protection for Venville's camera, has disappeared: "She left all of her belongings behind, even her statues and images of Santa Muerte. She just never came back" (41).[36] Similarly, the film *La muñeca fea* ends with a funeral for Reyna, and the women are all gathered at the gravesite saying their tear-filled farewells. But after that scene of collective grief, we see Carmen Muñoz, the home's founder and original director, the one whose vision and activism were the impetus for the creation of Casa Xochiquetzal, sitting in the plaza, walking the streets dressed in a flowered skirt with strappy silver heels, and finally standing on a street corner, alone. As the film nears its end, Carmen tells us that "el hambre y la necesidad" (hunger and need) have made her accept her return to the street. "Of course, not with the same success as before. Today, it's different. . . . At least when I started, I was doing it for my kids. I had vitality, I was young" (Lopez and Reyes 2016, 1:25:03).[37] But the scene ends with her saying, "As time goes on, all I can do is think that my place is here, forever."[38] She continues, "Al final, todos volvemos a la calle" (In the end, we all return to the street) (1:26:29).[39] Each of these documentaries highlights and occludes aspects of the house and the women in it, testifying to the fascination with seeing what is imagined to be an impossible juxtaposition between aging bodies and perverse sexuality, and always ending in tragedy.

Framing Friendship

The final project for consideration, the film *Plaza de la Soledad* (2016), by Mexican photographer and filmmaker Maya Goded, presents a wholly different mood. Goded is a widely recognized figure among feminist, activist, and artist circles in Mexico City and beyond. Her awards and recognitions include a W. Eugene Smith Award in 2001, a Guggenheim in 2003, and a Prince Claus Fund award in 2010. The daughter of a US anthropologist mother enamored with Mexico and a Communist father who was the son of Spanish exiles of Francisco Franco's dictatorship, Goded grew up among the leftist intelligentsia of Mexico City, and early on she worked with another famed feminist Mexican photographer, Graciela Iturbide. Unlike the previous accounts of the women of Casa Xochiquetzal, Goded's relationship with some of these subjects began decades earlier, starting in 1998 when she first began photographing sex workers and their clients in La Merced. That black-and-white photo series would eventually be published in 2006 under the same title, *La Plaza de la Soledad*, the title referencing a plaza in La Merced and the Catholic church for which it is named, Iglesia de la Santa Cruz y Soledad. In interviews, Goded states that although she grew up in Mexico City, the first time she spent any time in La Merced, this *barrio bravo*, was when she was in her twenties. In other words, while Goded is also from Mexico City, the world in which she grew up remains separated from these women by the distance of class, education, and perhaps the complicated ways that color and national origins shape social status in Mexico. Nevertheless, Goded returned to this neighborhood and the women she met there again and again. The resulting film, released eleven years after the first book, and almost twenty years after first forming these connections, documents these networks of social relations born of many years of exchange and friendship.

Although this film includes several of the women featured in these other accounts of Casa Xochiquetzal, and Goded was one of the original advocates involved in its founding, the house itself is never named. And although the advancing age of these women is frequently mentioned in Goded's interviews and media accounts of the film, the conceit of this documentary is less about the imagined curiosity or concern that aging sex workers might inspire and is focused instead on the interconnected lives of this small tightly bound community of women in La Merced. These are women who make their living as sex workers and who, like many of us, are looking for love and connection. There is no introductory text telling us what we are about to witness, no staff psychologist to explain how difficult these women's lives have been, no direct appeals to their rights to dignity. For several minutes into the film, aside from a carload of women singing "Amor de cabaret" (another bolero standard in the sex worker songbook), the dominant soundtrack we are offered is ripples of collective laughter.[40] Although none of the women are identified by name until the final frames of the film, I recognize their by-now-familiar faces.

Early in the film, we enter what appears to be a hotel room. Leti is naked on the bed, barely covered by a well-placed sheet; she is on her side, chatting to the director, telling her about a younger client who was particularly sweet to her, and grinning ear to ear (fig. 4.13). We enter the conversation midstream: "Y si llegamos a comprendernos, no importa la edad" (And if we come to understand each other, age doesn't matter) (Goded 2016, 7:44). Seconds later, the unseen female voice asks, "¿Y cómo estuvo, en el cuarto?"

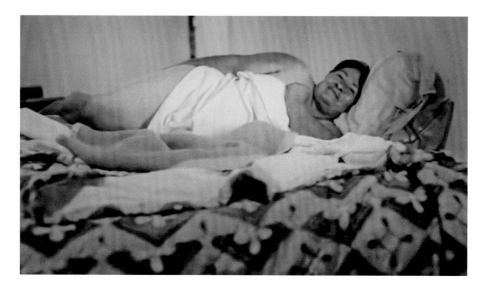

FIG 4.13 ▸ Leti, reclining in bed. Film still from *Plaza de la Soledad*, 2016.

(And how was it, in the room?), and Leti gushes about just how special he made her feel. He has promised to call. Eye level to a reclining Leti, as viewers we are positioned on the edge of the bed, like girlfriends at a sleepover eager to hear the details of a particularly promising rendezvous. There is an easy intimacy in the exchange: the relaxed posture of Leti's reclined pose, the cadence of Goded's voice full of tender concern for Leti's own desires, the giddiness of Leti's enthusiastic musings about amorous possibilities. Unlike the photograph of Norma wrapped in a sheet, this scene is less about demonstrating the director's access to Leti's exposed body and more about allowing us to enter a private moment of female friendship. The tag line for the film is "Todas buscamos amor" (We all look for love), and this scene allows us to imagine that it might be possible. Like Goded, I want Leti to find love and happiness; I also want this for myself—I'm looking for love too.

Even as the film revolves around a few central characters, it highlights the biographical threads that connect these women through diverse forms of love, kinship, labor, and the space of La Merced. If the Desrus / Gómez Ramos opening text emphasizes rivalry between these women and Stelley's documentary ends with an image of the inevitable solitude that is imagined to surround puta life, Goded's film foregrounds female friendship and connection. In another early scene, we see Raquel and Carmen plying their trade by the plaza that bears the name of the film, passing the time to-

FIG 4.14 ▸ Raquel and Carmen at work. Film still from *Plaza de la Soledad,* 2016.

gether, trying to make the best of a shitty job. They are laughing about the cold and their clients (fig. 4.14). As Carmen darts off to meet a customer she has spotted off-screen, she says, "Ahorita le voy a decir lo que le hago con la lengua y el dedito" (Now I'll tell him what I'm going to do with my tongue and my little finger) (Goded 2016, 12:08). They both crack up. The moments in Goded's film that focus on the business end of sex work frequently highlight the creative, emotional, and psychological labor of sex work, while the laughter and humor that punctuate many of these stories dislodges easy assumptions about tragedy or despair. In another scene, we see Leti on the street trying to appease one of her more elderly regulars who seems in a mood. As she reaches to give him a kiss on the cheek, she says, "You know I love you," while she rolls her eyes for Goded's nearby camera. If there is an element of the comedic to the stories of sex work these women share, they are the ones telling the joke.

Over the course of Goded's film, we meet these women's lovers, their clients, their children, their mothers, their friends. Carmen, the original founder of Casa Xochiquetzal, functions as a pivotal character in the film, connected to everyone and everything that happens in La Merced. As the camera follows her as she makes her way through the crowded streets, we meet Lupe, a young queer homeless teen whom Carmen accompanies to a prenatal appointment. After the doctor's visit (it's a boy!), they stop at a local taquería to get something to eat. Carmen asks Lupe about the first woman she fell in love with, but the conversation quickly turns to other more painful childhood memories, and Lupe recounts being held at gunpoint and raped. She was in elementary school. Lupe goes quiet; her eyes fill with tears that somehow manage not to fall. Carmen asks a few more questions while Lupe shakes her head in reply. Nobody was there to help her. She couldn't tell anyone. It still hurts to remember. As viewers, we sit in silence for thirty long seconds as the camera stays framed on Lupe's young face, her eyes cast down as she tries to hold back the ocean of sorrow inside her. I want to cry too. By the end of the film, we see her again with her infant son, Martín, laughing, smiling, joking, as she gleefully introduces him around the neighborhood, before settling into their sidewalk encampment that will serve as their shelter for the night. It is not that the tragic aspects of these women's lives are not made visible—they are, in devastating detail—but tragedy never fully settles into the defining narrative of the film; life in La Merced continues.

Throughout the course of the film, we hear that Carmen is having troubles in her fifteen-year relationship with her husband, Carlos, whom we also get to know over the course of the film, himself the son of a sex worker who grew up en el ambiente (in the life).[41] Carmen, whose own father was a pimp, recounts how Carlos began as her client but how she eventually fell in love with him because she didn't have to hide what she did from him. We also hear Carlos describe Carmen as the love of his life, as the camera offers us black-and-white images of them together, some from Goded's 2006 book and some from their wedding, which Goded also photographed (fig. 4.15). When it comes time to tell her own backstory, Carmen's narrative repeats the horrors of girlhood that permeate this archive: pregnant at twelve without a clue about what that meant, violently beaten and raped by her husband hours after giving birth, "como una bestia" (like a beast). "Of all the times he did that, that time was the worst," she tells us (Goded 2016, 19:38). As she recounts this episode in her life, the camera is tight on her face, even as she averts its gaze. This is a story she has told before. She does not cry. Instead, documentarian and subject sit together without speaking, and rather than dialogue, we hear the deep intake of air Carmen takes to calm herself. The connection between Goded and Carmen is made palpable through the long silence they share. At other times, such as in the scene with Lupe, it is Carmen asking the questions, serving in the role of interviewer, displacing Goded's role as director and documentarian. As the film screened, it was also Carmen who would most often appear with Goded in public presentations.[42]

FIG 4.15 ▸ Carmen and Carlos. Film still from *Plaza de la Soledad*, 2016.

As the film progresses, Goded introduces us to Esther (dressed in a huipil, a garment most often associated with the Indigenous women of Oaxaca), whom we meet as she is engaged in a cleansing ritual with Raquel. She is repeating a dialogue reminiscent of my own therapy sessions: "Cuando no tuvimos cariño de nuestros padres, nosotros nos encariñamos" (When we didn't receive loving affection from our parents, we lovingly care for ourselves) (Goded 2016, 25:29). They hug each other for a long time, smiling. Seconds later, Esther delivers a heartbreaking monologue directly into the camera about how she was abused at eight, the shame she felt from her family and her community about being sucia, and how her mother would tell her that todas las mujeres son putas (all women are whores) and that she regretted having her (fig. 4.16). Because parental shame is also the burden of puta life. Then the film takes us to meet Esther's mother. Esther has brought her mother the gift of an aquarium for her humble home. Sitting at a table together, they speak an Indigenous language. Esther gently weeps; her mother does not cry. Whatever intimacy might exist between Goded and Esther, her mother, who never looks into the camera, seems to want no part of it. The shift in language intentionally excludes non-Indigenous-language speakers, including Goded and most of her audience, from this moment of intra-familial and intra-ethnic drama.[43] Not everything is meant to be shared.

FIG 4.16 ▸ Esther. Film still from *Plaza de la Soledad*, 2016.

As a filmmaker, Goded is unafraid of silence, of having her audience sit with sadness and trauma. Goded is first and foremost a photographer, and this film frequently reproduces the quiet stillness of photography, more invested in registering feeling than educating an audience or making a point. Goded follows this tense scene of intergenerational trauma with a long, slow, wordless sequence in which Esther washes herself by an outdoor cistern. Like other pivotal scenes, here the film communicates through the senses without dialogue or narration. We see and hear the sudsy slathering of her face and body, the sounds of pail after pail of water washing away the thick soapy foam. Against a sonic background of cascading water, chirping birds, and piano notes, the camera plays in the water's reflection and drifts up to take in the blue of the sky framed in a canopy of trees before sliding back down to earth, providing a cinematic moment of sensory healing. However, the film also swerves away from easy notions about Indigenous identity and spiritual salvation. Later, we learn that Esther, this Indigenous spiritualist, therapist, scarred daughter, and abuse survivor, is also a sex worker and a dyke. And we meet Ángeles, her lover of thirteen years.

In a scene filmed in a hotel room, the two are observed preparing to go out for the evening. As Esther applies makeup, she declares, "Que chinga su madre la gente, yo no vivo de la gente, Maya, ni del machismo, vivo de mis nalgas" (People can fuck off, I don't live off of people, Maya, or from machismo, I live off my ass), bringing the director's presence into the scene

FIG 4.17 ▸ Ángeles. Film still from *Plaza de la Soledad*, 2016.

by invoking her first name. Ángeles then demonstrates the kind of private dance she might perform for a client, and speaking off camera, she dedicates it instead to her lover, Esther, "con todo el corazón en el alma" (with all the love in my soul), but not before Esther adjusts her outfit and prepares her for the solo dance number that follows. In a sequence that resembles a music video more than a scene in a documentary, Ángeles plays directly with and to Goded's camera to deliver the sexy. Standing against the two-toned wall, Ángeles stares boldly into the camera, visually re-creating the outline of an angel with outstretched wings, commanding attention (fig. 4.17).

As the scene shifts and the camera follows Esther and Ángeles into the street, we see their hands touch briefly before Ángeles yanks her hand away, while Esther's voice-over delivers another touching monologue—about how they have to hide from society and how nobody knows how much they love each other: "Cuando estamos solas nos amamos intensamente desde donde somos, desde quienes somos" (When we are alone, we love each other intensely from where we are, from who we are) (Goded 2016, 30:39). The entire sequence feels orchestrated as much by Esther and Ángeles as by Goded, intended to deliver a powerful message about what is unseen in the lives of these women and about the possibilities for queer love. But thankfully neither Goded nor Esther seems particularly interested in peddling a romantic narrative about idealized lesbian relationships. In a later scene, the couple are playfully bickering over money and drugs when Esther positions herself directly in front of Goded's camera while Ángeles

FIG 4.18 ▸ Maya, Esther, and Ángeles. Film still from *Plaza de la Soledad*, 2016.

finishes getting dressed to tell us what their lovers' quarrel was *really* about: "Ayer me pegó, se robó mi dinero y después . . . terminamos cogiendo" (Yesterday she hit me, took my money, and later . . . we ended up fucking). Esther, always pedagogical in her addresses to the camera, adds: "Pero lo goce mucho sexualmente" (But I enjoyed it very much sexually) (59:05). Everyone is laughing, including Goded, whose image is now captured in the mirror, along with a glimpse of Ángeles getting dressed nearby (fig. 4.18).

These moments where the director enters the scene, aurally or visually, serve to dislodge the imagined distance between the filmmaker and her subject to reveal the ways the image on the screen is being mutually constructed for us, the intended audience. But what also becomes dislodged are more sanitized ideas about lesbian sexuality, Indigenous identity, sex worker lives, and feminist politics.

A few of the articles that emerged after the film's release mention that Ángeles is a trans woman, but that detail is never brought out in Goded's film; it barely seems relevant to mention it here in my own account.[44] Similarly, Raquel, never one to be left out, also appears in Goded's film in her now established roles—demonstrating the arts of seduction, recounting her nighttime hallucinations, and singing; in the final scene, we see her singing wearing a new blonde wig, a gift from Goded. But importantly, she is presented without a diagnosis. Naming, categorizing, or explaining what transpires on the screen isn't part of Goded's intention. Instead, her cinematic practice is closer to what feminist filmmaker and theorist Trinh T.

Minh-ha terms "speaking nearby," resisting the authorial voice that might wish to elucidate a message. In her essay "Documentary Is/Not a Name," Trinh (1990, 89) emphasizes that "meaning can therefore be political only when it does not let itself be easily stabilized, and when it does not rely on any single source of authority, but, rather, empties or decentralizes it."[45] Meaning—about Mexican girlhood and misogyny; about sex, sexuality, and sex work; about the traumas of childhood and the agonies of aging; about spirituality and violence—swirls around these scenes, hovering but never settling into preformed narratives of tragedy, trauma, or survival. There is no overarching imperative to construct meaning from the snippets of these women's lives, yet Trinh reminds us that "to resist meaning does not necessarily lead to its mere denial" (76).

Like the other image-making projects that document the women who revolve around Casa Xochiquetzal, Goded's film reveals as much about the relationship between documentarian and subject as about the women themselves. Rather than project access or authenticity, Goded wants us to share in a feeling, and that feeling is the potential of female friendships, ones that offer the love, tenderness, and care that are so frequently denied by society. In interviews, Goded describes how the trajectory of the film changed over time and how she worked in collaboration with her subjects to present a chorus of different voices. Furthermore, she is upfront about having initially paid the women in that early volume for their time and later continuing to pay for their company with food, drinks, and incidental expenses. But her relationship with Carmen became something more: "With her, I established a longer relationship that was much deeper. I served as a witness at her wedding, I helped her with the down payment for her apartment, it seemed fair because she helped me establish many more relationships and also took care of me all that time" (Alcantara 2012, 87).[46] Carmen took care of Goded in the streets of La Merced; she brought her into this community and protected her. Goded was allowed entry into Carmen's mostly public life as a sex worker and advocate, allowed to share in her intimate friendships with this circle of women, and allowed to develop her own relationships with others that formed part of that community. In return, Goded cared for the fragility and power of these women's stories; for their ongoing social and political place in the material world; for their rights to self-expression, self-definition, and self-representation. And she expressed this commitment through a durational performance of care we might call friendship.

To write Goded into these networks of friendship and mutual affection, however, requires accounting for the power differentials of race, class, education, and access that also define the terms of creative production and distribution that surround the film. These imbalances in power, access, and resources surround my project as well; they require an unfaltering practice of negotiating care on an intimate level but also as an ongoing commitment to working for social change, including a redistribution of material resources. We might imagine what it has been like for Carmen, Raquel, Esther, Ángeles, Lupe, Leti, and the others who appear in this film, or indeed in any of these projects of documentation, to see their faces, their stories, their community valorized in the spaces of high culture, to have their voices be valued as worth hearing. But representation alone is never enough. Instead, Goded's decades-long project with this community of sex workers worked on multiple levels, providing material relief through her efforts to create and support Casa Xochiquetzal as well as individual women; her inclusive approach to representation without authorial explication; and the work's ability to mobilize others to demand more expansive and inclusive forms of care for sex workers.[47]

It seems ingenuous to suggest that Goded was drawn to these subjects out of purely altruistic motives, in part because I understand my own desires to linger with their faces and their stories as infinitely more complicated. On her website, Goded (n.d.) describes how she first began this project so many years ago: "I was raised in Mexico City, where female sexuality is dominated by Christian morality, by the idealized image of the good woman and the good wife, and an unquestioned mystification of motherhood. When I got pregnant, this need to understand women (and myself) grew." Like other artists, Goded used her photography to explore an aspect of her own life and circumstance. Similarly, I am drawn to these women and this project as a way to confront my own sexuality as I age. These women speak to me because I know they have something to teach me about the realities of *my* puta life. Their faces and their stories obligate me to sit with emotions that I might wish to expel, to ponder my own relationship to love and aging, desire and rejection, loneliness and heartbreak, to dwell in the dusk of my own archives of feeling.

Not all encounters with alterity are felicitous. Before I conclude, let me mention another artist who went to Casa Xochiquetzal looking to visually document this unique community and who responded quite differently to the complexity of these women's lives. The Argentinian photographer Ana Gallardo produced and exhibited several images of residents, including a wall-sized image of Raquel that I stumbled upon in El Museo Jumex in Mexico City in 2019.[48] In an interview, Gallardo is quoted as saying, "Fue una experiencia terrible, extenuante . . . porque aquella mujer era un ser balbuceante e inerme para quien era tan difícil coordinar las palabras como controlar sus esfínteres" (It was a terrible, exhausting experience because that woman was a stuttering and defenseless being for whom it was as difficult to coordinate words as to control her sphincters). Although the article doesn't reference exactly *whom* she was referring to, I have my suspicions. The article continues, "El trato cotidiano con las miserias de este despojo humano la llevó a cuestionarse seriamente qué hacía desempeñando un papel más propio de una enfermera o de un asistente social que de una artista, por lo menos en el sentido en el que habitualmente entendemos qué es una artista" (The daily dealings with the miseries of this human waste led her to seriously question what she was doing, playing a role more typical of a nurse or a social worker than an artist, at least in the sense in which we usually understand what an artist is). Neither the interviewer nor Gallardo elaborates on what exactly they believe is the role of the artist (Jiménez 2014).

Whether guided by an impulse toward authenticity, altruism, or aesthetic extraction, the different genres and modes of narrativity that this chapter chronicles are invested in producing emotional attachments to the subjects they depict, to inspiring different kinds of feelings. Perhaps these images call to mind the elderly women in our own lives and the conditions in which they live and love. Maybe their poverty, their age, or their circumstances make them seem wholly different, or frighteningly familiar. If we return to the Levinas quote with which we began, "In front of the face, I always demand more of myself," we might ask what kinds of demands we might make of ourselves in the presence of an archive seeping with the cruelest realities of what constitutes puta life. That these women deserve security, shelter, and autonomy seems clear enough, but can we also demand that they deserve love, dignity, and care? What kind of demand is a demand for care? And how can we learn to ask that of others and of ourselves? Even as these archives of puta life ask us to confront the everyday tragedies of those who live with the burdens stigma has etched into their skin, they also offer lessons on the value of femme friendship, durational care, and the possibilities for mutual aid across dynamics of difference. Moreover, in their ongoing demands for love, respect, and care, these women remind us of all the ways we are entangled in the radiance of the universe, united in our stubborn insistence to live on, for now.

Mi voz puede volar, puede atravesar
Cualquier herida, cualquier tiempo, cualquier soledad
Sin que la pueda controlar toma forma de canción
Así es mi voz que sale de mi corazón

Y volará sin yo querer
Por los caminos más lejanos, por los sueños que soñé
Será el reflejo del amor de lo que me tocó vivir
Será la música de fondo de lo mucho que sentí

CELIA CRUZ, "YO VIVIRÉ"

SEEING, SENSING, FEELING

Adela Vázquez's Amazing Past

Like the other women that you have met within the pages of this book, this final chapter is about a real person, Adela Vázquez, a living person with a scent and a style and an amazing past. Like the life stories of the women of Casa Xochiquetzal, like those of Vanessa del Rio herself, the story of Adela's life commands an archive that seeps out of any of the biographical containers to which it is assigned, producing an absence of all that we might know about her life and an excess of all that her life might mean to us. There is something inherently pedagogical about life narratives—they offer us working models for how others have navigated the circumstances that the inherited social order has provided. Biographical accounts have the power to ignite memories that are not uniquely our own, and they can activate novel ways of seeing the worlds around us. Through the promise of imagination and identification, life writing shares other conditions of being; it connects us to known and unknown others through the detail of a name, a date, an experience; it reminds us how we are bound to each other in unwitting ways through generation, gender, geography, and the accidents of history; and it brings into relief all the ways we are not the same. The promise of representation, recognition, and perhaps even reparative solace that life narratives offer can seem so comforting, helping us feel that we are not alone, that others have survived what we are still enduring. Yet what emerges most vividly in these narrations of life are the ways stories are mediated and constructed, not just by their subjects, authors, and editors but by the diverse readers who pour their desires for knowing and self-knowing into these biographical compositions to construct meaning there.

Whether composed as autobiography, memoir, biography, or an "as-told-to" testimonial account, these recitals of interior subjectivity are always relational, always directed to another, a reader who receives them: another sentient body outside the text who is intended to function as witness, confidant, ally, friend. Life narratives *do* things in the world. Through our willingness to engage with alterity, these intimate encounters with another's heartaches and hopes open us to the possibility of being transformed. As these texts craft unattainable sensual memories of someone else's past, they have the potential to ignite our own fantasies of a queer world-making future. Through the gift of imagination and identification, life narratives offer us the possibility of recognition and courage, allowing us to see our own lives in new ways, even as they provide a glimpse of other worlds we will never truly know. And sometimes, when those stories reveal injustice, brutality, and harm, that transformation is charged with the urgency of action.

Trans-everything

This chapter begins with the gift that is *Sexile/Sexilio*, a bilingual graphic life narrative by Jaime Cortez about the extraordinary life of Adela Vázquez.[1] In the introduction, Cortez (2004, vii) writes, "The life of Adela Vázquez is trans-everything—transnational, transgendered, transformative and fully transfixing." *Sexile/Sexilio* tells the story of Adela's journey of being assigned male at birth in Cuba, forming part of the Mariel boatlift, working briefly as a sex worker, and later becoming a sexual health educator and transgender advocate in San Francisco. Along the way, Adela shares her unique insights about life, sex, work, community, and care. As is the case for most people, Vázquez worked as a sex worker only briefly, although as the different narratives circulating around her life make clear, she has been working sex all her life.

Published in 2004 as the United States was on the cusp of being home to more than one million people living with HIV/AIDS, *Sexile/Sexilio* was imagined as an HIV-prevention project, funded through the Institute for

Gay Men's Health and AIDS Project Los Angeles (APLA). Published as a slim paperback, printed in English on one side and Spanish on the other, the printed volume was initially made available for free while copies lasted, and for years later it was offered as a free digital download in Spanish or in English on APLA's website. In his foreword, Patrick "Pato" Hebert, who was then working at APLA, writes, "HIV prevention is too often preoccupied with tiny pieces of what we do rather than the fullness of what we feel and the vastness of who we are becoming. *Sexile/Sexilio* is special because it reminds us of the power of storytelling" (2004, v).[2] Those words were written in the days before PreP and the medical management of HIV and AIDS, when stories, valued as medicine, were still being funded. It should be noted that Hebert, Cortez, and Vázquez are all part of what Hebert calls "the diasporic folk of Proyecto Village"—a reference to Proyecto ContraSIDA por Vida, a Latinx HIV-prevention agency founded in 1993 where I first met Adela, Jaime, Pato, and so many others.[3] Here, the intimacy and friendship that the text performs are shared by the subject, narrator, and critic, all of us bound together in a kind of queer kinship through our shared work with Proyecto.

Like many of the other personal narratives I have assembled in this book, Adela's story is narrated in the familiar "as-told-to-style," mediated through the creative and editorial vision of someone else who has been entrusted to translate oral speech into a published format. However, in this case, that process also involved shaping someone's words and memories into pictorial renderings, hand-crafted visual depictions that attempt to reproduce the events of a life span, embodying what cartoonist Amy Kurzweil (2021) describes as "the intimacy of the hand drawn line." More importantly, unlike the others I have profiled in this work, I know Adela the person, the one who lives outside the text. This further complicates my role as cultural critic—I know too much. Knowing Adela highlights my own entanglements and investments with her narrative, even as it makes me more attentive to the silences and shadows that hover around it—all that I don't know and all that I will never know weigh on that encounter and the interpretation of it that I am able to offer.

In the introduction, Jaime Cortez, a friend to both Adela and myself, narrates his insecurity as an "illustrator, writer, researcher and theorist" and outlines how he understands his role and responsibility as storyteller. He writes, "When the fear and uncertainty came a'knocking, I turned back to the transcripts of my interviews with Adela to remind myself why I need this story to be in the world. Not just because I'm a queer, a child of immigrants, or a lover of both comics and sexual narratives, but because this story is so fucked up, fabulous, raggedy and human that it opens a vast space where we can all ponder our own sense of risk, exile and home" (Cortez 2004, vii). Cortez sees his labor, all eight hundred hours of it, not as work of detached altruism designed to promote safer sex or the human rights of others but as part of his own desire, his urgent need, to create a capacious space for imagining his own life. Nevertheless, he also makes clear how any attempt to represent the life of another is invariably bound up with fears of misrepresentation, of failing in our role of adequately reproducing the contours of another's sense of self. The anxieties and desires that Cortez describes are ones that I also share. Like him, my motivation for seeing these stories of puta life circulate has as much to do with my own hopes for imagined community, for understanding the tours and detours of my own life, and for inspiring more just sexual futures than any belief that adequate representation might be possible. In fact, "fucked up, fabulous, raggedy and human" might serve as an apt descriptor for the stories of puta life I have assembled thus far, stories that carry the kernels of my own life, wishes, and heartaches within.

Erotic Encounters en el Campo

In *Sexile/Sexilio*, Adela's story begins: "Not to brag, but my birth was revolutionary" (Cortez 2004, 3). Adela was born in Camagüey, Cuba, in 1958, in the rural countryside of one of the country's interior provinces during the final months of Fulgencio Batista's dictatorship as the sugar mills burned with the promise of insurrection. I was born in the same province a few miles away and several months after the triumph of the revolution. Adela and I share a generation and a geography, even as our lives have been formed through different journeys of migration and gender, opportunities and obstacles. For all the ways our life trajectories have been marked by the same historical forces and the myriad ways our lives have been remarkably different, like Jaime Cortez, I, too, need Adela's life and lessons to circulate in the world. Like the other faces, figures, and narratives that have composed this book, Adela's life story is vital to my own desire for narratives that complicate sexual labor, migration, and understandings of the feminine, for theorizations of female sexuality that might account for the risks and pleasures of living a sexual life out loud.

The title of the first chapter of *Sexile/Sexilio*, "La infanta caliente" (The Hot Infanta), invokes both childhood and hints at the queen Adela would become.[4] It begins with a recounting of her childhood adventures growing up in the lush, tropical splendor of el campo, the Cuban countryside. For those coming of age surrounded by the wild abundance of nature, sexuality is seen and sensed outdoors, where the boundaries between human bodies and the natural world routinely come undone. Early on, Adela states, "I was fascinated by farm sex. Cow sex. Chicken sex. Insect sex" (Cortez 2004, 6). These opening scenes vividly call to mind the childhood memories of the novelist Reinaldo Arenas, another queer Cuban, in his memoir, *Before Night Falls* (1993). There, Arenas writes eloquently about the connection between emerging youthful eroticism and the landscape of the natural world. He explains, "One must remember life in the country is lived close to nature and, therefore, to sexuality. The animal world is always ruled by sexual urges. . . . In the country, sexual energy generally overcomes all prejudice, repression, and punishment. That force, the force of nature, dominates" (1993, 19). In his text, Arenas similarly describes scenes of carnal intimacies with the flora and fauna that shaped his sense of sexuality. In a section of his memoir titled "Eroticism," Arenas writes, "I think I always had a huge sexual appetite. Not only the mares, sows, hens, or turkeys but almost all animals were objects of my sexual passion" (18). And like Arenas, Adela's sexual initiation begins with fucking banana trees before turning her attention to fucking animals, and eventually boys. She states, "The tree got boring and I graduated to humans. I used farm temptations to get sex" (Cortez 2004, 7). In this early scene, Adela already sets the stage for the sexual adventures that follow. The panels describe how the young Adela would lure her schoolmates to the barn with the promise of sex with a goat and then offer herself in exchange: "You want to put your thing in me instead?" (7). Farther down, we get: "Nine years old and I was pimping a GOAT to get laid. And do you know what? The goat wasn't even that cute if you really look at the bitch! Ha! Ha! Ooh child, I was such a manipulating liar, but I couldn't help it, because even then, I would do anything for the sex. Besides, it was great revenge" (7) (fig. 5.1). How getting fucked by a boy who thought he was coming to fuck a goat is about getting revenge is never really spelled out in her account. In fact, it should already be clear that Adela is rarely invested in how *we*, her audience, might read her story, what sense or meaning *we* might make of the stories she tells. But perhaps, if we linger on this passage, we can imagine the ways the boys might have treated the nine-year-old who grew up to be Adela and conjure why she might want to exact revenge in this moment of her childhood or in the recitation of this scene of youthful sexuality years later.

FIG 5.1 ▸ Jaime Cortez, *Sexile/Sexilio*, 2004, 7.

In the bottom panel, Cortez allows us to visually step outside the time of the story and returns us to the present. We see Adela smoking a cigarette in the comfort of her San Francisco apartment, the tea and cookies suggesting this was a long, leisurely exchange between documentarian and speaking subject. Graphic narratives make possible the visual juxtaposition of different temporal registers coexisting on the same page. Within the pages of *Sexile/Sexilio*, those shifts transport us across not only time—illustrating a then and a now—but also genders and geographies, even as we remain within the narrative sphere of Adela's life story. As we enter the intimacy of a friendly afternoon exchange over tea, talking about sex, childhood, and the terms we use to shade the world, this panel visually performs the orality upon which the book is premised, an orality that registers the importance of friendship and storytelling in the formation of queer community.

Working Sex

Unlike this childhood story of lust and covert seduction, several passages in the book record the periods in Adela's life when sex was less about desire and more about sex as a commodity, something she could use and exchange. Adela recounts growing up as a "baby queer" in revolutionary Cuba, being taunted by her peers, and Cortez makes visual the words hurled at her to assign her a place in the social order: *puto, pájaro, pervertido, pato, maricón.*[5] And in an early episode, Adela recounts her strategy for psychic and social survival, seducing her bullies and then blackmailing them into silence: "At 11, the revolution did me a big favor. They sent me to boarding school. By that age I had lost my baby fat, so mama was looking real cute. Me and five hundred boys! HELLO! They all knew about me, and they wanted me. The students, the teachers, you name it. I fucked with them all, and that was how I learned that sex and beauty were power. My power" (Cortez 2004, 9). Unlike the previous scene between two schoolmates, this moment where Adela describes being a preteen having sex with adults—teachers, no less—makes me uncomfortable, but to be honest, that was not my initial reaction to the passage. I first read it with the same humor and sass that routinely emanate from Adela's stories and then was quieted by the shadow of all that scene suggests. Reading it now, I am mostly sad that a young person had to suffer the abuse and bullying that I know Adela must have endured or that she needed to exert this kind of sexual power to survive. But as with her stories about sex with trees and animals, she seems to attribute another set of queer cultural conventions, local to the time and place and circumstance, to these scenes of childhood sexual experience, proud of her own abilities to make the best of a bad situation.

Like Vanessa del Rio recounting her rape at the hands of the police, Adela narrates these scenes not through the language of victimization and sexual abuse but through the lens of power and revenge. As in my reading of del Rio's narrative, as the critic engaging Adela's account of her own life, this story requires me to wrestle with the messy emotions the scene inspires. How do I situate my unease and discomfort alongside her narrative without rewriting her felt experience through my own interpretive lens? My inability to fully grasp Adela's capacity to integrate these early memories into a larger lustful narrative of sexual agency and feminine power does not change the meaning of her memories for her, even as it does not ameliorate how I or you, another reader coming to this story, might engage this scene. However, in my role as critic, to whom should I address any interpretive intervention? To the Adela who exists on the page, to my adult friend Adela, or to the wounded reader who is shocked, hurt, and perhaps triggered by this scene of childhood abuse? However, another approach might ask, as a feminist critic, as a survivor of sexual abuse, what might *I* learn from these feminine sexual subjects about rescripting the misogyny and violence that surround puta life? If what is being recounted in this retelling is the surfacing of trauma, Adela locates the source of that trauma in the homophobia that surrounded her rather than in the coping mechanisms she used to get by. In fact, it seems important to note that both of these "victims" seem to skillfully externalize the harms that were inflicted on them. Neither Vanessa nor Adela are the least bit shy about telling their stories, already refusing to translate these experiences into shameful secrets. In fact, the accounts offered by Adela and Vanessa insightfully situate these scenes of violation as indicative of a larger corrupt social order rather than a personal tragedy or individual injury. As a reader and as an author, I try to register the lessons these women offer.[6] And because in narrative, as in life, the story continues, on the very same page we learn that by fifteen, the young Adela earned second prize in the boarding school's drag show competition.

After being drafted and rejected by the Cuban army for being a homosexual, Adela was educated and trained as a teacher but then later dismissed from her teaching post for wearing "a little foundation, some tasteful rouge, nothing wild" (Cortez 2004, 15). Therefore, by the time a bus

full of Cubans crashed into the Peruvian Embassy in Havana seeking political asylum, and Castro opened the Mariel Harbor to anyone who lacked
"revolutionary genes," Adela knew it was time to leave. Like many people
who arrived at the Peruvian Embassy seeking to leave the national experi-
ment of state socialism behind, Adela was brutally attacked and physically
beaten by bands of Cuban "patriots" to a chorus of "¡Que se vayan! ¡Abajo
la escoria!" (Let them leave! Down with the scum!), spurred on by Castro,
who called those wishing to leave their socialist homeland "escoria" (scum)
(Castro 1980). This scene of state-induced trauma is one that is repeated in
the numerous accounts told by Mariel refugees: of being surrounded by co-
workers, neighbors, and people they had once trusted as friends and being
physically beaten and abused.[7] It is a scene of a nation publicly turning on
and expelling those it has already rejected, those who had never really fit
in. As the refuse of the Cuban nation-state, Marielitos, as they came to be
known, arrived in the United States to find themselves equally vilified by
many of the Cuban Americans who received them. Taunted as homosexuals, prostitutes, and criminals, these new Cuban exiles were poorer, darker,
and queerer, more unruly and decidedly less grateful to their US hosts than
any previous generation of Cuban migrants. Many washing up on shore
were left living under the freeway in an improvised tent city in Miami, du-
biously named "Freedom Town"; others were dispersed to newly formed
refugee camps in Pennsylvania, Wisconsin, Puerto Rico, and Arkansas for
processing as they awaited sponsors; and no matter their location, everywhere they landed, they organized, protested, and in some cases rioted for
better treatment.[8]

As the story continues, we see Adela, having recently arrived in Fort
Chaffee, Arkansas, still bruised from the beating she suffered before leaving Havana. Sad and disillusioned after being unable to find a bed in the
overcrowded barracks, Adela sits on a bench under the stars. A stranger
approaches her, saying, "Hey mama, why's that nice face so sad tonight?"
(Cortez 2004, 39). Soon he informs her that having been in Fort Chaffee a
month, he is now the barracks czar, a position that includes the benefit of
a private shower (40) (fig. 5.2). On the opposite page, we see Adela naked on
her back with her legs up, holding her penis out of the way; the text reads,
"I got into bed and paid the rent" (41) (fig. 5.3).

In these moments of "seeing" Adela in masculine drag, I meet a person I
have never known. But I confess, this is another insight I came to in writing
about *Sexile/Sexilio*, not in my initial reading of it. Literature and fantasy
train us to jump back and forth into different temporal registers, to inhabit

FIG 5.2 ▶ Jaime Cortez, *Sexile/Sexilio*, 2004, 40.

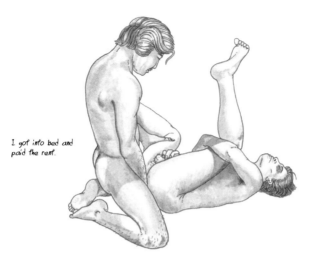

I got into bed and paid the rent.

FIG 5.3 ▸ Jaime Cortez, *Sexile/Sexilio*, 2004, 41.

different bodies and perspectives effortlessly. But the graphic layout, aside from reflecting back on her early days in Fort Chaffee, also provides a draw-ing on the bottom left of the Adela that I know, midsentence, gesturing to make a point, and readers get another monologue from Adela about sex and power. "I was a wreck, child. Tore up, beat down, dirty, hungry, tired, but after just forty-eight hours in the USA, I had a papi and a private crib. All I needed was a poodle and a picket fence. I was so exhausted, I almost didn't realize he was seducing me, but then I realized and I thought, 'I know this. It's beauty and sex getting me what I need.' Different country, same exchange. Pussy power, baby, pussy power" (Cortez 2004, 40). Here, Adela identifies in explicit terms the transnational, transactional value of femi-nine sexual labor and the material rewards of knowing how to work sex. If her language seems to essentialize a connection between feminine wiles and female genitalia, it is a gendered essentialism that she readily assigns to herself, a sexual power capable of making the American Dreams of a papi and a private crib come true, even if only for a night.

While the Cuban women who had greeted the new refugees had offered them Wrigley's gum, Coca-Cola, Bibles, and a bag full of donated clothes, as a queer refugee without a family and without a nation, Adela needed more. Like many of the other putas profiled in this book, part of what Adela needed and sought out was safety, security, and support. Most immediately, she needed a queer benefactor, someone to sponsor her out of the camps, someone to teach her the ways of this new place of dreams and nightmares. She found that in the person of Rolando Victoria, Adela's "alcoholic Angel in America," a gay Cuban sponsor with whom she lived, rent free, for two years and who imparted the six lessons of life in the United States. In this full-page panel, Cortez creates a queer version of the iconic image of la Caridad del Cobre, the patron saint of Cuba, with Rolando Victoria as the beneficent Cachita who cradles the baby Adela in her arms.[9] The knowledge about life in the United States that her sponsor imparted includes local customs concerning sexual practices as well as more difficult truths to assimilate. Lesson number six declares, "You are forever crowned by the pain of exile. Get used to it, girl" (Cortez 2004, 45) (fig. 5.4).

Pages later, in a chapter called "Legal Tender," Adela, now established in Los Angeles with her gay Cuban sponsor, begins a more formal relationship with sex work: "Makeup, drugs, clothes, hormones, food and a million other expenses. It was hard to keep up with the salary from my sewing work. I wasn't living rent free anymore, so mama needed to capitalize big time. . . . So I said 'fuck it' and went and took hoochie pictures and then I put an ad in the ho rag 'Hollywood Connections' to see if I'd get some business" (61). Modeling her entrepreneurial skills after the undocumented Mexican migrants and veteran trans women "working shit out" all around her, Adela learned how to navigate the underground economies and capitalist constraints of her new homeland. And, as she states, the response was off the hook, even if the "number one request" was for the "surprise down south" (61) (fig. 5.5).

In the top panel of this page, we see the actual ad Adela used to promote her sexual services. Capitalizing on her racialized exoticism and gendered difference, she describes herself as an "exotic Cuban she-male" and provides her numerical stats: "34A-26-38 and 8″." Here, rather than a graphic rendering, we see a photograph of Adela with long dark hair, crouching down in high heels and lingerie and staring directly at us, her penis hanging between her garter-and-stocking-covered thighs. The inclusion of an actual photograph within the context of a graphic narrative performs a kind of doubling, where the subject of representation is situated in the presence of her own image. Even as the text is certainly cringe-worthy, as Adela makes clear, it worked to pay the rent, and as in the episode with the goat, her readers can leave their judgments aside. By the time we reach the bottom-right panel, however, Cortez draws Adela rolling her eyes, and we

Rolando Victoria. That name is a sentence by itself for a reason, okay? He was the most bitchy, hilarious, faggoty faggot ever. I adored her. He opened his home to me as a sponsor. Rolando was a nurse and he had been a nurse in the United States for twenty one years. He was my alcoholic Angel in America. I stayed with him rent-free for two years. Like a good Cuban mama, and he taught me the six commandments of living in the U.S.A.

I:
STARE NOT AT THE CROTCHES OF MENFOLK. IT'S BAD MANNERS.

II:
A GOOD GARAGE SALE IS A GIFT FROM HEAVEN. DON'T WASTE IT.

III:
ALWAYS, ALWAYS PAY THE RENT ON TIME.

IV:
IN CUBA, WE LEARNED THAT GIVING HEAD IS LOWLY. THIS IS NOT CUBA.

V:
LEARN ENGLISH. YESTERDAY.

VI:
YOU ARE FOREVER CROWNED BY THE PAIN OF EXILE. GET USED TO IT, GIRL.

FIG 5.4 ▸ La Caridad del Cobre. Jaime Cortez, *Sexile/Sexilio*, 2004, 45.

Makeup, drugs, clothes, hormones, food
and a million other expenses. It was
hard to keep up with the salary from my
sewing work. I wasn't living rent free
anymore, so mama needed to capitalize big
time. I watched veteran transgenders and
especially the Mexican immigrants in
Los Angeles. They were geniuses at
working shit out in underground economies.
Labor for cash under the table,
live where you can and get over even
if you don't have no green card.

So I said "fuck it" and went and took
hoochie pictures and then I put in
an ad in the ho rag "Hollywood
Connections" to see if I'd get some
business.

EXOTIC CUBAN
★ **ADELLA** ★
SHE-MALE
34A-26-38 • 8"
(113) 859-1249
129-TS-

The response was off the hook.

Work it OUT!

RING
RING
RING
RING

The John's wanted company,
a partner for their
fantasies.

Be gentle,
oh Amazon
Avenger, I'm
only mortal!

The number one request was
for the "surprise down south."

Baby, you
are sooo
gorgeous.
Your eyes,
your face!

I just wanna
lick up your
hot pussy!

OMIGAWD!
What's this?
A cock!?!?!
Ooh and it's
so big and -
mmmmm...

SLURP
SLURP
SLURP

FIG 5.5 ▸ Jaime Cortez, *Sexile/Sexilio*, 2004, 61.

glimpse her boredom and frustration at performing the tired narrative of racialized transgender exoticism.[10]

By the next page, Adela tells us that "Mama figured out a whole menu and prices for everything"—"Ching, Cha Ching, Cha Cha Ching, Cha Ching Bling Bling!!!"—and outlines all the benefits of "whoring" (Cortez 2004, 62). But we quickly learn that Adela grew tired of having sex be her job. Within the context of a book on sexual labor, Adela's account of using sex to pay the bills at one point in her life reminds readers that sex work as a kind of temporary employment is actually the norm. Like Adela, most people use sex work to get by, to make it through a rough economic transition, or to earn a little extra cash. As Adela explains, "I was a great fuck but a lousy ho. I hated it when they wanted to have dinner first. I'm not trying to date your azz, sonso! So awkward. As a prostitute, I had no sexual freedom. I was a product, a service, an idea, but never really a human being. . . . Some people can deal with hoin' just fine, but it was so painful for me to live like that. Sometimes I'd think, 'My god, I used to be a math teacher'" (Cortez 2004, 62) (fig. 5.6). This last line serves to remind readers of just how different her life might have been if Adela had been allowed to stay in Cuba, to simply be a math teacher wearing a "little foundation and some tasteful rouge." The sense of alienation and objectification from her labor that Adela describes in this passage mirrors Karl Marx's thoughts on the estranged labor that permeates capitalist production. Marx writes, "The worker therefore only feels [herself] outside [her] work, and in [her] work feels outside [herself]" (Marx and Engels 1988, 74). We also see how the sexual market allows one to risk personal safety for a price, with customers willing to pay extra for sex without a condom.

Apart from how these stories speak to the labor of sex work, Adela's larger narrative articulates the other ways that we see Latinas work sex, as it illustrates the different kinds of things for which sex and sexuality can be exchanged: pleasure, safety, shelter, and of course money. In her book *Queen for a Day*, Marcia Ochoa (2014, 89), another queer child of Proyecto's diasporic village, writes, "Glamour, beauty, and femininity are technologies with specific practices that result in social legibility, intimate power, and potentially, physical survival in a hostile environment." As a sex worker, Adela's exotic good looks, feminine self-stylings, and flair for coquettish flirtation—her "social legibility"—functioned as a commodity that she could exchange for cash, but it also provided a particular kind of street currency and social capital, an additional coat of armor to paint over the harsh realities of life as an immigrant trans woman far from home.

Whoring has some pretty good benefits.
First of all, ho hours are flexible.
You can schedule your tricks around your
Ricky Lake show, pilates, laundry,
teeth cleaning or whatever your thing is.
Some Johns were nice, a few hella sexy.
The main thing was the money. Mama figured out
a whole menu and prices for everything.
I suck you.   Ching!
You suck me.   Cha Ching!
You fuck me.   Cha Cha Ching!
I fuck you.   Cha Ching Bling Bling!!!
Some of my tricks wanted to pay extra for
fucking with no condoms. HELL NO.

I was a great fuck but a lousy ho.
I hated it when they wanted to have
dinner first. I'm not trying to date
your azz, sonso! So awkward.
As a prostitute, I had no sexual freedom.
I was a product, a service, an idea, but
never a real human being.
You know what? It hurt. Some people
can deal with hoin' just fine, but it was
so painful for me to live like that.
Sometimes I'd think, "My god, I used to
be a math teacher."

FIG 5.6 ▶ Jaime Cortez, *Sexile/Sexilio*, 2004, 62.

Other Adelas

Representation matters, and portraiture and biographical documentation make real the lives and stories that are frequently out of view. Feminist art historian Milena Costa de Souza (2015, 255) writes, "The portrait is an image of a subject's face . . . which gives them the possibility of being more than a physical body. Therefore, the representation of the face confers historical and social existence to the person portrayed, as it allows them to exist even after their death."[11] Depictions of trans life, of the heartbreak of exile, of the daily wages of sexual labor are urgent and necessary precisely because these are not the faces and stories that get delivered to us through mass media. But while Adela may lack many things, most importantly a job at the moment, what she does not lack is representation. As with the other compelling life narratives I have shared over the course of this book, this is a story that will get repeated by Adela and by others, including myself, across a range of platforms for a range of diverse political purposes. In fact, even before the publication of *Sexile/Sexilio* in 2004, Adela was interviewed for a public radio program on transgender women in San Francisco, featured in Proyecto's promotional materials, and spotlighted in my own 2003 book, *Queer Latinidad*. In 2007 she was interviewed for an article by the late Salvadoran oral historian Horacio Roque Ramírez about her role in orchestrating the Afro-Caribbean vibes at another now defunct Latinx club space, Pan Dulce, where she performed under the stage name Adela Holyday (Roque Ramírez 2007).[12] In 2009 she also appeared in *Diagnosing Difference*, a documentary about transgender women in San Francisco that featured other transgender notables such as Susan Stryker, Dean Spade, and Cecilia Chung (Ophelian 2009). In the documentary, Adela's deep and deeply accented voice booms out of your speakers, adding the grain of her voice, the cadence of her English, and her conviction to representing the value of transgender lives to the sensory archive of Adela's biography.[13] That was 2009, and she seems to be performing mature matron for the camera: blond, including lightened eyebrows; more subdued makeup; and transparent pink reading glasses that mark the age of anyone over forty (fig. 5.7). The gesture captured in this shot might give you a sense of the authority Adela's presence commands. I recall Sandra Cisneros's short story about how when you are eleven, you are also ten, and nine, and eight, and seven, and six. Adela is now in her sixties, but she is also the thirtysomething performing at Esta Noche, the twenty-two-year-old Marielito washing up on shore, the nine-year-old pimping goats.

FIG 5.7 ▸ Adela Vázquez in *Diagnosing Difference,* 2009.

In 2013 Adela was featured in *SF Weekly,* the free weekly that is distributed all over the city, in a feature article by Julián Delgado that was later developed into a bilingual book of collected oral histories of queer Latinx immigrants (Delgado Lopera 2017).[14] The close-up photograph that graced the *SF Weekly* cover captures precisely the kinds of details that we might try to hide as we age: the weight of lines around the eyes, the texture of aging skin. But Adela's hair is purple, and it matches her lipstick perfectly, a punk puta who doesn't give a shit what you might think about how she looks (fig. 5.8). In the photograph inside the issue, Adela appears flawless, perched atop a wellworn leather coach, peering down at the viewer through a curtain of jet-black lashes, her hands expertly manicured and heavy with rings (fig. 5.9). In the photograph, she is positioned regally surrounded by Orientalist imagery. Adela is a Buddhist, and I am reminded of the Buddha she gifted me for my fiftieth birthday, a blessing of harmony and buenas vibras that today lives on my altar. And I remember sharing her giddy excitement at seeing her face peering out of newsstands on so many street corners of San Francisco.

When Delgado Lopera published those interviews a few years later as a bilingual book, *¡Cuéntamelo!,* the cover image chosen was another one of Adela's glam shots from years gone by, the arch of the eyebrow performing its own singular drama (fig. 5.10).[15] In 2015 Adela was once again the subject of an oral history for the book *Queer Brown Voices: Personal Narratives of Latina/o LGBT Activism,* edited by Uriel Quesada, Letitia Gomez, and Salvador Vidal-Ortiz. In her preface, Gomez talks about the problems of translation

FIG 5.8 ▸ Adela Vázquez. Cover, *SF Weekly*, June 26–July 2, 2013. Photograph by Gil Riego.

FIG 5.9 ▸ Adela Vázquez. *SF Weekly*, June 26–July 2, 2013. Photograph by Gil Riego.

FIG 5.10 ▸ Cover, Juliana Delgado Lopera, *¡Cúentamelo!*, 2017.

and meditation that oral history instantiates and specifically calls out editorial issues that arose with elements of Adela's oral history. It seems that at one point in the interview—conducted in Spanish and published in English—Adela talks about "women born-females" and "normal women" in ways that made the editors rightfully uncomfortable, producing another moment of Adela-authored cringe-worthy text (Gomez 2015, xii). Yet because those comments were voiced by a trans woman, the editors decided to faithfully reprint the interview. I try to imagine the interviewer wanting to interrupt Adela's monologue, perhaps trying to use her utterance as a pedagogical moment to make a point about language and transgender embodiment. But Adela is old school and stubborn, not fully versed in the critiques of normativity or up on the latest queer lingo of "cis-gendered," and most likely not in the mood to be schooled. A few years ago, I had students work on Wikipedia projects to document queer-of-color lives, the minor figures that mean so much to so many, and after reading *Sexile/Sexilio*, a student created a Wikipedia page for Adela because nothing says notable like having a Wikipedia page. More recently I heard Adela's story featured in a podcast called *Kickass Women of Color*, produced by Jandeliz, a high school student at Lawrence Academy in faraway Lawrence, Massachusetts, and we witness how stories can travel to inspire far-away lives (Jandeliz 2021). In fact, the stories about Adela just seem to multiply, each one a partial, problematic, rich, and imprecise attempt at biographical representation. Rather than capturing the subject's unique difference, these forms of biographical representation enact the inherent impossibility of fully capturing subjectivity. Representation invariably falls short, producing an absence that is never fully capable of capturing the psychic contours of embodied subjectivity and an excess, produced through the performative possibilities of interpretation and misinterpretation that nevertheless carries the promise of sparking something new.

Digital Turns

An imagined corrective to the shortcomings of biographical representation or misrepresentation is, of course, self-representation. Today, the social media platforms that surround us offer marginalized subjects, and indeed all of us with an internet connection, an endless array of ways to share who we are with others—Instagram, TikTok, SnapChat, Twitter, and, of course, the OG of social media platforms, Facebook, which recently underwent its own identity transformation as Meta, part of a newly conceived capitalist conglomerate Metaverse. What do bounded life narratives—memoirs, (auto)biography, testimonial literature—mean in a digital age, when so many of us are constantly documenting our own lives, capable of uploading old and new images, stories, and silences? These multimedia digital platforms empower us to curate emerging versions of ourselves that we might offer to others, allowing us to selectively approve the images and text, the sounds and sights, that function to define our lives, digitally. And Adela's Facebook page does not disappoint.

In a profile picture from 2017, her hair is blond and short, and her chosen Facebook name is Adela Cuba (fig. 5.11).[16] Here, the designer sunglasses perform their own kind of shade. And while her feed is cluttered with the usual collection of political and personal rants and raves about the political situation in Cuba, about transgender rights, and more recently assorted posts that speak to the challenges of feminine aging, Adela also maintains a photo album on her page that she has titled "The Amazing Past," a personal visual archive of her larger-than-life history. And because this is Facebook,

FIG 5.11 ▸ Screenshot of Adela Vázquez's Facebook page, November 11, 2017. Courtesy of Adela Vázquez.

where space for the past that is continually being produced is limitless, it offers a whole new self-curated visual archive of Adela's life.

Peering inside that folder opens onto another world of memory, feeling, and femme fabulosity. Figure 5.12 presents a candid photograph of Adela, working sex, translating what Marcia Ochoa (2014, 89) might term "transnational economies of desire and consumption" into a strapless outfit, a flowered up-do, a pink-and-orange makeup palette, a particularly feminine hand gesture of registering interest and aloofness simultaneously. The year is 1991. In contrast to Jaime Cortez's comic illustrations, this photograph captures a particular moment and style, thirteen years before the release of *Sexile/Sexilio*. What does it mean to see this younger version of Adela outside the illustrated story that Cortez has provided, or the more contemporary images of her I have offered? What might it mean to "read" her image, in all the queerest senses of the word, alongside her story? Perhaps like me, you find it hard to look away from the bowed arc of her brow, the blacklined curve of her almond-shaped eyes, or those perfectly lined magenta lips. The photograph also reveals how glamour functions as its own kind of sexual labor; this look took work. But like the other photographs of Adela we have seen, this image instantiates another encounter with the real, not the real of life narrative but the undeniable immediacy of presence that photographic forms promise to deliver. And this photographic archive of puta life, tucked into a Facebook profile, keeps delivering the looks.

FIG 5.12 ▸ Adela Vázquez, 1991. Captioned "Xmas at Leticia's like 1991." From "The Amazing Past" photo album on Adela's Facebook page. Courtesy of Adela Vázquez.

In figure 5.13 we see Adela strutting her stuff for the camera and her audience. This is Esta Noche, a broken-down dive queer Latino bar, the last queer Latino bar to close in San Francisco, a space that meant so much to so many, including to Adela. In another more recent interview, this time for a video presentation called "Legends, Monsters and Chosen Family," Adela describes what the scene *used* to be, when there were three queer Latinx bars on the corner of Sixteenth and Mission: "It was a great community, a community that is lost that I still miss. These were the places that people would go for more than dancing—it was a place to make community, to make friends, to find a dick, to find a roommate" (Still Here San Francisco 2021).[17] Esta Noche is gone now, another victim of San Francisco's unchecked gentrification, converted into a hipster hangout named the Bond Bar.[18] But in this photograph, we are transported to a time before gentrification and the white reterritorialization of San Francisco's Mission District; Esta Noche is open for business, packed with the possibility of action, and Adela is silently belting out a song.

FIG 5.13 ▸ Adela Vázquez, n.d. Captioned "Esta Noche Show." From "The Amazing Past" photo album on Adela's Facebook page. Courtesy of Adela Vázquez.

In this Facebook folder, most of the images seem to have been added in 2009, digitized from printed photographs with captions added through the haze of years gone by, offering a smattering of the mood and memories left behind. That these images required an additional level of labor, including affective labor, to digitize and caption marks them as special, even if that significance is never fully provided to those of us who stumble across them. Their importance, like the earlier moment of narrating revenge, is something we can only speculate. I am particularly glad that these photographs are safely preserved in the digital sphere because by now the original photographs have been lost to the detours of mobile lives in precarious times.

The images collected in that folder appear quite random, not necessarily organized by date or location or theme. In the comments, other friends, many from our shared days as part of the Proyecto village, wax nostalgic, and the comments are filled with much talk of "back in the day." In one, we see her without makeup and with rolos or curlers in her hair, a visual testament to both the labor and the magic of glamour (among her many other jobs, at one point in her life, Adela was a hairdresser). Another is captioned "Show @ Esta Noche giving away my crown" (fig. 5.14). One of my favorite photographs is of Adela with her friend Tina, delivering face and attitude for the ages (fig. 5.15). Tina was another Cubana who also hustled and who would eventually die in jail but not before selling salacious pictures of Adela to her jail mates. This too is puta life. What does Adela see in these younger images of herself that she wants to share or remember or document? Is it just the glow of youth? A testament to friendship? Or do these archived photographs capture a moment when another future seemed possible? If the digital space of social media—with its overload of sights, sounds, and snippets of the special and the mundane—doesn't necessarily get us any closer to the real, what does it instantiate? Perhaps we need to look more closely, to linger longer, to listen more attentively to the possibilities that these images also announce.

In many of these images, we see Adela *werk*, conjuring the African American trans term that signals the vitality, vigor, and verve that are continually demanded of transfemme lives, the endless hustle to werk it out. But Adela also includes a candid photo of herself working, sitting at her cluttered desk from her days as an outreach coordinator at Proyecto ContraSIDA por Vida, smiling at whoever stopped by with a camera to interrupt her work day (fig. 5.16). Adela was very good at her job and is rightfully

FIG 5.14 ▸ Adela Vázquez, 1993. Captioned "Show @ Esta Noche giving away my crown." From "The Amazing Past" photo album on Adela's Facebook page. Courtesy of Adela Vázquez.

FIG 5.15 ▸ Adela Vázquez and Acasio de León, a.k.a. Tina, n.d. From "Photos of Adela" photo album on Adela's Facebook page. Courtesy of Adela Vázquez.

FIG 5.16 ▸ Adela Vázquez, 1995. Captioned "Apple days lol at PCPV 1995." From "The Amazing Past" photo album on Adela's Facebook page. Courtesy of Adela Vázquez.

proud of the life-changing work she did at Proyecto, recruiting other trans Latinas, many sex workers like herself, to protect themselves against HIV but also inviting them to form part of a community dedicated to living, to self- and community empowerment. The very name Proyecto ContraSIDA por Vida politicizes the value of affirming life for those for whom survival was never promised.

That single photograph of Adela sitting at her desk within the offices of Proyecto also makes another point undeniably clear: trans women, particularly trans women of color, need more than representation and documentation; they need jobs that provide health insurance, sick days, vacation time, and access to an appropriate toilet—indeed, a job like my own that offers a pension so that one can also stop working when the time comes. In the absence of these most basic forms of care, Black Brazilian transgender scholar Dora Santana describes the practices of survival and community formed within Black transfemme spaces of impossibility, a practice she calls "mais viva" (more alive). She writes, "*Mais viva!* more alert, more alive, [it] is that embodied knowledge developed within that liminal space of not forgetting the imbrications between experiences of violence and the ways we find joy and acknowledgment and support, even if that comes in a micro-intimate level" (2019, 214, 215). Contained within Santana's invocation of *mais viva* is also a political demand for *mas vida*, more life and more expansive life chances.

By now we know the brutality that statistics document. Transrespect versus Transphobia reported that 2021 was set to be the deadliest year for transgender people worldwide: by November 20, 2021, International Trans Day of Remembrance, 375 trans people had been murdered, 96 percent were trans women, more than half were known sex workers, and the majority were racialized minorities or migrants (TvT 2021).[19] These numbers speak to the deadly intersection of transphobia, xenophobia, racialized misogyny, and the stigma that attaches to sex workers and those who work sex. Yet, in her insistence on naming, joy, acknowledgment, and support, Santana reminds us that survival is always more than simple protection from physical harm, though it must include that; it is about attending to the weight of a world intent on denying the beauty of your humanity and the psychic scars that stigma leaves behind, and it is about the possibilities for recognition and repair that friendship and community can engender. *Mais viva* announces "the strategies we, as trans and black people, use to not be broken at the end of the day" (Santana 2019, 214).

Lately on Facebook, Adela has taken to manipulating photographs old and new, applying Warholian filters, smoothing the edges of age (fig. 5.17). In most of the images on Facebook, she appears as glamorous as ever, affirming Ochoa's (2014, 89) assertion that "glamour allows its practitioners to conjure a contingent space of being and belonging." But Adela's ability to produce her own images or control how they might circulate is not quite the point. All of us struggle to be seen, heard, and recognized by those around us, even as we stumble in our efforts to fully represent the fullness of our lives or the feelings they inspire.

Even on Facebook, even within the virtual spaces she has carefully curated to represent herself, Adela is unable to fully capture all she is and all that her life might signify to others or herself. The hardest part, or perhaps the most comforting, is that even in the corporeal presence of the compelling biographical subjects I have presented, even if Adela, Vanessa, Raquel, or indeed any of the women I have profiled over the course of this book were here with us now, representing themselves, we wouldn't really know them, not fully. And that is as it should be. Butler (2005, 42–43) writes, "As we ask to know the other, or ask that the other say, finally or definitively, who he or she is, it will be important not to expect an answer that will ever satisfy. By not pursuing satisfaction and letting the question remain open, even enduring, we let the other live, since life might be understood as precisely that which exceeds any account we may try to give of it."

Adela is unemployed now; the nonprofit jobs have run dry or been taken over by a bright new crew of young queer and trans activists who know how to speak the new lingo that these jobs require. Gentrification has made San Francisco unaffordable, and the incursion of privileged whiteness has made it unlivable, in no small part because of the influx of tech giants like Facebook. Adela tried to leave; she went to Florida but had to come back to San Francisco to an uncertain future in a city that seems to have no place for her. Perhaps for now, the place of glamour in Adela's life, the contingent space of being and belonging, *is* Facebook, a place to contain the elsewhere of youth and the memory of sexual futures that could have been, even as the strain and heartbreak of living remain out of sight. Adela maintains another image folder on Facebook she has titled "My Friends and I," another digital album of photos of curated memories, and tucked into that folder is a photograph of Adela and me, taken at the book launch of ¡*Cuéntamelo!* (fig. 5.18).

Adela and I are friends but not besties; we certainly don't see each other as much as when we shared time at Proyecto, when I still lived in San Fran-

FIG 5.17 ▸ Adela Vázquez, n.d. Courtesy
of Adela Vázquez.

FIG 5.18 ▸ Adela Vázquez with the author,
June 20, 2014. From "My Friends and I"
photo album on Adela's Facebook page.
Courtesy of Adela Vázquez.

cisco, before both of us grew wearier from life's travails. Whenever we see each other, I like to believe that we both feel a connection, femme friendship, Cuban camaraderie, the queer kinship that Proyecto etched into our skin, our shared belief that another future is possible. When we get together now, we talk about the old days, catch up on our current amores, desamores y aventuras, but mostly we commiserate about how awful feminine aging is, how impossible the situation—in San Francisco, Cuba, the world—has become, and like the matronly roles we have aged into, we talk about the children we share: that younger generation of queer and trans artists and activists who have taken up the charge to make things better. I was nervous sharing a draft of this book with Adela, in part because I remember her astute and pointed comments when I shared a copy of my dissertation chapter on Proyecto with her so many years ago. But her reply made me smile: "Me ha encantado tu interpretación de quien soy yo" (I love your interpretation of who I am). It makes clear that she understands the limits that surround representation; she knows that my partial and flawed offering is only one interpretation among many. Even as we both know that the "yo" of Adela will forever defy any attempt to offer an account of her life, I struggle to name all the ways my own life has been enriched through Adela's presence in it, and I share her desire to document the singular importance of her life as a transgender immigrant Latina woman werking it out, her impulse to give her memories material substance.

As a scholar with the security of tenure, I have tried to do right by Adela; to compensate her monetarily for her photos, her stories, her time; to offer other opportunities for extracting wages from her labor, her wisdom, and her extraordinary puta life. She knows that I try, but we both know it is never enough; the world we live in needs to change. Doing right, therefore, also means committing to making it better for Adela, as well as those I don't know, those unnamed others who might likewise have stories to tell and nowhere to go; those who also long to be recognized as precious and divine. It means claiming activist work in its myriad of forms to end the stigma that surrounds sex work and all forms of sexual exchange; a commitment to advocate for lives of dignity for all, where shelter, care, and community is a given and friendship is a way of life; a shared quest for affirming life as a way of conjuring another world together.

EPILOGUE

Toward a Conclusion That Does Not Die or a Subject That Is Allowed to Live

Writing against the captive impulses of criminalizing states and the judgmental stares of petty publics, this book is my small contribution to the political project of affirming puta life, of refusing the stigma that surrounds sex work and lingering instead in the life lessons it might offer. Toward that end, I have resisted authorial claims to knowledge production and shared instead the words and faces of those mujeres públicas who have been my teachers and my guides, who have challenged me to look and listen more closely in order to sense other ways of knowing the labor of sex. As method, I have offered a slow sensory encounter that is allowed to ferment over time, stirred by the soft strokes of queer poetics and the felt force of friendship under the protective veil of the spirits that hover near by. In the process, I have tried to model a femme practice of receptivity, opening myself to other ways of knowing and unknowing, allowing myself to be transformed by the possibilities that connection engenders, and attentive to what remains outside. Along the way, I have shared pieces of myself with you, parts that are also tender and prone to misinterpretation, fragments that are scattered within and beyond memory. Books take time; I have grown older sitting with this archive of faces and figures. Spending time with my age mates, I have tried to make peace with my own conflicted thoughts about aging, sexuality, and what might come next. As I have watched my own body grow more fragile as life has rubbed raw the bruised places in my heart, I have seen the women I have profiled in this text model different ways to come to terms with the final phase of this journey and the always uncertain paths to arrive there.

In the end, those instances where I have tried to reach for the touch of recognition or repair have revealed the anxious authorial urges and contradictory desires that representation splays open as well as the strain and friction of the wildest hopes they also hide. The truth is that I am wary of the authority I have assumed in composing this text, all the ways I feel inadequate to the task that I have laid out for myself: the impossible task of the translator; the documentarian; the scholar who aspires to change hearts, laws, worlds; the aging puta who seeks connection and community. I have sought out ways of knowing that might guide us toward other modes of relationality capable of extending friendship and care across the differences that separate us. I have tried to be gentle, to leave air for distrust and doubt, knowing that many times I am exhuming another's vulnerability and heartache across an insurmountable chasm of space and time and flesh. Yet to say that the differences that divide us are too deep or too difficult is to refuse the work of affirming life, not as a singular enterprise of survival but as a collective dream about what Denise Ferreira da Silva calls "entangled worlds." Ferreira da Silva (2017, 58) writes, "What if, instead of The Ordered World, we could image The World as a Plenum, an infinite composition in which each existant's singularity is contingent upon its becoming one possible expression of all the other existants, with which it is entangled beyond space and time." This text has invited you to become entangled with puta life because you already are. Fantastic projections that depict sex workers as either dangerous manipulative vixens or perpetually lamentable victims make it harder to recognize your ancestors, your communities, or yourself as impacted by the ongoing criminalization and stigma that surrounds every aspect of sexual labor. But sex workers are all around you; they are your students and your professors, the mom at your day care, and the tamal vendor on your block. If you care about mass incarceration, police brutality, immigrant detention, sexual violence, state surveillance, reproductive rights, freedom of expression, child care, elder care, poverty, education, refugee rights, housing, health care, and the life chances of those who were never meant to survive, I want you to care about sex workers. The ongoing stigmatization and criminalization of sex work is a feminist issue, a racial justice issue, a queer and trans issue, an immigrant rights issue, a labor issue, a disability justice issue, an issue that touches on the very rights of bodily autonomy, yet too often the stigma that surrounds sexual labor has kept it from forming part of our ongoing demands for justice for all. And what we know for certain is that criminalization makes everything bad about sex work worse. Even if I fail in my efforts to represent the fullness of these women's lives, to register my own entanglement with the putas who surround me and the puta who I am, I have tried to convey the innumerable ways that their lives, our lives, are informed by the nefarious forms of sexual regulation and social stigma that surround us all. This book is a call to sit with the weight of testimony, to demand more of ourselves, to do the work and the werk of changing the world, of making puta life more livable for all of us.[1]

NOTES

Introduction

1 Curiously, the OED *Online* provides an audio file for the word that replaces the hard middle sound of the Spanish "t" with a soft "də," "pudə," which completely deflates the sonic power of the word, making it sound closer to *pura*, or pure, rendering it almost comical. See *Oxford English Dictionary*, s.v. "puta, n.," accessed August 5, 2020, http://www.oed.com.

2 The debates about the etymology of the word *puta* register their own terse tensions—either tracing it back to the benign feminine form of the Latin word *putus*, meaning boy, or alternately suggesting its origins relate to the Latin *pūtidus*, meaning rotten, spoiled, or fetid.

3 In *Labyrinth of Solitude*, Octavio Paz (1994, 75) famously performs a deconstruction of the word *chingada*, the fucked one, and names the Mexican people "hijos de la chingada," where *chingada* serves as a synonym for *whore*. See also Norma Alarcón's "Tradductora, Traditora" (1989), which speaks back to Paz.

4 Leite organized the first national gathering of sex workers in Brazil in 1987; five years later, she organized Davida, one of the first activist groups in Latin America to advocate for the rights of sex workers. In addition to the Murray documentary *Um beijo para Gabriela* (2013), see Lenz 2014.

5 For an indispensable historical account of sex worker movements in Latin America, see Cabezas 2019. Despite the contemporary examples offered here, Amalia Cabezas rightly locates the origins of the sex worker movement in Latin America in the nineteenth century, a discussion I take up in the following chapter.

6 In San Francisco, Margo St. James, another iconic sex worker advocate, ran unsuccessfully for San Francisco's Board of Supervisors in 1996. St. James is credited with starting the organizations COYOTE (Call Off Your Old Tired Ethics) and WHO (Whores, Housewives, and Others) and later founded the St. James Infirmary in San Francisco, a "peer-based occupational health and safety clinic for sex workers of all genders" that continues to this day. St. James died in 2021 (Kukura 2021).

7   The group is named Miluska in honor of Villón's friend and colleague who was murdered while working in 1998.

8   For more on Sylvia Rivera, including STAR, the organization she cofounded with Marsha P. Johnson, see La Fountain-Stokes's (2021) powerful portrait of her life as a street hustler. See also Gan 2007. For more on the Compton's Cafeteria riot, see the film *Screaming Queens: The Riot at Compton's Cafeteria* (Silverman and Stryker 2005). For more on the sex workers in the LGBTQ movement, see Shah 2011–12; for more on the role of queers in sex worker movements, see Chateauvert 2015.

9   See the Institute of Development Studies' "Map of Sex Work Law" (n.d.), an indispensable guide for understanding legal approaches, law enforcement, and characteristics of enforcement related to sex work around the world.

10 See Frances Aparicio's *Listening to Salsa* (1998, 45–56), in which she discusses a popular plena (a traditional Puerto Rican musical form) that references Luberza Oppenheimer alongside readings of two literary references to this story. Those two short stories—"Cuando las mujeres quieren a los hombres," by Rosario Ferré (2000), considered the First Lady of Puerto Rican letters; and "La última plena que bailó Luberza," by Manuel Ramos Otero (1979), known as one of the most celebrated openly gay writers of Puerto Rico—represent the broad-ranging reach of this iconic figure. Another historical Afro-Latina sex worker and madam who became enshrined in popular culture is María de la Caridad Norberta Pacheco Sánchez of Cartagena Spain, known as Caridad la Negra (1879–1960). Her life served as the inspiration for Darío Fernández Flórez's 1951 novel, *Lola, espejo oscuro*, which was later adapted into a film of the same name (Merino and Sáenz de Heredia 1966), as well as other cultural texts of tragedy inspired by her life. My given name, in honor of my grandmothers and the patron saint of Cuba, is Juana María de la Caridad, marking this as one of numerous instances of finding an echo of my name in the archive. Both of these historical figures have incredibly well sourced Wikipedia pages that provide more biographical details. See also the Heaux History Project, a twitter account (@HeauxHistory) and Patreon website that documents Black, Brown, and Indigenous erotic labor and sex worker history (Heaux History Project, n.d.).

11 This is not to claim that this is the first novel that deploys this trope, just to suggest its long history within the genre regionally. The figure of the prostitute with a heart of gold is rooted in the mythologized biblical legacies of Mary Magdalene.

12 Eréndira and her heartless grandmother also make an appearance in García Márquez's *One Hundred Years of Solitude*.

13 It bears emphasizing that within my own text, the term *woman* refers to anyone who uses that term to define themselves.

14 See the Department of Homeland Security's "Blue Campaign," accessed December 22, 2014, https://www.dhs.gov/blue-campaign. This approach is further complicated by a policy of "Continued Presence," a temporary immigration sta-

tus that provides some relief for those who may be potential witnesses, making "victims" eligible for such government relief programs as those offered to refugees and thereby incentivizing the use of the term. On her blog, *The Naked Anthropologist*, Agustín (n.d.) uses the term *rescue industry* to name an "ever-larger social sector dedicated to helping and saving prostitutes, sex workers, fallen women." She argues that by "defining women as victims Rescuers find their own identity and meaning in life."

15   See LaShawn Harris's (2016) insightful book *Sex Workers, Psychics, and Numbers Runners*, in which she delineates how the criminalization of sex work in the early part of the twentieth century was used as a tactic of racialized and gendered control and exploitation and details how African American women created underground economic and social systems of support.

16   These include *We Too: Essays on Sex Work and Survival*, edited by Natalie West (2021); *Porn Work: Sex, Labor, and Late Capitalism*, by Heather Berg (2021); *A Whore's Manifesto: An Anthology of Writing and Artwork by Sex Workers*, edited by Kay Kassirer (2019); *Hustling Verse: An Anthology of Sex Worker Poetry*, edited by Amber Dawn and Justin Ducharme (2019); *Revolting Prostitutes: The Fight for Sex Workers' Rights*, by Molly Smith and Juno Mac (2018); *Coming Out like a Porn Star: Essays on Pornography, Protection, and Privacy*, edited by Jiz Lee (2015); and *Playing the Whore: The Work of Sex Work*, by Melissa Gira Grant (2014). See also the helpful guide *Thriving in Sex Work: Heartfelt Advice for Staying Sane in the Sex Industry; A Self-Help Book for Sex Workers*, by Lola Davina (2017). In Spanish, see the recent texts *Puta Feminista: Historias de una trabajadora sexual*, by Georgina Orellano (2022), and *Prostitución/Trabajo Sexual: Las Protagonistas Hablan*, edited by Diana Maffía and Claudia Korol (2021). In Portuguese, the anthology *Feminilidades: Corpos e Sexualidades em Debate*, edited by Daniele Andrade da Silva et. al (2013), includes several first-person accounts from sex workers.

17   There are several helpful guides that attempt to directly address best practices for academics researching and teaching about sex work. My own work is indebted and informed by these efforts. See specifically the incredibly comprehensive "Sex Worker Syllabus and Toolkit for Academics," compiled and curated by Heather Berg, Angela Jones, and PJ Patella-Reya (n.d.), which defines best practices and offers extensive readings. See also "Sex Work Centered Guide for Academics," by the collective Support Ho(s)es (2021), which also publishes guides for media and journalism professionals, health and wellness professionals, as well as a sex work–centered guide for writing to incarcerated populations.

18   See Caleb Luna's (2022) important work on how fatness comes to be associated with sexual excess. See also Yessica Garcia Hernandez's (2021) work on gordibuenas and the erotics of fatness.

19   Several new collections have taken up the role of photography and visual culture in colonial mappings of the world. See the excellent volume *Ethnopornography: Sexuality, Colonialism, and Archival Knowledge*, edited by Pete Sigal, Zeb

Tortorici, and Neil L. Whitehead (2019); *Orientalism, Eroticism and Modern Visuality in Global Cultures*, edited by Joan DelPlato and Julie Codell (2016); and *Photography's Other Histories*, edited by Christopher Pinney and Nicolas Peterson (2003). See also *An Eye for the Tropics: Tourism, Photography, and Framing the Caribbean Picturesque*, by Krista Thompson (2007); *Camera Orientalis: Reflections on Photography of the Middle East*, by Ali Behdad (2016); and *Vision, Race, and Modernity: A Visual Economy of the Andean World*, by Deborah Poole (1997). Malek Alloula's *The Colonial Harem* (1986) remains a touchstone for the field, as does earlier work on Native American photography compiled by Lucy Lippard in *Partial Recall: With Essays on Photographs of Native North Americans* (1993).

20　The phrase *ruins of representation* is borrowed from Gerald Vizenor's (1994) book *Manifest Manners*, a gift of language from my dearly loved teacher that I return to again and again.

21　The essay "Erotic Storytelling: Sexual Experience and Fantasy Letters in *Forum Magazine*," by Dee L. McEntire (1992), considers these letters as a form of folklore for documenting sexual experiences.

22　Readers should be reminded that at the time, the legal drinking age was eighteen and many gay bars were controlled by the Mafia, which had little interest in policing age or other illegal activities. I make brief mention of the Warehouse in *Queer Latinidad* (2003, 153) and *Sexual Futures* (2014, 103–4). The mood of that moment is also relived in my poem "Brujería" (2015).

23　It bears mentioning, in the interest of greater transparency and as a commentary on queer sexual cultures, that Julia and I *had* been sexual playmates for a minute and that we are still best friends.

24　*Sudaca* is a slur used to designate women from Latin America.

25　For example, see García-Peña's (2015) "Translating Blackness" for the ways that Black Dominican women articulate their experience of racialization in Italy.

26　See *Urban Dictionary*, s.v. "cubana," accessed August 5, 2021, https://www.urban dictionary.com/define.php?term=cubana.

27　See Albert et al.'s (2020) "FOSTA in Legal Context" for a sociological account of these effects. They conclude: "The result is that people in the sex trades, who work in legal, semilegal, and criminalized industries, have been forced into dangerous and potentially life-threatening scenarios. Many no longer have access to affordable methods of advertising and have returned to outdoor work or to in-person client-seeking in bars and clubs, where screening of the type that occurs online is impossible, and where workers are more vulnerable to both clients and law enforcement. These effects have been most impactful on sex workers facing multiple forms of marginalization, including Black, brown, and Indigenous workers, trans workers, and workers from lower socio-economic classes, who are prohibited from or unable to access more expensive advertising sites that may not be as impacted by FOSTA" (1089–90). For a more personal account of how the stigma surrounding sexual labor informs the lived possibilities of those in academia, see Mistress Snow's (2019) powerful piece in the

Chronicle of Higher Education about how coming out as a sex worker to her academic adviser impacted her as a graduate student.

28 The *New York Times* reported, "OnlyFans has become a source of income for two million creators, including sex workers, during the pandemic. The company said it had helped to democratize sex work, in part by letting creators effectively run their own businesses and own the content that they post on the site. Creators have collectively earned more than $4.5 billion since OnlyFans started nearly five years ago, the company said" (Lorenz and Lukpat 2021).

29 In the notorious Robert Pickton case in Canada that involved the murder of forty-nine women, mostly Indigenous women and most from Vancouver's Downtown Eastside, one woman managed to escape Pickton's grip, slashing his jugular vein in the process, and entered the police station near death with multiple stab wounds before falling unconscious for four days. That night in 1997, both Pickton and his victim lost more than three liters of blood, and both were treated in the same local hospital; the key to the handcuffs she was still wearing was found in Pickton's pocket. But because the victim was a sex worker and a heroin addict, "the Crown considered the woman too unstable to testify"; charges against him were eventually dropped, and his killing spree continued for thirteen years (Culbert 2010). Coincidentally or not, during that same time period, fashion photographer Lincoln Clarkes was also luring heroin-addicted sex workers from Vancouver's impoverished Eastside to pose for his camera. Clarkes (2002) eventually published a book titled *Heroines*, which included images of Pickton's victims, another contribution to the photographic archive of puta life. See also Shari Huhndorf's (2021) essay "Scenes from the Fringe: Gendered Violence and the Geographies of Indigenous Feminism," which opens with a discussion of the Pickton murders and explores the response of Indigenous feminist artists to the larger ongoing epidemic of missing and murdered Indigenous women.

30 In media reports of the 2021 massacre at massage parlors in Atlanta, there was considerable back-and-forth about whether the victims were actually sex workers, an attempt to distance these women from historical associations of Asian women as sexual servants and massage parlors as sites of sexual commerce. What we know for certain is that the six murdered Asian American victims were between the ages of forty-four and seventy-four. Soon Chung Park was seventy-four, Suncha Kim was sixty-nine, Yong Ae Yue was sixty-three, Hyun Jung Grant was fifty-one, Xiaojie Tan was forty-nine, and the youngest, Daoyou Feng, was forty-four—confounding stereotypes of who is employed at these facilities.

One. Women in Public

1 I am indebted to the warmth and collegiality of Natalia López López, chief librarian at the Instituto Nacional de Salúd Pública and dedicated conservator

of this unique tome. She and her staff were extraordinarily generous in sharing their knowledge of the public health terminology of the period and pointing me to the available relevant literature. My thanks also to Michelle Velasquez-Potts, my research assistant extraordinaire, for all her efforts in helping me document this archive.

2 Less than two decades later, a whole host of concerted zoning laws, hygiene regulations, and additional public policies came to be instituted under the decidedly less euphemistic title *Reglamento de prostitución 1878* (Ríos de la Torre 2008).

3 Among the definitions listed by the Real Academia Española: "Título o despacho real para el goce de un empleo, honor o privilegio" (Title or office for the enjoyment of a job, honor, or privilege); "Cédula que dan algunas cofradías o sociedades a sus miembros para que conste que lo son" (Certificate that some societies give to their members to establish who they are); and "Documento expedido por la Hacienda pública, que acredita haber satisfecho determinada persona la cantidad que la ley exige para el ejercicio de algunas profesiones o industrias" (Document issued by the Public Treasury, which proves that a certain person has satisfied the amount that the law requires for the exercise of some professions or industries). The discursive connection to the Public Treasury confirms that this was as much a project of collecting revenue for the state as it was about protecting the health of sex workers or their clients. There is an additional usage of *patente* that seems worth noting: the phrase *patente de sanidad*, a health certificate issued to sea-faring vessels that indicates whether there is plague or contagion at the place of departure, establishes these women, rather than their clients, as potentially disease-carrying vessels needing authorization from the state to move from port to port. One of the definitions of the English word *patent* also bears noting; the first definition that *Merriam-Webster's* offers is "open to public inspection." See Real Academia Española, s.v. "patente," *Diccionario de la lengua española*, Edición del Tricentenario, accessed September 29, 2021, https://dle.rae.es/patente; *Merriam-Webster's*, s.v. "patent," accessed September 29, 2021, https://www.merriam-webster.com/dictionary/patent.

4 All translations are mine unless otherwise indicated.

5 See specifically Deborah Poole's important work *Vision, Race, and Modernity*, in which she connects the carte de visite to the study of "racial physiology" and Alphonse Bertillon's systems of documenting criminality, noting that Bertillon was himself a member of an early French anthropological society and used cartes de visite as illustrations for his 1883 book *Les races sauvages* (Poole 1997, 139–41).

6 For more on early photography in Latin America, including a discussion of photography studios, see *Negros no estúdio do fotógrafo*, by Sandra Sofia Machado Koutsoukos (2010). Machado Koutsoukos outlines the ways that studio photography functioned to "perform freedom" for free Black people in Brazil. The author makes a point of discussing how Black and mulata concubines of elite

white Brazilians used portraiture as a way to show off their material wealth and as evidence of their status. See also the first volume of *Historia de la fotografía dominicana*, by Jeannette Miller (2010), for considerable discussion of the role of photography in nation building; and Sara Facio's (1997) *La fotografía en la Argentina*.

7 In the subsequent direct quotes from the *Registro*, I have corrected spelling and added accents as needed for readability.

8 As I note later, these registries began popping up around Mexico, Latin America, and other parts of the world; therefore, the conventions—how categories were assigned or determined—might very well have varied in different local contexts produced later. Furthermore, some scholars, relying on a variety of secondary sources, seem to mix photographs and details from similar archives and ascribe them to the original 1865 archive I focus on here.

9 Ngram suggests that the name Juana enjoyed considerable popularity in the eighteenth and nineteenth centuries. Search for "Juana," 1600–2019, Spanish (2019), Google Books Ngram Viewer, accessed September 5, 2022, https://books.google.com/ngrams/graph?content=Juana&year_start=1600&year_end=2019&corpus=32&smoothing=3.

10 The contemporary researchers, Claudia I. Damián Guillén et al. (2010), who coauthored this carefully researched article offer a detailed breakdown of several aspects of the seven books they review, specifically a precise accounting of the poses, props, expressions, and clothes that appear. The specific details they track are quite curious; for example, they make note of those who are cross-eyed or who wear braids, ties, mantillas, rebozos, fans, or short hair. They catalog facial expressions as "gesto serio, poco expresivo" (serious, non-expressive look), "gesto duro con ceño fruncido" (hard look with furrowed brow), and "sonriendo" (smiling). They also make note of the number of times that the same dress is worn by different women, suggesting it was one of the props available at the photography studio.

11 *Encyclopedia Britannica*, s.v. "sumptuary law," accessed July 11, 2018, https://www.britannica.com/topic/sumptuary-law. In her book *Profit and Passion: Transactional Sex in Colonial Mexico*, Nicole von Germeten (2018, 109) notes how in the early nineteenth century in New Spain, there starts to be a shift in terminology, with the words *prostitute* and *prostitution* appearing more frequently. She cites this shift in usage as co-constitutive of attempts to regulate and control sexual labor and punish the public flouting of moral codes. For a curious historical account of these laws in Mexico, see Patricia Anawalt's (1980) essay "Costume and Control: Aztec Sumptuary Laws."

12 For more discussion on casta paintings and racial categories in colonial New Spain, see Deans-Smith 2005.

13 Several of the photographs of Storyville, the red-light district of early twentieth-century New Orleans taken by photographer Ernest Bellocq and discussed briefly in the next chapter, have suffered a similar fate; many of the

faces have been scratched off. It is suggested that Bellocq's brother—a Catholic priest—might be responsible for damaging these prints. See Rose 1974.

14 A port city central to commercial and military interests in the region, Havana received an influx of soldiers from the Iberian Peninsula following the 1865 War of Santo Domingo. Using census data from 1900, Cuban historian Mayra Beers (2003, 103) claims that the war had left almost half of the women on the island widows and estimates that during this postwar period more than 2,440 women engaged in prostitution, making it the "fourth largest source of employment" for women on the island. During this time, "prostitute" was listed as an occupation in the census, in immigration records, and in other state documents, suggesting the way it was understood as a legitimate if stigmatized occupation. Immigrant women feature quite prominently in the available archives in ways that suggest that they were at the forefront of the sex worker movement in Cuba. This might have to do with their perceived status as Europeans or with the possibilities afforded by the distance from their own homes and communities.

15 My most sincere thanks to my cherished colega Amalia Cabezas for pointing me to this fascinating historical record. See her captivating essay (2019) on how the historical record demonstrates a long history of sex worker movements in Latin America as well as her important work on contemporary sex work in Cuba and the Dominican Republic, *Economies of Desire* (2009). Other accounts of *La Cebolla* include Barcia Zequeira 1993; Beers 2003; Calvo Peña 2005; and Sippial 2013. Calvo Peña's essay does a wonderful job of situating *La Cebolla* within the larger political discourse around race, colonialism, and the labor movements of the period. Both Beers and Sippial explore the role of sex work and sexuality in the formation of national identity and state control in the early days of nation building in Cuba. Sippial devotes an entire chapter to las horizontales, situating them within the context of print media, with astute attention to the role of racial discourse postabolition. Calvo Peña provides evidence to warrant suspicion about the actual author(s) of this newspaper, suggesting that most of the entries were authored by the newspaper's male editor, Victorino Reineri, producing a transgendered performance of a kind. However, other accounts complicate that conclusion. Barcia Zequeira's research suggests that wealthy prostitutes financed and contributed to the articles.

16 Beers describes how the first attempts at regulating prostitution in Cuba date back to an 1873 registry, when the state registered more than four hundred sex workers. This early Cuban registry did not involve photography. At that time, the state charged sex workers a yearly quota for a license to work, obligating them to receive weekly medical exams, including internal exams with a speculum. These quotas were then used to fund the hospitals and public health system (Beers 2003, 104). In her essay, Calvo Peña (2005) suggests that in Cuba at the time, those that did not register might have suffered less at the hands of the police.

17 Cuban women were granted the right to vote in 1933.

18 Without additional information, it is difficult to ascribe any specific significance to the racialized name La Conga in this archive, although the name
appears on more than one occasion in *La Cebolla*. In Cuba, a frequent adage intended to address the prevalence of racial mixture in the population is "el que
no tiene del Congo tiene del Carabalí" (those who don't have Congo [blood or
heritage] have Carabalí), referencing two of the major ethnic groups of African
slaves brought to Cuba. Congo references the ancient empire located around
the Congo River and is associated in Cuba with the secret religious practices of
Palo Monte or Palo Congo. Carabalí refers to the people of the Calabar region
of southern Nigeria. See Ortíz Álvarez 2020 for more references to Africa in
phrases and idiomatic expressions used in Cuba and Brazil.

Two. Colonial Echoes and Aesthetic Allure

1 Numerous art historians have written about the visual function of the Black
maid in Manet's *Olympia*. I direct readers to the early 1985 essay by Sander L.
Gilman and the 2001 essay by Jennifer DeVere Brody.

2 In *Wayward Lives, Beautiful Experiments*, Saidiya Hartman (2019, 25) claims that
the odalisque "conjoins two distinct categories of the commodity: the slave and
the prostitute." She writes, "The odalisque is a forensic image that details the
violence to which the black female body can be subjected. It is a durational image of intimate violence" (27). My own reading suggests the differences between
these forms of sexual commodities.

3 The nameless model depicted in figure 2.3 is the same model who appears on
the cover of Natasha Trethewey's (2002) Pulitzer Prize–winning collection of
poetry, *Bellocq's Ophelia*. This stunning poetry collection, itself a work of critical
fabulation, imagines the Storyville archive from the point of view of one of Bellocq's subjects.

4 Another self-described "acquaintance" of Bellocq from that period interviewed
(he didn't appear to have any friends), fellow photographer Dan Leyrer, re-
marked: "The girls liked him yes, but the men didn't like him. They didn't dis-
like him, I mean, but they had no use for him. His men friends thought he was
queer, but he wasn't queer with men" (quoted in Szarkowski 1970, 15).

5 The quote continues, "but I know he done a few months in the ice house, so
you can't tell" (Leyrer, quoted in Szarkowski 1970, 15). Unable to find a reliable
referent for what "a few months in the ice house" might reveal about Bellocq's
sexuality, I am left to wonder about what took him out of circulation. Among
the most plausible possibilities that I encountered for this reference is that "ice
houses" used to serve as temporary holding jails in smaller southern counties,
although the reference to "a few months" complicates that claim.

6 Before being sold to the United States in the Louisiana Purchase in 1803, New

Orleans had long received immigrants from the Caribbean, particularly Haiti and Cuba, including white creoles, enslaved Africans and African Americans, and free people of color. After the Haitian Revolution, New Orleans received more than ten thousand refugees from both Haiti and Cuba, where many had previously fled, causing the city's population to almost double in size (Fussell 2007).

7 Using census reports from that period, Craig Foster (1990) details that in 1900, the Black population in Storyville was 38 percent, but by 1910, the combined Black and mulatto population had decreased to 28 percent, with 16 percent of those being mulattoes. This drop in numbers might be explained in two ways: Storyville as a designated red-light district might have resulted in the displacement of African American communities that had previously lived there before it was overrun by brothels; or many sex workers might have self-reported mulatta, lighter-skinned women earning considerably more. Foster notes that the age range for women in Storyville was between twelve and fifty-seven, with a median age of twenty-six. In noting differences between the 1900 and 1910 censuses, he also noted an increasing trend toward older prostitutes.

8 This grouping of diverse ethnic and national categories under the misnomer of a singular ethnic or national naming calls to mind the ways all Asians become "chino" (Chinese) in Latin America, those from the diverse lands of the Middle East become "turcos" (Turks), and South Asians, regardless of faith, become uniformly identified as "hindús" (Hindus).

9 Atget used a view camera with a bellows placed on a tripod and worked with eighteen-by-twenty-four-centimeter negative glass plates. Like Bellocq, Atget made all his own photographic prints using a "print-out" technique in which light-sensitive paper, in contact with the glass negative, was printed out in natural light before being washed, gold-toned, fixed, and washed again.

10 While that book, titled *La Femme criminelle*, never emerged, figure 2.6, produced at least three years later, suggests an ongoing interest in that project that exceeded the motivation of Dignimont's commission (Metropolitan Museum of Art, n.d.).

11 Man Ray (b. Emmanuel Radnitzky, 1890–1976), the artist and photographer known for his contributions to Dadaism and Surrealism, was an early collector of Atget's photography.

12 Cartier-Bresson's biography evidences the impact of changes in image-making technology. His first camera was a Brownie Box; introduced in 1900 and initially marketed to children, it was a simple and inexpensive camera that would make photography available to ordinary people, moving it outside the studio and into the larger spaces of the public. The Brownie, and the handheld portable cameras that would follow, helped inaugurate the snapshot, the family photo album, photojournalism, travel photography, and war photography. Small enough to be carried into war zones, innocuous enough to move through public spaces discreetly, these cameras transformed the kinds of photographic

images that were able to circulate and helped make possible the genre that would become street photography. Cartier-Bresson took full advantage of these advances, eventually acquiring the 50 mm Leica that would accompany him on his travels for much of his early career.

13 *Vu* premiered in Paris in 1928, and *Regards*, the Communist Party pictorial, launched in 1932. In Brazil, the short-lived illustrated magazine *S. Paulo* premiered in 1936, and *Rotofoto* was inaugurated in Mexico in 1938. In the United States, *Life* turned from a regular light-news format to a platform for photography when Henry Luce bought the company in 1936; *Look*, its most obvious competitor, launched in 1937; and the British equivalent *Picture Post* first appeared in 1938. According to Beth Wilson (2016), 1938 is also the first time the word *photojournalist* appeared, in an article authored by Alfred Eisenstadt, a staff writer for *Life*.

14 On both Magnum's website and in the Metropolitan Museum of Art in New York, detailing the photograph's exhibition history, the photograph is titled simply *Calle Cuauhtemoctzin, Mexico City, 1934*. However, the caption identified on Magnum's licensing catalog and their permissions invoice provides the following description: "MEXICO. Mexico City. Prostituées. Calle Cuauhtemoctzin. 1934." In her book *Compromised Positions: Prostitution, Public Health, and Gender Politics in Revolutionary Mexico City*, Katherine Elaine Bliss (2010, 156) describes Calle Cuauhtemoctzin as the "site of the cheapest sexual commerce in the capital," where "foreign and Mexican prostitutes alike solicit customers by hanging out *accesoria* windows and calling out to passersby."

15 The other photographer of that period who merits mentioning is Brassaï (1899–1984), born in Hungary to an Armenian mother and a Hungarian father. Himself an immigrant to Paris, he became famous for his photographs of the Parisian demimonde—where sexual adventure and racial exoticism ruled the night. Two of his most widely circulated books of photography feature street walkers, bar girls, cabaret dancers, madams, and brothels quite prominently. Brassaï's *Paris by Night*, published in 1933, does so in a more coded manner, while *The Secret Paris of the '30s*, published decades later in 1976, does so more brazenly. In fact, Brassaï's photographic archive is crowded with images titled simply *Fille de joie* (Girl of joy), some staged, others not.

It should be noted that Brassaï's Paris was the Paris of a thriving international ex-pat community; African American figures like Josephine Baker and Langston Hughes were fleeing the racism of the United States, but also Cubans like Wifredo Lam and Alejo Carpentier were escaping the tyranny and censorship of Cuban dictator Gerardo Machado. *The Secret Paris of the '30s* devotes chapters to "Street Fairs" where we are introduced to the "graceful Conchita . . . her breasts firm as those of a white negress"; "Sodom and Gomorrah," which describes the many places where "the cream of Parisian inverts was to meet without distinction as to class, race, or age"; "Le Bal Nègre in the Rue Blomet," a Black Ball "where a kind of hysterical sorcery permeated the night club";

"An Opium Den," replete with reclined bodies afloat in Orientalist iconography; or "The Bal Des Quat'z Arts," the arts students' ball "where the theme was changed every year—Incas, Aztecs, Phoenicians, Egyptians, Gauls—the costumes were always practically nonexistent" (Brassaï 1976, n.p.).

16 Malek Alloula, in his work *The Colonial Harem*, also remarks on the use of windows and door frames. Alloula (1986, 21) positions his reading within the context of colonial Algeria to argue that windows, particularly those with latticed bars so common in the Arab world, are intended to register confinement and the theme of "the woman imprisoned in her own home," just as she is imagined to be imprisoned by the veil. I am reading something slightly different in these images taken in Europe and the United States.

17 In interviews, Cartier-Bresson mentions another photograph from that film role in which the Black woman is absent, and the madam and the homosexual are seen touching, staring directly at the viewer. But the image looks forced; the pair make an odd heterosexual couple, and the image simply doesn't contain the visual dynamism and curiosity that the photograph with the triangulated figures inspires.

18 The original reads: "En 1934, en México, fui muy afortunado. Sólo tuve que empujar una puerta y ahí estaban dos lesbianas haciendo el amor. ¡Qué voluptuosidad, qué sensualidad! No se veían sus rostros. Disparé. Haber podido verlo fue un milagro. Eso nada tiene de obsceno. Es el amor físico en plenitud. Nunca habría logrado que posaran."

19 Arnold's first success came while taking a photography class at the New School for Social Research taught by Alexey Brodovitch, the art director of *Harper's Bazaar*. For an assignment on fashion photography, she traveled uptown to Abyssinian Baptist Church in Harlem, already a hub of civil rights activism, to photograph an African American fashion show, eventually selling her "behind the scenes" images of the event to the British photo magazine *Picture Post* for a feature titled "Fashion Show in Harlem." These included images of Charlotte "Fabulous" Stribing, an already established model within the Black community, and other women dressing backstage. This practice of watching models and later actresses and starlets prepare themselves, performing the rites of femininity supposedly unencumbered by the presence of men, would later become a signature element of her work. That in 1954 Arnold might record the Black model's name seems a small yet significant detail and performs the slide from street photographer, in the vein of Cartier-Bresson and others, to photojournalist. While Arnold produced the images that accompanied the article on Harlem fashion shows, the writer who crafted the text that would surround her images was working across the ocean, with only the details that Arnold had provided. Arnold protested later that the writer "misrepresented what she had done and sounded patronizing toward the models"; the incident is said to have sparked her interest in controlling the rights not only to the photographs she produced but also to the captions and text that would surround them (di Giovanni 2015,

26). In photojournalism, the image and the text are intended to work together to craft a story that neither medium is supposedly fully capable of accomplishing on its own. This is another example of a visual appetite for the foreign or unknown, except now it was a white woman traveling to the uncharted visual landscapes of Harlem to bring back to white audiences what the Black press and the Black public had already known. Although Arnold is credited as being the "first" woman at Magnum, another woman, Inge Morath, was hired at the Paris office of Magnum around the same time (di Giovanni 2015, 18–26).

20 For more on the figure of the mulata, see Melissa Blanco Borelli's (2015) *She Is Cuba: A Genealogy of the Mulata Body*. Blanco Borelli writes of this feminine figure, too often imagined as always already sexually available: "Her lived reality troubles the rumors that make claims about her racial and sexual identity, that commodified her body, and that associate her with tragedy, veneration, vilification in the history and cultural imaginary of Cuba" (5).

21 Years later, in 2015, Spanish Belgian photographer Cristina de Middel began a global photographic project, Gentlemen's Club, that began in Rio de Janeiro and focused on the men who pay for sex, photographing them in the hotel rooms where sex workers take their clients. On the website for the series, she states, "I have tried to publish this series in different media but there seems to be no interest (so far) in getting to understand the whole dimension of the business" (Middel, n.d.).

22 Decades later, Meiselas revisited the project when it moved online and published images from this book alongside audio recordings taken from these earlier interviews. The addition of sound—and with it the vocal particularities, regional slang of the period, and the carnival scene—and the background noise that depicts the sonic textures of the space introduce another sensory element to this now digital text. Inserting the discarded technology of a tape-cassette recording alongside these images on a new digital platform attaches a human voice to puta life. The recordings animate the black-and-white photographic series, sonically reinserting this remnant of the body back into the temporal auditory space from which these images and these interviews were extracted. See Meiselas 2013.

23 As part of this photojournalistic project, Meiseles, not content to merely provide a photographic account of the place and the people within it, also includes interviews and letters from workers and clients and, once again, is particularly attentive to perspective and the technologies of capture at play in a scene.

24 My appreciation to Achy Obejas, translator, writer, poet, and friend, for her keen eye in helping me with this translation.

25 To be clear, I certainly do not believe it bears any actual correlation to what kinds of sexual exchange might be happening in the world. Instead, it simply supports my claim about the Latin American world as where you would go to look for these sexualized "hot zones."

26 Used in Europe does include some mention of sex work, but the majority of the

reports focus on labor abuses in agriculture, construction, manufacturing, and small businesses.

27 The website seems to have been altered in 2021 and this language removed; however, in the article "Monitoring the Margins: Street Views of Sex Workers," Wolthers (2016) records the same text.

28 See Louise Wolthers's (2016) outstanding essay on this phenomenon, "Monitoring the Margins: Street Views of Sex Workers." There, Wolthers also discusses the Belgian artist Mishka Henner, who creates archival prints of these images, shot mostly in isolated and deserted areas of Italy and Spain, in order to emphasize the isolation and vulnerability sex workers face as criminalized and often undocumented workers.

29 Once you zoom in, each page offers the legal status of prostitution in that country, often through links to Wikipedia pages.

Three. Carnal Knowledge, Interpretive Practices

1 The bibliography for porn studies has been growing exponentially since Linda Williams's groundbreaking text *Hard Core: Power, Pleasure, and the "Frenzy of the Visible,"* originally published in 1989 (repr., 1999). For intersections of race and pornography, Miller-Young 2014, Nash 2014, Nguyen 2014, and Shimizu 2007 remain indispensable. See also Ariana Cruz's (2016) *The Color of Kink.* Useful edited volumes include *Porn Archives* (Dean, Ruszczycky, and Squires 2014); *The Feminist Porn Book: The Politics of Producing Pleasure* (Taormino et al. 2013); *Porn Studies* (Williams 2004); *New Views on Pornography: Sexuality, Politics, and the Law* (Comella and Tarrant 2015); and *Coming Out like a Porn Star: Essays on Pornography, Protection, and Privacy* (Lee 2015). An academic journal, *Porn Studies,* devoted to this burgeoning field of academic inquiry was launched in 2014.

2 What I reference as the "golden age of porn" refers to a period, roughly from 1970 to 1985, in which some adult feature films were screened in movie theaters and reviewed in the mainstream press, including the *New York Times* and *Variety.* That heightened publicity allowed a star system to develop and also generated more elaborate marketing campaigns oriented around specific actors. The rise of the home video marks the end of this period.

3 There are numerous compilation videos, including *Vanessa's Hot Nights* (1980), *The Erotic World of Vanessa #1* (1981), *Hot Shorts: Vanessa del Rio* (1986), *Vanessa Obsession* (1987), *Best of Vanessa del Rio* (1988), and *Taste of Vanessa del Rio* (1990). More recent compilations include *Vanessa del Rio—Dirty Deeds* (2001), *Vanessa's Anal Fiesta* (2004), and *Strokin' to the Oldies* (2004).

4 Directed by Thomas Mignone, the film stars Vivian Lamolli. Her biography on IMDb (2022) identifies her as "a Latin American actress, singer and dancer born and raised in Miami, Florida."

5 Readers will note the dedications on the photos included in figure 3.2; in one,

she signs, "Puta Life! Vanessa del Rio" and then underneath writes, "AKA Ana María," a sonic echo of my name that she commented on in our first email exchange. In another, she dedicates the image to "mi amiga dulce," and I melt at the joy of femme friendship with my favorite puta icon.

6   This is not to suggest that her audience consists solely of white men or others who have no connection to stories of racial and gendered violence; her fan base is quite diverse. Yet being reminded of these more realistic aspects of del Rio's story may complicate a merely sexually inflected viewing of the film.

7   Testimonial literature is a decidedly broad category that could be said to include slave narratives such as *Incidents in the Life of a Slave Girl* but also texts like *Black Elk Speaks* and, of course, *I, Rigoberta Menchú*. For more on the politics and performance of testimonial literature in Latin American letters, see Beverley 1993 and the 1996 anthology *The Real Thing*, edited by Georg M. Gugelberger.

8   Amnesty International, Human Rights Watch, and Open Society have all come out in support of the decriminalization of sex work as part of an effort to address human rights violations against sex workers. In its *World Report 2014*, Human Rights Watch (2014) links the decriminalization of sex work to a parallel effort to decriminalize simple drug use and possession. The report states, "Criminalization in both cases can cause or exacerbate a host of ancillary human rights violations, including exposure to violence from private actors, police abuse, discriminatory law enforcement, and vulnerability to blackmail, control, and abuse by criminals. These severe and common consequences, and the strong personal interest that people have in making decisions about their own bodies, mean it is unreasonable and disproportionate for the state to use criminal punishment to discourage either practice" (47).

9   In her acknowledgments in the book, del Rio (2010, n.p) refers to Hanson as "my sister-slut-goddess" and describes her as being "my sexual anthropologist as well as a close friend."

10 As of this writing, the trade version is sold out.

11 In this chapter, I cite the specific source, either the book or the DVD, and mention any notable discrepancies in the notes.

12 As we saw in my discussion of New Orleans in chapter 1, for racially marked Caribbean subjects, claiming "Spanish" functions to create a cultural distance from African American blackness while erasing potential associations with Caribbean slavery. It also serves to mark a linguistic difference from other Caribbean islanders. In the US Southwest, claims to "Spanish" are generally rooted more in ancestry than in language or culture and articulate a distinction between populations descended from the Spanish in the region and those descended from Indigenous or mestizo communities. In some Caribbean contexts, claiming "Indigenous" or Indian roots can be a way to explain nonwhite lineage while refusing possible attachments to African ancestry. Finally, it bears noting that while in a US racial system of the period del Rio might have been

classified as mulata or as simply Black, within a local Cuban or Puerto Rican syntax, she would more likely be classified as trigueña, morena, or dark-haired.

13 Miller-Young's (2014) text *A Taste of Brown Sugar: Black Women in Pornography* provides an indispensable historical account of how niche racial markets in pornography developed. She found that Vanessa's films were marketed to both Black and Latino men in the 1980s and claims that a separate niche market for Latino pornography did not develop until the late 1990s (297n23).

14 In a curious twist on stereotypes that associate Black and Latinx racial difference with "rhythm," in this film, del Rio auditions for the role but is booed off stage for dancing badly.

15 The chapter "Laughing Matters" in Jennifer Nash's (2014) *The Black Body in Ecstasy* illustrates the way humor in pornography can make visible the absurdity of racist and gendered fictions surrounding sexual pleasure. That text is particularly useful in reading how humor functions in del Rio's films, some of which are quite hilarious. But Nash's insights on humor are also useful for reading the narrative accounts of her life that she provides.

16 This is reminiscent of another famous "Puerto Rican" who was also of mixed Puerto Rican and Cuban parentage, Piri Thomas. His coming-of-age and coming into consciousness autobiography *Down These Mean Streets* ([1967] 1997) is frequently cited as the quintessential novel of the Afro-Puerto Rican experience, even as he was of mixed Afro-Cuban and Puerto Rican parentage. In that iconic Latinx autobiography, his father's Afro-Cuban heritage, and therefore his connection to the African diaspora, one of the central themes of the book, is erased.

17 The bibliography on Afro-Latina identity has expanded considerably in recent years; for a general overview, as well as foundational texts in the field, see the outstanding volume *The Afro-Latin@ Reader*, by Miriam Jiménez Román and Juan Flores (2010). For historical perspectives, see Nancy Mirabal's (2017) *Suspect Freedoms*, about Afro-Cubans in the United States during the nineteenth and twentieth centuries, and Christine Arce's (2018) *México's Nobodies: The Cultural Legacy of the Soldaderas and Afro-Mexican Women*. See also Borelli 2015; Figueroa 2020; García-Peña 2015; Hernandez 2020; Santana 2019; and Zamora 2022.

18 In her text, she refers to this magazine as simply *Belle*.

19 It might also be said that the ways African Americans have taken up del Rio as one of their own reveal particular attachments to lighter skin and the foreign exoticism associated with the Caribbean and Latin America.

20 In *A Taste for Brown Sugar*, Miller-Young (2014) points out that in del Rio's 1984 film *Maid in Manhattan*, sometimes referenced as *Vanessa: Maid in Manhattan*, del Rio plays a maid named Juanita yet received star billing, and the film, including its title, is centered on her character, even though she appears in only two scenes. In 2002 Jennifer Lopez, another famous Puerto Rican, starred in a film of the same name.

21 See Xandra Ibarra's website, xandraibarra.com. On that site, it states that

"Ibarra performed hundreds of live 'spictacles' under the alias of La Chica boom. In this 10 year project, she embodied her own racial and sexual abjection and directly engaged the politics of racialized sexuality to discover queer forms of pleasure" (Ibarra, n.d.). In Ibarra's performance piece *FML: F*ck My Life* (2012), she famously kills off her alter-ego La Chica Boom after being exhausted by the reception of the work by white audiences. See Christina León's (2017) insightful article on that performance and the aesthetic "failure" of "spictacles."

22 Nicknamed "Coca" by her lover Armando Bó, Sarli went on to become a pop cultural idol. Queer film icon John Waters also credits Sarli's films as an early influence for his camp aesthetics (Misiones 2018). For more on Sarli, see Ruétalo 2004, Foster 2008, the documentary film on her life *Carne sobre carne* (Curubeto 2007), and the 1999 interview by Thibon. The other Latin American vixen who rose from the genre of Latin American sexploitation films in the 1980s is Xuxa (Maria da Graça Xuxa Meneghel), the Brazilian singer, children's television host, and media personality. A more contemporary example of a Latina using sex work to launch a more mainstream career is Cardi B (Belcalis Marlenis Almánzar), a Dominican, Trinidadian New Yorker who has become a rap icon. For more on Cardi B, particularly about her life as a stripper, see Jaime 2022 and Zamora 2022.

23 *Putísima* is an intensifier for the word *puta*, meaning very, very puta. The remainder of the quote reads: "Coca is such a whore that she becomes a lesbian, a revolutionary and almost militant expression about the oppressed condition of women." The original longer quote reads: "'Fuego' ¡de 1969! donde la pobre Coca sufre de una fiebre uterina o ninfomanía o simplemente es putísima; condición o enfermedad que Alba Mujica aprovecha para establecer una relación lésbica con la joven, o sea la mujer pulposa—Coca es tan puta que se hace lesbiana, una idea revolucionaria y casi militante sobre la condición oprimida de las mujeres."

24 More recently the genre of porn star memoir has exploded, including more texts by women of color. See recent titles by Asa Akira (2015), India Morel (2013), and Roxy Reynolds (2014).

25 Without a hint of irony, in Jameson's text, rather than chapter titles, each section is divided into books with Roman numerals, preceded by an epigraph from a Shakespearean sonnet.

26 Del Rio's decision to leave porn and try her hand at bodybuilding was prompted by the panic around AIDS that circulated among adult entertainers and by a short period in jail.

27 *Oxford English Dictionary*, s.v. "victim," accessed April 28, 2022, http://www.oed.com.

28 In his essay "The Fact of Blackness," in *Black Skin, White Masks*, Frantz Fanon (1967, 109) writes of the colonial gaze: "The glances of the other fixed me there, in the sense in which a chemical solution is fixed by a dye."

29 For additional readings at the nexus of race, abjection, and sexualized forms of power relations, see Hoang Tan Nguyen's (2014) *A View from the Bottom: Asian American Masculinity and Sexual Representation*; Darieck Scott's (2010) *Extravagant Abjection: Blackness, Power, and Sexuality in the African American Literary Imagination*, and my own *Sexual Futures, Queer Gestures, and Other Latina Longings* (2014).

30 This is an instance where the recorded audio and the "transcribed" interview are not quite identical. In the recorded interview, there is no mention of him being "handsome, blond, and ruggedly studly." In both the written version and the on-screen interview, the story itself is quite long and detailed. The written account is more than three paragraphs long and appears in a section about run-ins with the police. I have elected to cite the textual version for clarity.

31 Once again, the language in the film clip is slightly different from what is printed in the book. In the DVD, there is no mention of it being "so theatrical, such a humiliating adventure" and also no mention of "Ooh, I felt like such a dirty girl for enjoying it!" These additions appear to have been added later to facilitate readability.

32 In that scene, del Rio's character is being punished for trying to start a prison riot in which she repeatedly calls the police "pigs," reflecting the politics of the moment and the ongoing antagonism sex workers have toward police.

33 In a list included in the book titled "The Basic Vanessa," in addition to listing leopard as a favorite color, she lists her favorite book/author as *Macho Sluts* by Pat Califia and her hero as Muhammad Ali (del Rio 2010, 258). Vanessa, like this author, identifies as bisexual.

34 The physical changes to her face, hair, genitals, and body, brought about through self-styling, photographic manipulation, age, and technologies of the body, are quite evident throughout the book. In the chapter "Gym Rat," she describes a brief period where she began to take steroids, developing both her muscles and the size of her clitoris, which is reported to be more than five centimeters long (del Rio 2010, 224). Later in her life, she also underwent breast augmentation and various genital piercings, and the newer images include several colorful tattoos.

35 In this chapter, we get quite a few passages that seem to be from a contemporary interview with Stout. In my conversations with del Rio, she indicated that he died before the publication of the book.

Four. Touching Alterity

1   Other names mentioned are Isela Vega, Rosalba Ríos, and Jesica Vargas, who along with Jesusa Rodríguez founded Mujeres, Xochiquetzal en Lucha por su Dignidad as a nongovernmental organization authorized to receive donations for the house. Donations can be made at https://casaxochiquetzal.wordpress .com/donaciones/.

2   The Spanish-language book *Las amorosas más bravas* (Desrus and Gómez Ramos 2014) is not paginated. An English-language insert under the title *Tough Love* provides a translation of the text without the photographs and does include page numbers. In my text, I use the English translations from *Tough Love* and provide the Spanish original in the notes in those moments when the original and the translation are less than exact or in order to reveal a particularity of language.

3   Bénédicte Desrus focuses much of her work on forms of social stigma, including projects about homosexuals in Uganda; albinos in Tanzania; Muxe in Oaxaca, Mexico; and global obesity. Her website is http://www.benedictedesrus .com/. Celia Gómez Ramos currently authors a regular column called "Mujeres en busca de sexo" (Women in search of sex) for *El Sol de México*, a daily newspaper.

4   The Consejo Nacional para la Cultura y las Artes (Conaculta, National Council for Culture and Arts) is a government agency of the Mexican state in charge of promoting and protecting the arts and managing the national archives.

5   "Convivir no ha sido fácil, aunque varias de las residentes de la Casa Xochiquetzal se conocían, no eran amigas, pues siempre compitieron por los clientes. Quizá hoy tampoco lo sean. La supervivencia las hizo bravas. Son sabias, divertidas, buenas narradoras y de imaginación vigorosa. Están acostumbradas a desconfiar, a no generar lazos duraderos, a analizar los puntos débiles y fuertes de los demás. Son observadoras natas, psicólogas prácticas. Se comen el mundo a cucharadas o a mordidas, como sea necesario" (n.p.).

6   The building that would become Casa Xochiquetzal was donated by the Mexican state and had once been the Hall of Fame Museum. When it was first acquired, it was full of a mishmash of national memorabilia, including clothes belonging to Pedro Infante and a pair of huaraches once worn by the legendary *lucha libra* rival of El Santo, Pedro Aguayo.

7   Given Desrus's meticulous recording of names on her Sipa USA website, this decision to not caption the photographs might involve editorial and layout considerations from the publisher or privacy concerns related to photographic permissions.

8   Online I have seen another image of Desrus and Gómez Ramos's book that uses this image as the cover.

9   "Mis tatuajes, sí, uno en cada brazo. El primero me lo hice a los 16 años, es la cara de una pantera, y el otro es el torso de una mujer con los pechos descubier-

tos y en el tope mi nombre, Norma. Otras marcas en mi cuerpo son la cicatriz que dejó el desarmador en la ceja, tres navajazos y un piquete en el pecho, de asaltos; un par de mordidas bravas en el brazo izquierdo, recuerdo de Rosa; un navajazo en el brazo derecho, de un pleito, y el de mi infancia" (n.p.).

10   These colorful nicknames appear untranslated in the English version. Some rough translations might be la Sombra (the shadow), la Güera (the light-skinned one), la Juguitos (a reference to frozen juice pops), Cachetes de Gatito (kitten cheeks); la Jefa (the boss, gendered feminine), el Gordo (the fat one, gendered masculine), la Sinaloense (the one from Sinaloa), Maria Machetes (Maria Machete, which has a sonic resonance with *marimacha*, a popular term for lesbians), and Normota (which rather than the more common diminutive that is frequently used in Spanish-language names is an augmentative, big Norma). Nicknames serve as their own form of narrative. For more on nicknames, see my own discussion of naming as an identity practice in *Queer Latinidad* (2003, 12–13).

11   "Un día me di veintitantos cortes en la muñeca izquierda con una navaja de afeitar porque no le encontraban gran sentido a la vida" (n.p.). In their sociological account of Casa Xochiquetzal, Flores Castillo, Cabello, and Cavalli (2017) mention the frequency with which suicide is mentioned in the residents' biographical accounts.

12   "Tengo mis clientes frecuentes . . . estaré ya viejita, estaré como estaré, pero las mañas no se olvidan" (n.p.). Translated as "tricks" in the original, *mañas* can also mean a vice or bad habit.

13   Venville is the author of two other books of photography, *Layers* (2003) and *Lucha Loco* (2006), the second of which is also based in Mexico about lucha libre wrestlers. In addition to commercial work, he is the director of two feature films, *44 Inch Chest* (2009) and *Henry's Crime* (2010).

14   Curiously, Venville and I share a birthday, September 5.

15   The Ebony 4×5 camera is a wooden field camera known for producing an exceptionally high level of detail. Originally designed and manufactured by Hiromi Sakanashi in Japan in 1981, these cameras ceased to be produced in 2016. The name comes from the aged ebony hardwood used in its construction and the size of the negative.

16   A shrine to la Santa Muerte, located at 12 Alfarería Street in Tepito, is maintained by Enriqueta Romero, and a procession to her that begins there is celebrated every year on November 1. Frequently associated with narco culture and the notorious street gang Mara Salvatrucha, the cult of la Santa Muerte is now practiced by believers from around the world.

17   Wiechmann's article in *Stern*, cited here, includes a link for donations. *Stern* funds projects related to their news through their Star Foundation. As of June 11, 2022, they had registered ten thousand euros as having been donated to Casa Xochiquetzal (see https://www.stern.de/stiftung/9491556-9491556.html).

18   "Las mujeres tienen discursos aprendidos que manejan de manera repetitiva y

que no siempre muestran una afirmación positiva de su propia persona" (The women have learned discourses that they repeat, often in ways that do not affirm a positive self-image) (11). Flores Castillo also confirmed to me that a few transgender women have passed through the house in its many years of operation.

19 It is worth noting that the Spanish-language term *sexo servidoras* emphasizes service, echoing what I have argued elsewhere is a cultural value whereby being of service to another is seen as a positive attribute rather than an indication of inferiority (Rodríguez 2014, 127), in contrast to the English term, *sex worker*, which emphasizes labor. Of course, neither *service* nor *work* necessarily connotes monetary compensation.

20 Sonia's preferred terms are *chica del tacón dorado*, girl with the golden heel; *mariposilla*, a variant of butterfly; *cusca*, a more informal, particularly Mexican word for "whore"; *mujer de cascos ligeros*, women of a light shell, helmet, or head, meaning reckless or foolhardy; and the ever popular term *puta*.

21 Santiago Stelley was born in Madrid and studied Latin American studies and comparative literature at the State University of New York at Buffalo and the University of Havana before becoming the creative director for Vice.com.

22 George Reyes studied at Harvard University before attending film school at New York University. Claudia Lopez is a native of Mexico City and graduated from the Department of Communications at Technológico de Estudios Superiores de Monterrey.

23 As the documentary continues, it begins to highlight the conflict that developed between the original founder and the first director of the house, Carmen Muñoz, and the psychologist identified only as Rosalba. Rosalba appears in both the Stelley and the Lopez/Reyes documentaries. Rosalba would later become the director of the house, displacing Carmen, whose husband had been accused of embezzling money from the house. By the end of *La muñeca fea*, Carmen tells us that she is back working the streets. At the time *Las amorosas más bravas* was published, there was another woman credited as being the house psychologist, Argelia Yadhira Bravo Hernández, but Rosalba Ríos Martinez is also credited. Given the time required to produce films and books, it becomes difficult to ascertain a chronology of the exact time of production for these diverse images and texts.

24 I suspect this is related to several factors. Given the way that sex workers continue to be stigmatized, it should not be surprising that many of the residents are simply not comfortable revealing their faces and stories on camera. Second, even as the house frequently serves as a temporary shelter for women, some of the residents are clearly longtime residents appearing in texts that were produced across a longer time period.

25 "I've never been a whore ever. I ended up in Casa Xochiquetzal because my daughter brought me here. I didn't know it was for whores, but here I am and what are you going to do? If these other women run around selling ass, well,

to each her own. It's nothing I'm going to see but I don't feel comfortable with them, I don't want men thinking I'm a whore too" (Venville and de la Rosa 2013, 28). Reyna is one of several women included in that project who does not undress for Venville's camera.

26 "Tiene un leve retraso mental, pero sus compañeras nunca hablan del tema" (n.p.). "Acaba de regresar a la Casa, luego de haber intentado darle una oportunidad al amor, a los 72 años, aunque ella prefiere no sentir" (n.p.).

27 "Amalia se desborda de felicidad imaginando que podría participar en una película" (n.p.). In the original Sipa USA website from which I secured permissions, this person is identified as Amalia in the captions that accompany the photographs. On Desrus's website, she is identified as Amalia in the section that discusses the photography project behind Casa Xochiquetzal, and is identified as Raquel on the section of her website that sells prints, including the photograph in figure 4.2 (Benédicte Desrus Photography, n.d.). I assume no malice on the part of Desrus and suspect she simply used the name that was given to her at the time.

28 "A Amalia le hablan por las noches. Lucha por no salirse de la realidad, pero escucha los susurros que no la dejan dormir, siente que le avientan tierra y agua sucia por los orificios de la pared y, en ocasiones, que la quieren matar. Por eso, siempre usa su peluca y se protege cobijada en esa cama" (n.p.).

29 "Si me llaman el loco / Porque el mundo es así / La verdad sí estoy loco / Pero loco por ti."

30 "El sexo es muy bonito pero tienes que saber las posiciones."

31 "Me libre yo del polvo, de tierra, de drenaje, agua de drenaje, orines de animal, orines de borracho. Todo eso me avientan aquí."

32 This song is one of several that is included in Monste Neira's blog *Museo de la prostitución*, dedicated to collecting cultural artifacts such as songs, photographs, films, music, literature, poetry, and comics related to sex work. It also includes a small collection of sex worker posters and slogans advocating for the rights of sex workers.

33 Numerous musical scholars have taken up what has become a timeless and endlessly repeated musical genre. My favorite reading of the affective impact of boleros remains José Quiroga's (2000) hauntingly lyrical chapter "Tears at the Nightclub" in *Tropics of Desire*.

34 Along with Paola's earlier mention of Santería, this functions as another instance of what Laura Gutiérrez (2019, 15) terms "archipelagic concatenation," a way to think Mexican culture and cultural production in ways that accentuate its connection to an Afrodiasporic Caribbean. See also Gutierrez's indispensable 2010 book that explores cabaret as a queer feminist cultural practice in Mexico and its diasporas.

35 "Un domingo por la tarde murió Carmelita" (n.p.).

36 "Dejó todas sus pertenencias, hasta su estatua e imágines de La Santa Muerte. Simplemente no regresó" (n.p.).

37 "Claro no con el éxito de antes, antes era una cosa, hoy es otra. . . . Cuando empecé, pues estaba llena de hijos, es cierto, pero tenía vitalidad, estaba joven." The English translation of doing it "for my kids" seems to carry a slightly different resonance than the statement of her being "llena de hijos," which is more about the burden of having multiple children without the same implication of maternal sacrifice.

38 "Los años han ido pasando, y lo único que puedo pensar es que mi lugar es este. Y que aquí voy a permanecer, siempre."

39 The English subtitles translate this line as "In the end, we do return to the street," which projects a slightly different meaning from "todos volvemos," which translates to "we all return."

40 "Amor de cabaret," by Sonora Santanera, includes these lyrics:

> Amor de cabaret que no es sincero
> Amor de cabaret que se paga con dinero
> Amor de cabaret que poco a poco me mata
> Sin embargo, yo quiero amor de cabaret.

> [Cabaret love that is not sincere
> Cabaret love that is paid for with money
> Cabaret love that kills me little by little
> However, I still want cabaret love.]

41 In Spanish as in English, the phrase *en el ambiente*, or "in the life," doubly signifies queerness and sex work, marking a life that exists outside normal circuits of sociality, marking the linguistic, cultural, and social convergences of these overlapping communities.

42 In one YouTube video, Carmen and Maya are seen viewing the documentary in a private screening in advance of the 2016 Sundance film festival. As the opening scenes roll, they are seen crying and hugging each other (Remezcla 2016). In another video, Carmen, Carlos, Esther, Ángeles, Lupe, and Goded address an audience after seeing themselves on the big screen (Cinépolis Distribución 2017).

43 Rather than attempt to decode or translate these passages, I am reminded of Manuel Cuellar's productive insights on indigeneity in which he locates "indigeneity as a position or rather a positioning of their lived experience—a location that refers to a place but also a position in relation to the non-Indigenous" (forthcoming).

44 References to Ángeles as a transsexual, a travesti, and/or a transgender woman are mentioned in several of the media accounts that emerged afterward, including by Paul Julian Smith (2017), Abel Muñoz Hénonin (2017), and Sofía Ochoa Rodríguez (2016). That Goded seems wholly uninterested in engaging this aspect of Ángeles's narrative is the reason I mention it here.

45 For additional critical analysis of the relationship between documentary form

and ethics, see Iván Ramos's (2017) essay "Slow Encounters: Chantal Akerman's *From the Other Side*, Queer Form, and the Mexican Migrant."

46 "Con ella también establecí una relación de mucho tiempo y mucho más estrecha. Fui testigo de su boda, le ayudé con el adelanto de su departamento, me parecía justo porque ella me ayudó a establecer muchas más relaciones y además me cuidó todo ese tiempo."

47 In his essay "Solidarity Not Charity," Dean Spade (2020, 133) outlines what he sees as the criteria for evaluating tactics of redress, asking, "Does it provide material relief? Does it leave out an especially marginalized part of the affected group (e.g., people with criminal records, people without immigration status)? Does it legitimize or expand a system we are trying to dismantle? Does it mobilize people, especially those most directly impacted, for ongoing struggle?" While projects of representation are not the same as the projects of intervention or reform that Spade is discussing, like Goded, in addition to using my platform to advocate for the rights of sex workers, I also contribute to groups organized by and for sex workers internationally.

48 The wall plaque that accompanies the image which is part of the La Colección Jumez reads: "Ana Gallardo developed this project at Casa Xochiquetzal, a residence for senior women who used to be sex workers. Here, Gallardo blows up the scale of the women's image so they become part of the viewers' personal space, bringing us closer to them. Her work, which often involves her emotionally with her collaborators during long periods of time, invites us to reflect on the conditions of precariousness and marginality which are part of women's lives. According to the artist, 'affective relationships, encounters with others, the appropriation of life histories, of feelings, doubts, certain mysteries, failures, disagreements, those are my prime materials'" (Gallardo 2014). The contrast between the wall plaque and the quoted interview is striking. While I do not have the complete details of Gallardo's encounter with the women at Casa Xochiquetzal or the context of this interview, the language, particularly in Spanish, is too disturbing to ignore.

Five. Seeing, Sensing, Feeling

Epigraph: This song serves as the Spanish-language version of Gloria Gaynor's disco classic "I Will Survive"; however, note that the lyrics of the Spanish version, which became one of Celia Cruz's signature songs, are radically different.

My voice can fly, it can traverse
Any wound, any time, any loneliness
Without being able to control it, it takes the form of a song
This is my voice, it comes from my heart
And it will fly without me wanting to
Along the farthest roads I've traveled, along the dreams that I dreamed

It will be the reflection of the love of what I had to live
It will be the background music of how much I felt.

1 Jaime Cortez is a talented writer, illustrator, and performer. In addition to writing and illustrating *Sexile/Sexilio* (2004), he is the editor of *Virgins, Guerillas and Locas: Gay Latinos Writing about Love* (1999) and the author of *Gordo* (2021).

2 Patrick "Pato" Hebert, artist, activist, and educator, is also associate professor of the arts at New York University's Tisch School of the Arts. His current work engages the ongoing lingering personal and collective impact of the coronavirus crisis.

3 These were and are my friends, and while academic convention might prefer that I refer to the subject of this chapter as Vázquez, part of what I wish to convey in this chapter is precisely the intimacy of friendship. Adela is Adela to me. See the chapter "Activism and Identity in the Ruins of Representation" from my book *Queer Latinidad* (2003) to read my discussion of this unique and influential Latinx HIV service provider. A shorter, more condensed version of that chapter that includes a short postscript was reprinted in the exceptional 2020 volume *AIDS and the Distribution of Crises*, edited by Jih-Fei Cheng, Alexandra Juhasz, and Nishant Shahini. The archives of Proyecto ContraSIDA por Vida are housed in the Ethnic Studies Library at UC Berkeley.

4 This is the title that appears in both the Spanish and English versions. All quotes are taken from the original English in which the interview was conducted.

5 In the text, these words appear in Spanish in both the Spanish and the English versions: *puto* (a masculine form of puta), *pájaro* (a bird, another slang term for gay men), *pervertido* (pervert), *pato* (duck, but also another slang word for gay men), *maricón* (faggot).

6 For a touching personal account of another author, academic, friend, translating the childhood stories of another transwoman in Lima, Peru, see Cornejo 2014.

7 For more on the many queers, predominately gay men, who arrived as part of the Mariel boatlift, see Susana Peña's (2013) *Oye Loca: From the Mariel Boatlift to Gay Cuban Miami*. See also Lázaro González González's new video project in process, *Sexile*, a transmedia project that documents queer stories from the Mariel. A recent queer Cuban exile currently completing a PhD at Berkeley, González González combines archival footage with oral histories filmed in both Cuba and the United States (González, n.d.). For an account of the political turmoil that moment created for the queer left at the time, see the 1984 article coauthored by Lourdes Arguelles and Ruby Rich.

8 Educated in Cuba to value collective organizing, and inculcated with a revolutionary spirit of protest, Mariel refugees became legendary for organizing, protesting, and rioting for better conditions in these US refugee camps. At Fort Chaffee, where nineteen thousand were detained, a riot broke out on June 1, 1980, that destroyed four barracks and left sixty-two refugees injured: "After

the riots, Gov. Bill Clinton and President Jimmy Carter ensured that the lightly fortified camp was turned into a prison, encircled with miles of concertina wire and 2,000 heavily-armed federal troops." See Arkansas Times Staff 2004 for local reporting. Jailed indefinitely without trial and threatened with deportation to Cuba, Mariel refugees were also implicated in prison riots in both Atlanta and Louisiana in 1987. See Pear 1987.

9   Cachita, as she is affectionately called, is also my patron saint; my full name is Juana María de la Caridad Rodríguez Hernández. La Caridad del Cobre is syncretized in Santería traditions as the Yoruba goddess Ochún, a river goddess of femininity, sensuality, beauty, and love.

10   It should be noted that Adela is quite content to be a trans woman with a penis.

11   My translation from the original Portuguese: "O retrato é uma imagem da face de um sujeito, criada por um/a artista e/ou fotógrafo/a, a qual lhe confere a possibilidade de ser mais que corpo físico. Por isso, a representação da face confere existência históricosocialao/à retratado/a, pois permite que ele/ela exista mesmo após a sua morte."

12   Horacio is another member of Proyecto's diasporic crew of queers. He died on Christmas Day 2015 and is still missed by all who loved him.

13   A video uploaded to YouTube in 2009, "Diagnosing Difference—'Passing,'" https://www.youtube.com/watch?v=NIbwnx-Bw5w, provides a clip from the documentary that includes an on-camera interview with Adela.

14   In addition to *¡Cuéntamelo!* (2017), Delgado Lopera is the author of *Fiebre Tropical* (2020), a lively and quirky Spanglish novel about growing up immigrant and queer in an evangelical household in Miami. They were my student at UC Berkeley and first met Adela, whom they now describe as their queer mama, when I invited Adela to speak to my class after assigning *Sexile/Sexilio* (Cortez 2004). Delgado Lopero changed their first name to Julián after the initial publication of these texts.

15   The book includes seven brief first-person narratives, and each story is accompanied by an illustrated drawing by the artist Laura Cerón. The format of this bilingual book, which you flip to access the other language, has two different photographs of Adela's face gracing the Spanish and the English covers of the text.

16   Like many of us, Adela changes her profile pictures frequently.

17   This video is an homage to another *veterana* from Proyecto's diasporic village, Valentin "Tina" Aguirre, who, along with Augie Robles, was one of the original filmmakers of the powerful 1994 independent documentary *¡Viva 16!* (Aguirre and Robles 1994).

18   For more on the impact of gentrification in San Francisco for queer communities of color, see my essay "Public Notice from the Fucked Peepo: Xandra Ibarra's 'The Hookup/Displacement/Barhopping/Drama Tour'" in the anthology *Queer Night Life* (Rodríguez 2021). That piece discussed Ibarra's inspired 2017 pop-up performance piece that visited queer and Latinx sites that have closed

due to gentrification. See also Iván Ramos's (2015) "The Dirt That Haunts: Looking at Esta Noche" and the archival video gem *¡Viva 16!* (Aguirre and Robles 1994), about the thriving Latinx sexual cultures that flourished on that corner.

19 This information, sourced from a range of media accounts, mostly from countries that have established LGBTQ networks, states, "Brazil remains the country that reported the majority of the murders (125), followed by Mexico (65) and the United States (53)." Moreover, it mentions that "murders of trans people in the United States have doubled from last year; people of colour make up 89% of the 53 trans people murdered" and indicates that the "average age of those murdered is 30 years old; the youngest being 13 years old and the oldest 68 years old" (TvT 2021).

Epilogue

1 Proceeds from the publication of this book will be donated to organizations that provide direct services to sex workers.

REFERENCES

Film and TV

Aguirre, Valentin, and Augie Robles, dirs. 1994. *¡Viva 16!* Documentary. San Francisco: Independent Production.

Baker, Steven, executive producer. 2021. *OnlyFans: Selling Sexy*. Documentary. New York: ABC News Originals.

Bauer, Jill, and Ronna Gradus, dirs. 2015. *Hot Girls Wanted*. Documentary. Miami Beach, FL: Two to Tangle Productions.

Cathouse: The Series. 2005–14. Henderson, NV: By George Productions (II).

Curubeto, Diego, dir. 2007. *Carne sobre carne: Intimidades de Isabel Sarli*. Documentary. Buenos Aires: Flesh and Fire.

The Deuce. 2017–19. Baltimore, MD: Blown Deadline Productions.

Dona Beija. 1986. Rio de Janeiro, Brazil: Rede Manchete.

Doña Bella. 2010–11. Marsella, Colombia: RCN and Telefutura.

The Girlfriend Experience. 2016–. New York: Transactional Pictures.

Goded, Maya, dir. 2016. *Plaza de la Soledad*. Documentary. Mexico City: Monstro Films, La Sombra del Guayabo, Alebrije Cine y Video, Estudios Splendor Omnia.

Harlots. 2017–19. London: Monumental Pictures, ITV (Independent Television).

Lopez, Claudia, and George Reyes, dirs. 2016. *La muñeca fea*. Documentary. Pride Films.

Me Chama de Bruna. 2016–19. Rio de Janeiro, Brazil: TV Zero.

Merino, Fernando, and José Luis Sáenz de Heredia, dirs. 1966. *Lola, espejo oscuro*. Madrid: Ágata Films S.A.

Murray, Laura, dir. 2013. *Um beijo para Gabriela / A Kiss for Gabriela*. New York: Rattapallax Production Company.

O Negócio. 2013–18. São Paulo, Brazil: Mixer Films, HBO Latin America Originals, Home Box Office (HBO).

Ophelian, Annalise, dir. 2009. *Diagnosing Difference*. San Francisco: Floating Ophelia Productions.

Rua Augusta. 2018–. São Paulo, Brazil: O2 Filmes.

Silverman, Victor, and Susan Stryker, dirs. 2005. *Screaming Queens: The Riot at Compton's Cafeteria*. Documentary. San Francisco: Frameline Films.

Sin senos no hay paraíso. 2008–9. Bogotá, Colombia: RTI Televisión, Telemundo Studios.

Stelley, Santiago, dir. 2008. *Vice Guide to Sex: House of the Setting Sun*. New York: Vice Media.

Venville, Malcolm, dir. 2009. *44 Inch Chest*. Culver City, CA: Anonymous Content.

Venville, Malcolm, dir. 2010. *Henry's Crime*. West Hollywood, CA: Company Films.

Other Works

Aguilar Ochoa, Arturo. 1996. *La fotografía durante el imperio de Maximiliano*. Mexico City: Universidad Nacional Autónoma de México.

Agustín, Laura María. 2007. *Sex at the Margins: Migration, Labour Markets and the Rescue Industry*. London: Zed Books.

Agustín, Laura María. n.d. "Category Archive: Rescue Industry." *The Naked Anthropologist*. Accessed June 1, 2021. https://www.lauraagustin.com/category/rescue-industry-2.

Akira, Asa. 2015. *Insatiable: Porn—a Love Story*. New York: Grove.

Alarcón, Norma. 1989. "Traddutora, Traditora: A Paradigmatic Figure of Chicana Feminism." *Cultural Critique*, no. 13, 57–87.

Albert, Kendra, Emily Armbruster, Elizabeth Brundige, Elizabeth Denning, Kimberly Kim, Lorelei Lee, Lindsey Ruff, Korica Simon, and Yueyu Yang. 2020. "FOSTA in Legal Context." *Columbia Human Rights Law Review* 52, no. 3 (July): 1084–158.

Alcantara, Benjamin. 2012. "Paradojas en la Representación Documental: El Trabajo de Maya Goded." Tesis de Maestría en Historia del Arte, Universidad Nacional Autónoma de México.

Alloula, Malek. 1986. *The Colonial Harem*. Minneapolis: University of Minnesota Press.

Anawalt, Patricia. 1980. "Costume and Control: Aztec Sumptuary Laws." *Archaeology* 33, no. 1 (January/February): 33–43.

AP Archive. 2016. "Sex Workers Runs for Congress in Peru." YouTube, November 16, 2016. https://www.youtube.com/watch?v=JnfYT50W580.

Aparicio, Frances R. 1998. *Listening to Salsa: Gender, Latin Popular Music, and Puerto Rican Cultures*. Hanover, NH: University Press of New England.

Araki, Nobuyoshi. 2007. *Nobuyoshi Araki: Bondage*. London: Taschen.

Arce, B. Christine. 2018. *México's Nobodies: The Cultural Legacy of the Soldadera and Afro-Mexican Women*. Reprint ed. New York: SUNY Press.

Arenas, Reinaldo. 1993. *Before Night Falls*. Translated by Dolores M. Koch. New York: Viking.

Arguelles, Lourdes, and B. Ruby Rich. 1984. "Homosexuality, Homophobia, and

Revolution: Notes toward an Understanding of the Cuban Lesbian and Gay Male Experience, Part I." *Signs: Journal of Women in Culture and Society* 9, no. 4 (July): 683–99.

Arkansas Times Staff. 2004. "1980—Crisis at Ft. Chaffee." *Arkansas Times*, September 23, 2004. https://arktimes.com/news/cover-stories/2004/09/23/1980-crisis-at -ft-chaffee.

Ashly, Jaclynn. 2021. "Sex Worker Turned Congresswoman Opens New Horizons." *New Frame*, September 30, 2021. https://www.newframe.com/sex-worker-turned -congresswoman-opens-new-horizons/.

Assouline, Pierre. 1998. "Un instante tan pleno." *La Nacion*, August 12, 1998.

Bailón Vásquez, Fabiola. 2016. "Reglamentarismo y prostitución en la ciudad de México, 1865–1940." *Revista de la Dirección de Estudios Históricos*, no. 93 (April): 79–97.

Barcia Zequeira, María del Carmen. 1993. "Entre el poder y la crisis: Las prostitutas se defienden." *Contrastes*, nos. 7–8, 7–20.

Barthes, Roland. 2010. *Camera Lucida: Reflections on Photography*. Translated by Richard Howard. New York: Hill and Wang.

Beers, Mayra. 2003. "Murder in San Isidro: Crime and Culture during the Second Cuban Republic." *Cuban Studies* 34, no. 1 (January): 97–129.

Behdad, Ali. 2016. *Camera Orientalis: Reflections on Photography of the Middle East*. Chicago: University of Chicago Press.

Bénédicte Desrus Photography. n.d. "About | Bénédicte Desrus Photography." Accessed June 10, 2022. https://benedictedesrus.photoshelter.com/about/index.

Berg, Heather. 2021. *Porn Work: Sex, Labor, and Late Capitalism*. Chapel Hill: University of North Carolina Press.

Berg, Heather, Angela Jones, and PJ Patella-Rey. n.d. "Sex Worker Syllabus and Toolkit for Academics." Google Doc. Accessed September 10, 2021. https://docs.google .com/document/d/1ziubffIk5wqueSDB6p0OfsajfyyscYsNyWSzT0bXuDc/edit.

Bertillon, Alphonse. 1883. *Les races sauvages*. Paris: G. Masson.

Beverley, John. 1993. *Against Literature*. Minneapolis: University of Minnesota Press.

Bliss, Katherine Elaine. 2010. *Compromised Positions: Prostitution, Public Health, and Gender Politics in Revolutionary Mexico City*. University Park: Pennsylvania State University Press.

Body-Rockin. n.d. "Body-Rockin: Model Details: Vanessa Del Rio." Accessed November 3, 2021. https://www.body-rockin.com/user/model_details.php?id =434&navpage=feature&fid=62.

Borelli, Melissa Blanco. 2015. *She Is Cuba: A Genealogy of the Mulata Body*. New York: Oxford University Press.

Brackes, Lucía. 2012. "El último Bo." *Los Andes*, October 25, 2012. https://www .losandes.com.ar/article/ultimo-675698.

Brassaï. 1976. *The Secret Paris of the '30s*. Translated by Richard Miller. New York: Pantheon Books. Originally published as *Le Paris secret des années 30* (Paris: Gallimard, 1976).

Brassaï. 2001. *Paris by Night*. Translated by Stuart Gilbert. Boston: Bulfinch. Originally published as *Paris de nuit* (Paris: Édition Arts et Métiers Graphiques, 1933).

Brizuela, Natalia, and Jodi Roberts. 2018. *The Matter of Photography in the Americas*. Stanford: Stanford University Press.

Brody, Jennifer DeVere. 2001. "Black Cat Fever: Manifestations of Manet's 'Olympia.'" *Theatre Journal* 53, no. 1 (March): 95–118.

Brown, Elspeth H., and Thy Phu. 2014. Introduction to *Feeling Photography*, edited by Elspeth H. Brown and Thy Phu, 1–28. Durham, NC: Duke University Press.

Butler, Judith P. 2005. *Giving an Account of Oneself*. New York: Fordham University Press.

Cabezas, Amalia L. 2009. *Economies of Desire: Sex and Tourism in Cuba and the Dominican Republic*. Philadelphia: Temple University Press.

Cabezas, Amalia L. 2019. "Latin American and Caribbean Sex Workers: Gains and Challenges in the Movement." *Anti-trafficking Review*, no. 12 (April 29): 37–56.

Calvo Peña, Beatriz. 2005. "Prensa, politica y prostitucion en La Habana finisecular: El caso de 'La Cebolla' y la 'polemica de las meretrices.'" *Cuban Studies* 36 (1): 23–49.

Campt, Tina M. 2017. *Listening to Images*. Durham, NC: Duke University Press.

Cano, David. 2011. "Prostitutas por Fernell Franco." *Memoriando Fotografía* (blog), July 4. http://memoriandofotografia.blogspot.com/2011/07/prostitutas-por-fernell-franco.html.

Cartier-Bresson, Henri. 2015. *Henri Cartier-Bresson: The Decisive Moment*. Göttingen: Steidl.

Castro, Fidel. 1980. "May Day Rally." Latin American Network Information Center (LANIC), Castro Speech Data Base. http://lanic.utexas.edu/project/castro/db/1980/19800501-1.html.

Chateauvert, Melinda. 2015. *Sex Workers Unite: A History of the Movement from Stonewall to SlutWalk*. Boston: Beacon.

Cinépolis Distribución. 2017. "Plaza de la Soledad: Función Especial Con Sus Protagonistas." YouTube, April 28, 2017. https://www.youtube.com/watch?v=clı_zKaAviY.

Clarkes, Lincoln. 2002. *Heroines: The Photographs of Lincoln Clarkes*. Vancouver: Anvil.

Comella, Lynn, and Shira Tarrant, eds. 2015. *New Views on Pornography: Sexuality, Politics, and the Law*. Santa Barbara, CA: Praeger.

Cornejo, Giancarlo. 2014. "For a Queer Pedagogy of Friendship." *TSQ: Transgender Studies Quarterly* 1, no. 3 (August): 352–67.

Cortés Rocca, Paola. 2005. "Subjectivities and Techniques of Control in Late Nineteenth-Century Mexico: Emperor Maximilian's 'Registro De Mujeres Públicas.'" *Journal of Latin American Cultural Studies* 14, no. 2 (August): 211–22.

Cortez, Jaime, ed. 1999. *Virgins, Guerillas and Locas: Gay Latinos Writing about Love*. San Francisco: Cleis.

Cortez, Jaime. 2004. *Sexile/Sexilio*. Translated by Omar Baños. Los Angeles: Institute for Gay Men's Health.

Cortez, Jaime. 2021. *Gordo*. New York: Grove.

Costa de Souza, Milena. 2015. "Ao encontro das queer faces." *Estudos Feministas* 23, no. 1 (January): 249–58.

Cruz, Ariane. 2016. *The Color of Kink: Black Women, BDSM, and Pornography*. New York: New York University Press.

Cuellar, Manuel. Forthcoming. "*Los mecos de Veracruz*: Queer Gestures and the Performance of Nahua Indigeneity." *Journal of Latin American Cultural Studies*.

Culbert, Lori. 2010. "Bloody Knife Fight Left One Pickton Victim Clinging to Life." *Calgary Herald*, August 4, 2010. http://www.calgaryherald.com/news /pickton+jurors+never+heard+from+trade+worker+taken+farm/3360169 /story.html.

Damián Guillén, Claudia I., Paola G. Ortega, Abigail Pasillas Mendoza, and Adriana Ramírez Salgago. 2010. "Ejercicio y construcción de identidades en los retratos de prostitutas del Archivo General Municipal de Puebla." *Antropología: Boletín Oficial Del INAH*, no. 89 (May–August): 46–63.

da Silva, Daniele Andrade, Jimena de Garay Hernández, Aureliano Lopes da Silva Jr., and Anna Paula Uziel, eds. 2013. *Feminilidades: Corpos e Sexualidades em Debate*. Rio de Janeiro: Universidade do Estado do Rio de Janiero.

Davina, Lola. 2017. *Thriving in Sex Work: Heartfelt Advice for Staying Sane in the Sex Industry; A Self-Help Book for Sex Workers*. Oakland, CA: Erotic as Power.

Davina, Lola (@Lola_Davina). 2020. "I deeply believe that so much of the root of #whorephobia (and by that I mean fear and hatred of sex workers) . . ." Twitter, August 21, 2020. https://twitter.com/Lola_Davina/status/1296953996226297861.

Dawn, Amber, and Justin Ducharme, eds. 2019. *Hustling Verse: An Anthology of Sex Workers' Poetry*. Vancouver: Arsenal Pulp.

Dean, Tim, Steven Ruszczycky, and David Squires, eds. 2014. *Porn Archives*. Durham, NC: Duke University Press.

Deans-Smith, Susan. 2005. "Creating the Colonial Subject: Casta Paintings, Collectors, and Critics in Eighteenth-Century Mexico and Spain." *Colonial Latin American Review* 14, no. 2 (December): 169–204.

Delgado, Juliana. 2013. "¡Cuéntamelo! An Oral History of Queer Latin@ Immigrants in San Francisco." *SF Weekly*, June 26–July 2, 2013.

Delgado Lopera, Juliana. 2017. *¡Cuéntamelo! Oral Histories by LGBT Latino Immigrants. / ¡Cuéntamelo! Testimonios de Inmigrantes Latinos LGBT*. San Francisco: Aunt Lute Books.

Delgado Lopera, Juliana. 2020. *Fiebre Tropical*. New York: Amethyst Editions.

DelPlato, Joan. 2002. *Multiple Wives, Multiple Pleasures: Representing the Harem, 1800–1875*. Madison, NJ: Fairleigh Dickinson University Press.

DelPlato, Joan, and Julie Codell, eds. 2016. *Orientalism, Eroticism and Modern Visuality in Global Cultures*. New York: Routledge.

del Rio, Vanessa. 2010. *Vanessa del Rio: Fifty Years of Slightly Slutty Behavior*. As told to Dian Hanson. Cologne: Taschen.

Desrus, Bénédicte, and Celia Gómez Ramos. 2014. *Las amorosas más bravas / Tough*

Love. English translation by Michael Parker-Stainback. Mexico City: Libros del sargento.

d'Halmar, Augusto. (1902) 1998. *Juana Lucero*. 5th ed. Santiago: Andrés Bello.

di Giovanni, Janine. 2015. *Eve Arnold: Magnum Legacy*. New York: Prestel.

Dyer, Richard. 2013. *Heavenly Bodies: Film Stars and Society*. New York: Routledge.

Facio, Sara. 1997. *La fotografía en la Argentina: Desde 1840 a nuestros días*. Buenos Aires: La Azotea.

Fanon, Frantz. 1967. "The Fact of Blackness." In *Black Skin, White Masks*, translated by Charles Lam Markmann, 109–40. New York: Grove.

Feinberg, Leslie. 2017. "Interview: Sylvia Rivera by Leslie Feinberg." The Queer Bible. October 8. https://www.queerbible.com/queerbible/2017/10/8/interview -sylvia-rivera-by-leslie-feinberg.

Fernández Flórez, Darío. 1951. *Lola, Espejo Oscuro*. Madrid: Editorial Plentitud.

Ferré, Rosario. 2000. "Cuando las mujeres quieren a los hombres." In *Papeles de Pandora*, 22–41. New York: Vintage Español.

Ferreira da Silva, Denise. 2017. "On Difference without Separability." Catalog. 32nd Bienal de São Paulo: Incerteza Viva. São Paolo: 32a São Paulo Art Bienal.

Figueroa, Yomaira C. 2020. "Your Lips: Mapping Afro-Boricua Feminist Becomings." *Frontiers: A Journal of Women Studies* 41 (1): 1–11.

Fleetwood, Nicole R. 2011. *Troubling Vision: Performance, Visuality, and Blackness*. Chicago: University of Chicago Press.

Fleetwood, Nicole R. 2012. "The Case of Rihanna: Erotic Violence and Black Female Desire." *African American Review* 45, no. 3 (Fall): 419–35.

Flores Castillo, Nancy, Marta Cabello, and Stefano Cavalli. 2017. "Autonomía y empoderamiento de las 'Amorosas más Bravas.'" Paper presented at III Congreso Internacional de Ciencias Sociales, Universidad Autónoma del Estado de Morelos Facultad de Estudios Superiores de Cuautla, October 25, 2017.

Foster, Craig L. 1990. "Tarnished Angels: Prostitution in Storyville, New Orleans, 1900–1910." *Louisiana History: The Journal of the Louisiana Historical Association* 31, no. 4 (Winter): 387–97.

Foster, David William. 2008. "Las lolas de la Coca: El cuerpo femenino en el cine de Isabel Sarli." *Karpa: Dissident Theatricalities, Visual Arts and Culture* 1, no. 2 (Summer): n.p.

Foucault, Michel. 1978. *The History of Sexuality*. Vol. 1. Translated by Robert Hurley. New York: Vintage.

Foucault, Michel. 2003. *Society Must Be Defended: Lectures at the Collège de France, 1975–76*. Edited by Mauro Bertani and Alessandro Fontana. Translated by David Macey. New York: Picador.

Foucault, Michel. 2006. *Psychiatric Power: Lectures at the Collège de France, 1973–74*. Translated by Jacques Lagrange. New York: Palgrave Macmillan.

Fregosa, Juliana. 2018. "El detallado registro fotográfico de las prostitutas mexicanas que realizó el emperador Maximiliano I en el siglo XIX." Infobae, June 17, 2018. https://www.infobae.com/america/mexico/2018/06/17/el-detallado

-registro-fotografico-de-las-prostitutas-mexicanas-que-realizo-el-emperador
-maximiliano-i-en-el-siglo-xix/.

Fussell, Elizabeth. 2007. "Constructing New Orleans, Constructing Race: A Population History of New Orleans." *Journal of American History* 94, no. 3 (December):
846–55.

Gallardo, Ana. 2014. "Sin Título." Print on Wallpaper. La Colección Jumex. Museo
Jumex, Mexico City, Mexico.

Gan, Jessi. 2007. "'Still at the Back of the Bus': Sylvia Rivera's Struggle." *Centro Journal* 19 (1): 124–39.

Garcia Hernandez, Yessica. 2021. "The Making of Fat Erotics: The Cultural Work
and Pleasures of *Gordibuena* Activists." *Fat Studies* 10, no. 3 (May 25): 237–52.

García Márquez, Gabriel. 2005. *Innocent Erendira and Other Stories*. New York: Harper
Perennial.

García Márquez, Gabriel. 2006. *Memories of My Melancholy Whores*. Translated by
Edith Grossman. New York: Vintage.

García-Peña, Lorgia. 2015. "Translating Blackness." *Black Scholar* 45, no. 2 (April 3):
10–20.

Germeten, Nicole von. 2018. *Profit and Passion: Transactional Sex in Colonial Mexico*.
Berkeley: University of California Press.

Gilman, Sander L. 1985. "Black Bodies, White Bodies: Toward an Iconography of
Female Sexuality in Late Nineteenth-Century Art, Medicine, and Literature."
Critical Inquiry 12, no. 1 (October): 204–42.

Glissant, Édouard. 1997. *Poetics of Relation*. Translated by Betsy Wing. Ann Arbor:
University of Michigan Press.

Goded, Maya. 2006. *Plaza de la Soledad*. Barcelona: Lunwerg Editores.

Goded, Maya. n.d. "Plaza de la Soledad | Maya Goded." Accessed June 8, 2022.
https://mayagoded.net/en/plaza-de-la-soledad-documentary.

Goffman, Erving. 2009. *Stigma: Notes on the Management of Spoiled Identity*. New York:
Simon and Schuster.

Gomez, Letitia. 2015. Preface to *Queer Brown Voices: Personal Narratives of Latina/o
LGBT Activism*, edited by Uriel Quesada, Letitia Gomez, and Salvador Vidal-
Ortiz, ix–xv. Austin: University of Texas Press.

González, Lázaro. n.d. *Sexile*. lazarogonzalezfilms. Accessed September 15, 2021.
https://www.lazarogonzalezfilms.com/current-project.

Grant, Melissa Gira. 2014. *Playing the Whore: The Work of Sex Work*. New York: Verso.

Guerrin, Michel. 1993. "An Interview with Henri Cartier-Bresson." *Visual Anthropol-
ogy* 5, nos. 3–4 (January): 331–37.

Gugelberger, Georg M., ed. 1996. *The Real Thing: Testimonial Discourse and Latin America*. Durham NC: Duke University Press.

Gutiérrez, Laura G. 2010. *Performing Mexicanidad: Vendidas y Cabareteras on the Transnational Stage*. Chicana Matters Series. Austin: University of Texas Press.

Gutiérrez, Laura G. 2019. "Afrodiasporic Visual and Sonic Assemblages: Racialized
Anxieties and the Disruption of Mexicanidad in Cine de Rumberas." In *Decen-

tering the Nation: Music, Mexicanidad, and Globalization, edited by Jesús A. Ramos-Kittrell, 1–22. Lanham, MD: Rowman and Littlefield.

Guzmán, Joshua Javier, and Christina A. León. 2015. "Cuts and Impressions: The Aesthetic Work of Lingering in Latinidad." *Women and Performance: A Journal of Feminist Theory* 25, no. 3 (September): 261–76.

Hanson, Dian, ed. 2009. *Tom of Finland XXL*. Cologne: Taschen.

Hanson, Dian, ed. 2011. *The Big Book of Breasts 3D*. Cologne: Taschen.

Harris, LaShawn. 2016. *Sex Workers, Psychics, and Numbers Runners: Black Women in New York City's Underground Economy*. Urbana: University of Illinois Press.

Hartman, Saidiya. 2008. "Venus in Two Acts." *Small Axe* 12, no. 2 (June): 1–14.

Hartman, Saidiya. 2019. *Wayward Lives, Beautiful Experiments: Intimate Histories of Social Upheaval*. New York: W. W. Norton.

Heaux History Project. n.d. Accessed June 15, 2022. https://www.patreon.com/heauxhistory.

Hebert, Patrick "Pato." 2004. Foreword to *Sexile/Sexilio*, by Jaime Cortez, translated by Omar Baños. Los Angeles: Institute for Gay Men's Health.

Hénonin, Abel Muñoz. 2017. "Plaza de la Soledad." *Revista Icónica*, May 4, 2017. http://revistaiconica.com/plaza-de-la-soledad/.

Hernandez, Jillian. 2020. *Aesthetics of Excess: The Art and Politics of Black and Latina Embodiment*. Durham, NC: Duke University Press.

Holmes, Helen. 2021. "'First They Come for Sex Workers, Then They Come for Everyone,' Including Artists." *Observer*, January 27, 2021. https://observer.com/2021/01/first-they-come-for-sex-workers-then-they-come-for-everyone-including-artists/.

Huhndorf, Shari M. 2021. "Scenes from the Fringe: Gendered Violence and the Geographies of Indigenous Feminism." *Signs: Journal of Women in Culture and Society* 46, no. 3 (March): 561–87.

Human Rights Watch. 2014. *World Report 2014*. New York: Seven Stories. https://www.hrw.org/world-report/2014.

Ibarra, Xandra. n.d. "Spictacles." *Xandra Ibarra* (blog). Accessed July 3, 2021. https://www.xandraibarra.com/spictacles/.

IMDb. n.d. "Vivian Lamolli." Accessed June 2, 2022. http://www.imdb.com/name/nm4796168/bio.

Institute of Development Studies. n.d. "Map of Sex Work Law." Sexuality, Poverty and Law Programme. Accessed September 28, 2021. http://spl.ids.ac.uk/sexworklaw.

Jaime, Karen. 2022. "'I'm a Stripper, Ho': The Sonics of Cardi B's Ratchet, Diasporic Feminism." *Performance Matters* 8, no. 1 (May 28): 83–96.

Jandeliz. 2021. "1.3: Adela Vazquez." *Kickass Women of Color* (podcast), February 26, 2021. https://www.listennotes.com/podcasts/kickass-women-of/13-adela-vazquez-3MYTdS_kP-Z/.

Jiménez, Carlos. 2014. "Un Desamparo redimible: Ana Gallarado." *M-Arte y Cultura*

Visual (blog), June 16, 2014. http://www.m-arteyculturavisual.com/2014/06/16
/un-desamparo-irredimible-ana-gallardo/.

Kafer, Alison. 2013. *Feminist, Queer, Crip*. Bloomington: Indiana University Press.

Kassirer, Kay, ed. 2019. *A Whore's Manifesto: An Anthology of Writing and Artwork by Sex Workers*. Portland, OR: Thorntree.

Kukura, Joe. 2021. "SF's Trailblazing Sex Worker Activist Margo St. James Has Died." *SFist*, January 20, 2021. https://sfist.com/2021/01/20/sfs-trailblazing-sex -worker-activist-margo-st-james-has-died/.

Kuppers, Gaby, and Amanda Thow, eds. 1993. *Companeras: Voices from the Latin American Women's Movement*. London: Latin America Bureau.

Kurzweil, Amy. 2021. "The Art of Graphic Resurrection." Presentation given at the American Academy in Berlin, October 26, 2021, Berlin, Germany.

La Fountain-Stokes, Lawrence. 2021. "The Life and Times of Trans Activist Sylvia Rivera." In *Critical Dialogues in Latinx Studies: A Reader*, edited by Ana Y. Ramos-Zayas and Mérida M. Rúa, 241–53. New York: New York University Press.

Landau, Emily Epstein. 2013. *Spectacular Wickedness: Sex, Race, and Memory in Storyville, New Orleans*. New Orleans: Louisiana State University Press.

Lawrenson, Helen. 1955. "The Sexiest City in the World." *Esquire*, February 1, 1955.

Lee, Jiz, ed. 2015. *Coming Out like a Porn Star: Essays on Pornography, Protection, and Privacy*. Berkeley, CA: ThreeL Media.

Lenz, Flavio. 2014. "Gabriela Leite, prostituta que viveu e promoveu a liberdade." *Revista Em Pauta: Teoria social e realidade contemporânea* 12, no. 34 (December): 208–15.

León, Christina A. 2017. "Forms of Opacity: Roaches, Blood, and Being Stuck in Xandra Ibarra's Corpus." *ASAP/Journal* 2, no. 2 (July 31): 369–94.

Levinas, Emmanuel. 1997. *Difficult Freedom: Essays on Judaism*. Translated by Seán Hand. Baltimore, MD: Johns Hopkins University Press.

Lippard, Lucy R., ed. 1993. *Partial Recall: With Essays on Photographs of Native North Americans*. New York: New Press.

Lorenz, Taylor, and Alyssa Lukpat. 2021. "OnlyFans Says It Is Banning Sexually Explicit Content." *New York Times*, August 19, 2021.

Luna, Caleb. 2022. "Undisciplined Bodies: Race, Sexuality and Size in U.S. Media and Culture." PhD diss., University of California, Berkeley.

Machado Koutsoukos, Sandra Sofia. 2010. *Negros no estúdio do fotógrafo*. Artes e Cultura edition. Campinas, SP, Brazil: Universidade Estadual de Campinas (UNICAMP).

Maffía, Diana, and Claudia Korol, eds. 2021. *Prostitución/Trabajo Sexual: Las Protagonistas Hablan*. Buenos Aires: Paidós.

Magnum Photos. 2017. "Henri Cartier-Bresson's Mexico." *Magnum Photos* (blog), September 16, 2017. https://www.magnumphotos.com/arts-culture/travel /henri-cartier-bresson-mexico/.

Manalansan, Martin F. 2014. "The 'Stuff' of Archives: Mess, Migration, and Queer Lives." *Radical History Review* 2014, no. 120 (October): 94–107.

Marx, Karl, and Friedrich Engels. 1988. *The Economic and Philosophic Manuscripts of 1844 and the Communist Manifesto.* Translated by Martin Milligan. Amherst, NY: Prometheus Books.

McEntire, Dee L. 1992. "Erotic Storytelling: Sexual Experience and Fantasy Letters in *Forum Magazine.*" *Western Folklore* 51 (1): 81–96.

Meiselas, Susan. 1976. *Carnival Strippers.* New York: Noonday.

Meiselas, Susan. 2002. *Pandora's Box.* London: Trebruk.

Meiselas, Susan. 2013. "Susan Meiselas Carnival Strippers Audio." YouTube, September 4, 2013. https://www.youtube.com/watch?v=3z4illGQFbQ.

Metropolitan Museum of Art. n.d. "Eugène Atget | Rue Asselin." Accessed September 29, 2021. https://www.metmuseum.org/art/collection/search/283266.

Middel, Cristina de. n.d. "Gentlemen's Club." Accessed March 15, 2020. http://www.lademiddel.com/gentlemans-club.html.

Miller, Jeannette. 2010. *Historia de la fotografía dominicana.* Vol. 1, *1851–1961.* Santo Domingo, Dominican Republic: Grupo León Jimenes.

Miller-Young, Mireille. 2014. *A Taste for Brown Sugar: Black Women in Pornography.* Durham, NC: Duke University Press.

Mirabal, Nancy Raquel. 2017. *Suspect Freedoms: The Racial and Sexual Politics of Cubanidad in New York, 1823–1957.* New York: New York University Press.

Misiones Cuatro. 2018. "John Waters: 'Conocer a Coca Sarli va a ser como conocer al Papa.'" April 4, 2018. https://misionescuatro.com/espectaculos/john-waters-conocer-coca-sarli-va-conocer-al-papa/.

Mistress Snow. 2019. "I Told My Mentor I Was a Dominatrix." *Chronicle of Higher Education,* December 5, 2019. http://www.chronicle.com/article/i-told-my-mentor-i-was-a-dominatrix/.

Montero, Jacqueline (@jacquelin2924). 2017. "feliz con la cominidad GLBT." Twitter, July 10, 2017. https://twitter.com/jacquelin2924/status/884438716542046208.

Morel, India. 2013. *Infamous: Memoirs of a xxx Star.* CreateSpace Independent Publishing Platform.

Moulin, Félix Jacques Antoine. 2014. *Félix Moulin (1802–1879) and l'Algérie photographiée.* Edited by Pierre Zaragozi. Paris: P. Zaragozi.

Muñoz, José Esteban. 2019. *Cruising Utopia: The Then and There of Queer Futurity.* New York: New York University Press.

Muñoz, José Esteban. 2020. *The Sense of Brown.* Edited by Joshua Chambers-Letson and Tavia Nyong'o. Durham, NC: Duke University Press.

Musée d'Orsay. n.d. "La Villette, rue Asselin, fille publique faisant le quart devant sa porte." Accessed October 10, 2019. https://www.musee-orsay.fr/fr/oeuvres/la-villette-rue-asselin-fille-publique-faisant-le-quart-devant-sa-porte-39016.

Musser, Amber Jamilla. 2014. *Sensational Flesh: Race, Power, and Masochism.* New York: New York University Press.

Nash, Jennifer Christine. 2014. *The Black Body in Ecstasy: Reading Race, Reading Pornography.* Durham, NC: Duke University Press.

National Press Photographers Association. n.d. "Code of Ethics." Accessed June 28, 2017. https://nppa.org/code-ethics.

Nazarieff, Serge. 2002. *Early Erotic Photography*. Cologne: Taschen.

Nead, Lynda. 1990. "The Female Nude: Pornography, Art, and Sexuality." *Signs: Journal of Women in Culture and Society* 15, no. 2 (Winter): 323–35.

Negrón-Muntaner, Frances. 2004. *Boricua Pop: Puerto Ricans and the Latinization of American Culture*. New York: New York University Press.

Neira, Montse. n.d. *Museo de la prostitución* (blog). Accessed July 13, 2021. http://museodelaprostitucion.blogspot.com/.

Nguyen, Hoang Tan. 2014. *A View from the Bottom: Asian American Masculinity and Sexual Representation*. Durham, NC: Duke University Press.

Ochoa, Marcia. 2014. *Queen for a Day: Transformistas, Beauty Queens, and the Performance of Femininity in Venezuela*. Durham, NC: Duke University Press.

Ochoa Rodríguez, Sofia. 2016. "Plaza de la Soledad." EnFilme: Cine Todo el Tiempo, April 3, 2016. https://enfilme.com/en-cartelera/plaza-de-la-soledad.

Orellano, Georgina. 2022. *Puta feminista: Historias de una trabajadora sexual*. Buenos Aires: Sudamericana.

Ortíz Álvarez, María Luisa. 2020. "'Se formó el bembé' / 'Bater o bembé': La influencia africana en el léxico y en las expresiones idiomáticas del español de Cuba y el portugués de Brasil." In *De aquí a Lima: Estudios fraseológicos del español de España e Hispanoamérica*, edited by Elena Dal Maso, 139–51. Venice: Fondazione Università Ca' Foscari.

Patzán, Marta Lidia Nij, ed. 2021. *O trabalho dos trabalhadores do sexo para a autodeterminação: Reconhecimento dos seus direitos laborais; "Trabalhadores sexuais e os seus direitos laborais."* n.p.: Edições Nosso Conhecimento.

Paz, Octavio. 1994. *The Labyrinth of Solitude: The Other Mexico, Return to the Labyrinth of Solitude, Mexico and the United States, the Philanthropic Ogre*. Underlining ed. New York: Grove.

Pear, Robert. 1987. "Behind the Prison Riots: Precautions Not Taken." *New York Times*, December 6, 1987. http://timesmachine.nytimes.com/timesmachine/1987/12/06/691287.html.

Peña, Susana. 2013. *Oye Loca: From the Mariel Boatlift to Gay Cuban Miami*. Minneapolis: University of Minnesota Press.

Pinney, Christopher, and Nicolas Peterson, eds. 2003. *Photography's Other Histories*. Durham, NC: Duke University Press.

Poole, Deborah. 1997. *Vision, Race, and Modernity: A Visual Economy of the Andean World*. Princeton, NJ: Princeton University Press.

Project DoxySpotting. n.d. "DoxySpotting—the Streetview Prostitution Archive." Accessed September 19, 2020. http://doxyspotting.com/.

Quesada, Uriel, Letitia Gomez, and Salvador Vidal-Ortiz, eds. 2015. *Queer Brown Voices: Personal Narratives of Latina/o LGBT Activism*. Austin: University of Texas Press.

Quiroga, Jose. 2000. *Tropics of Desire: Interventions from Queer Latino America*. New York: New York University Press.

Raiford, Leigh. 2013. *Imprisoned in a Luminous Glare: Photography and the African American Freedom Struggle*. Chapel Hill: University of North Carolina Press.

Ramos, Iván A. 2015. "The Dirt That Haunts: Looking at Esta Noche." *Studies in Gender and Sexuality* 16, no. 2 (April 3): 135–36.

Ramos, Iván A. 2017. "Slow Encounters: Chantal Akerman's *From the Other Side*, Queer Form, and the Mexican Migrant." *ASAP/Journal* 2, no. 2 (May): 423–48.

Ramos Otero, Manuel. 1979. "La última plena que bailó Luberza." In *El cuento de la mujer del mar*, 47–68. Rio Piedras, Puerto Rico: Ediciones Huracan.

Reineri Gimeno, Victorino. 1888. "Carta Abierta." *La Cebolla: Órgano Oficial del Partido de Su Nombre*, no. 3 (September 23). University of Florida Digital Collections. https://ufdc.ufl.edu/AA00020045/00003/2x.

Remezcla. 2016. "Carmen Reacts to Watching 'Plaza de la Soledad' Doc." YouTube, February 2, 2016. https://www.youtube.com/watch?v=Rn8156p30uk.

Restrepo Zapata, Camilo. 2002. *La foto de idéntidad: Fragmentos para una estética*. Medellín: Fondo Editorial Universidad EAFIT.

Reynolds, Roxy. 2014. *Secrets of a Porn Star*. Stockbridge, GA: G Street Chronicles.

Ríos de la Torre, Guadalupe. 2008. "Burdeles modernos y mujeres públicas: El trabajo sexual en México." *Letra: Salud, Sexualidad, SIDA*, September 4, 2008. https://www.jornada.com.mx/2008/09/04/ls-jovenes.html.

RLJE Films. 2010. "44 Inch Chest—MALCOLM VENVILLE INTERVIEW." YouTube, February 16, 2010. https://www.youtube.com/watch?v=BezpdfHIEEM.

Rodríguez, Juana María. 2003. *Queer Latinidad: Identity Practices, Discursive Spaces*. New York: New York University Press.

Rodríguez, Juana María. 2014. *Sexual Futures, Queer Gestures, and Other Latina Longings*. New York: New York University Press.

Rodríguez, Juana María. 2015. "Brujería, the Queer Karaoke Remix." *Chicana/Latina Studies* 14, no. 2 (Spring): 58–59.

Rodríguez, Juana María. 2020. "Activism and Identity in the Ruins of Representation." In *AIDS and the Distribution of Crises*, edited by Jih-Fei Cheng, Alexandra Juhasz, and Nishant Shahani, 352–87. Durham, NC: Duke University Press.

Rodríguez, Juana María. 2021. "Public Notice from the Fucked Peepo: Xandra Ibarra's 'The Hookup/Displacement/Barhopping/Drama Tour.'" In *Queer Nightlife*, edited by Kemi Adeyemi, Kareem Khubchandani, and Ramón H. Rivera-Servera, 211–21. Ann Arbor: University of Michigan Press.

Román, Miriam Jiménez, and Juan Flores, eds. 2010. *The Afro-Latin@ Reader: History and Culture in the United States*. Durham, NC: Duke University Press.

Roque Ramírez, Horacio N. 2007. "'Mira, Yo Soy Boricua y Estoy Aquí': Rafa Negrón's Pan Dulce and the Queer Sonic Latinaje of San Francisco." *Centro Journal* 19 (1): 275–313.

Rose, Al. 1974. *Storyville, New Orleans: Being an Authentic, Illustrated Account of the Notorious Red-Light District*. Tuscaloosa: University of Alabama Press.

Ruétalo, Victoria. 2004. "Temptations: Isabel Sarli Exposed." *Journal of Latin American Cultural Studies* 13, no. 1 (March): 79–95.

Ruiz, Jason. 2014. *Americans in the Treasure House: Travel to Porfirian Mexico and the Cultural Politics of Empire*. Austin: University of Texas Press.

Sabsay, Leticia. 2016. *The Political Imaginary of Sexual Freedom: Subjectivity and Power in the New Sexual Democratic Turn*. New York: Palgrave Macmillan.

Salamon, Gayle. 2010. *Assuming a Body: Transgender and Rhetorics of Materiality*. New York: Columbia University Press.

Santana, Dora Silva. 2019. "Mais Viva! Reassembling Transness, Blackness, and Feminism." *TSQ: Transgender Studies Quarterly* 6, no. 2 (May): 210–22.

Scott, Clive. 2007. *Street Photography: From Atget to Cartier-Bresson*. London: I. B. Tauris.

Scott, Darieck. 2010. *Extravagant Abjection: Blackness, Power, and Sexuality in the African American Literary Imagination*. New York: New York University Press.

Scott, Joan. 1993. "The Evidence of Experience." In *The Lesbian and Gay Studies Reader*, edited by Henry Abelove, Michèle Aina Barale, and David Halperin, 397–415. New York: Routledge.

Sekula, Allan. 1981. "The Traffic in Photographs." *Art Journal* 41, no. 1 (Spring): 15–25.

Shah, Svati P. 2011–12. "Sex Work and Queer Politics in Three Acts." *S&F Online* 10, nos. 1–2 (Fall/Spring). http://sfonline.barnard.edu/a-new-queer-agenda/sex-work-and-queer-politics-in-three-acts/0/.

Shannon, K., T. Kerr, S. A. Strathdee, J. Shoveller, J. S. Montaner, and M. W. Tyndall. 2009. "Prevalence and Structural Correlates of Gender Based Violence among a Prospective Cohort of Female Sex Workers." *BMJ* 2009, no. 339 (August 11): b2939.

Shimizu, Celine Parreñas. 2007. *The Hypersexuality of Race: Performing Asian/American Women on Screen and Scene*. Durham, NC: Duke University Press.

Sigal, Pete, Zeb Tortorici, and Neil L. Whitehead, eds. 2019. *Ethnopornography: Sexuality, Colonialism, and Archival Knowledge*. Durham, NC: Duke University Press.

Sippial, Tiffany A. 2013. *Prostitution, Modernity, and the Making of the Cuban Republic, 1840–1920*. Chapel Hill: University of North Carolina Press.

Smith, Molly, and Juno Mac. 2018. *Revolting Prostitutes: The Fight for Sex Workers' Rights*. New York: Verso.

Smith, Paul Julian. 2017. "Of Stars and Solitude: Two Mexican Documentaries." *Film Quarterly* 71, no. 1 (September): 73–79.

Spade, Dean. 2020. "Solidarity Not Charity: Mutual Aid for Mobilization and Survival." *Social Text* 38, no. 1 (142): 131–51.

Stardust, Zahra Zsuzanna. 2015. "Coming Out, Coming Hard: Privacy, Exhibitionism and Running for Parliament." In *Coming Out like a Porn Star: Essays on Pornography, Protection and Privacy*, 300–305. San Francisco: ThreeL Media.

stern.de. n.d. "Unsere Projekte in Aller Welt." Accessed October 25, 2021. https://www.stern.de/stiftung/9491556-9491556.html.

Still Here San Francisco. 2021. "Legends, Monsters and Chosen Family: An Evening with Tina V. Aguirre." YouTube, February 15, 2021. https://www.youtube.com/watch?v=jMXsnwNcMtA.

Strauss, Neil. 2004. "How to Make Love like a Porn Star: A Cautionary Tale." Book review, *Publishers Weekly*, August 9, 2004. http://www.publishersweekly.com/978-0-06-053909-2.

Support Ho(s)e Collective. 2021. "Support Ho(s)e: Sex Work Centered Guide for Academics." https://sxhxcollective.org/wp-content/uploads/2021/03/SxHx-academic-guide-final.pdf.

Szarkowski, John, ed. 1970. *Storyville Portraits: Photographs from the New Orleans Red-Light District, circa 1912*. New York: Museum of Modern Art.

Taormino, Tristan, Constance Penley, Celine Parrenas Shimizu, and Mireille Miller-Young, eds. 2013. *The Feminist Porn Book: The Politics of Producing Pleasure*. New York: Feminist Press at the City University of New York, 2013.

Taschen. 2008. "Interview with Vanessa Del Rio, by Dian Hanson." YouTube, January 28, 2008. https://www.youtube.com/watch?v=bniQ8-5R434.

Thibon, Placer, Isabel Sarli, and Luis Gruss. 1999. "Isabel Sarli: 'Me Acusaron de Obscena y Promarxista' / On m'a Accusée d'être Obscène et pro-Marxiste." *Cinémas d'Amérique Latine*, no. 7, 53–57.

Thomas, Piri. (1967) 1997. *Down These Mean Streets*. Thirtieth Anniversary ed. New York: Vintage.

Thompson, Krista A. 2007. *An Eye for the Tropics: Tourism, Photography, and Framing the Caribbean Picturesque*. Durham, NC: Duke University Press.

Trethewey, Natasha. 2002. *Bellocq's Ophelia: Poems*. Saint Paul, MN: Graywolf.

Trinh T. Minh-ha. 1990. "Documentary Is/Not a Name." *October* 52 (Spring): 76–98.

Trombadore, Cara E. "Police Officer Sexual Misconduct: An Urgent Call to Action in a Context Disproportionately Threatening Women of Color." *Harvard Journal on Racial and Ethnic Justice* 32 (2016): 153–88.

TvT. 2021. "TMM Update TDoR 2021." November 11, 2021. https://transrespect.org/en/tmm-update-tdor-2021/.

Tyburczy, Jennifer. 2016. *Sex Museums: The Politics and Performance of Display*. Chicago: University of Chicago Press.

Valencia, Loana D. P. 1996. "Wanna Be a Puta." *Conmoción: Revista y Red Revolucionarias de Lesbianas Latinas*, no. 3, 38–39.

Vargas, Deborah R. 2014. "Ruminations on *Lo Sucio* as a Latino Queer Analytic." *American Quarterly* 66, no. 3 (September): 715–26.

Venville, Malcolm. 2003. *Layers*. London: Spine.

Venville, Malcolm. 2006. *Lucha Loco*. London: AMMO Books.

Venville, Malcolm, and Amanda de la Rosa. 2013. *The Women of Casa X*. Amsterdam: Schilt.

Vizenor, Gerald. 1994. *Manifest Manners: Postindian Warriors of Survivance*. Hanover, NH: Wesleyan University Press.

Wallis, Brian. 1996. "Black Bodies, White Science: The Slave Daguerreotypes of Louis Agassiz." *Journal of Blacks in Higher Education*, no. 12 (Summer): 102–6.

West, Natalie, ed. 2021. *We Too: Essays on Sex Work and Survival*. New York: Feminist Press at the City University of New York, 2021.

Wiechmann, Jan Christoph. 2019. "Jahrelang verkauften sie ihren Körper. Jetzt sind sie alt und bekommen, wonach sie sich sehnten." *Stern*, February 23, 2019. https://www.stern.de/panorama/weltgeschehen/mexiko--ein-besuch-im-weltweit-ersten-altenheim-fuer-prostituierte-8589518.html.

Williams, Linda. 1999. *Hard Core: Power, Pleasure, and the "Frenzy of the Visible."* Expanded ed. Berkeley: University of California Press.

Williams, Linda, ed. 2004. *Porn Studies*. Durham, NC: Duke University Press.

Wilson, Beth E. 2016. "The Corporate Creation of the Photojournalist: *Life* Magazine and Margaret Bourke-White in World War II." *Journal of War and Culture Studies* 9, no. 2 (April 2): 133–50.

Wolthers, Louise. 2016. "Monitoring the Margins: Street Views of Sex Workers." *Photography and Culture* 9, no. 3 (September): 239–54.

Zamora, Omaris Z. 2022. "Before Bodak Yellow and Beyond the Post-soul." *Black Scholar* 52, no. 1 (January 2): 53–63.

Zehbrauskas, Adriana. 2018. "Retired from the Brutal Streets of Mexico, Sex Workers Find a Haven." *New York Times*, January 9, 2018. https://www.nytimes.com/2018/01/09/world/americas/mexico-prostitutes-shelter.html.

INDEX

Note: Page numbers in italics refer to figures.